Supporting Difficult Transitions

Transitions in Childhood and Youth

Series editors: Marilyn Fleer, Mariane Hedegaard and Megan Adams

The series brings together books that present and explore empirical research and theoretical discussion on the themes of childhood and youth transitions. Special attention is directed to conceptualizing transitions holistically so that societal, institutional and personal perspectives are featured within and across books. Key to the series is presenting the processes of transitions between practices or activities and their relationship to the person, in contexts such as intergenerational family practices, the processes of care, a person's development, the learning of individuals, groups and systems, personal health, labour and birthing and aging. All books take a broad cultural-historical approach of transitions across a range of contexts and countries and when brought together in one place make an important contribution to better understanding transitions globally. Books in the *Transitions in Childhood and Youth* series offer an excellent resource for postgraduate students, researchers, policy writers and academics.

Also available in the series

Children's Transitions in Everyday Life and Institutions, edited by Mariane Hedegaard and Marilyn Fleer

Supporting Difficult Transitions

Children, Young People and Their Carers

Edited by
Mariane Hedegaard and Anne Edwards

BLOOMSBURY ACADEMIC
LONDON • NEW YORK • OXFORD • NEW DELHI • SYDNEY

BLOOMSBURY ACADEMIC
Bloomsbury Publishing Plc
50 Bedford Square, London, WC1B 3DP, UK
1385 Broadway, New York, NY 10018, USA
29 Earlsfort Terrace, Dublin 2, Ireland

BLOOMSBURY, BLOOMSBURY ACADEMIC and the Diana logo
are trademarks of Bloomsbury Publishing Plc

First published in Great Britain 2019
Paperback edition first published 2021

Copyright © Mariane Hedegaard, Anne Edwards and Contributors, 2019

Mariane Hedegaard, Anne Edwards and Contributors have asserted their right under the Copyright, Designs and Patents Act, 1988, to be identified as Authors of this work.

For legal purposes the Acknowledgements on p. vii constitute
an extension of this copyright page.

Series design by Joshua Fanning
Cover image: mactrunk/iStock

All rights reserved. No part of this publication may be reproduced or transmitted in any form or by any means, electronic or mechanical, including photocopying, recording, or any information storage or retrieval system, without prior permission in writing from the publishers.

Bloomsbury Publishing Plc does not have any control over, or responsibility for, any third-party websites referred to or in this book. All internet addresses given in this book were correct at the time of going to press. The author and publisher regret any inconvenience caused if addresses have changed or sites have ceased to exist, but can accept no responsibility for any such changes.

A catalogue record for this book is available from the British Library.

A catalog record for this book is available from the Library of Congress.

ISBN: HB: 978-1-3500-5276-5
PB: 978-1-3502-1223-7
ePDF: 978-1-3500-5277-2
eBook: 978-1-3500-5278-9

Series: Transitions in Childhood and Youth

Typeset by Deanta Global Publishing Services

To find out more about our authors and books visit
www.bloomsbury.com and sign up for our newsletters.

Contents

Notes on Contributors   vii
Series Editors' Foreword   xii

1   Rethinking Professional Support for Challenging Transitions: Enabling the Agency of Children, Young People and Their Families *Anne Edwards and Mariane Hedegaard*   1

Part One   A Fresh Look at Professional Work with Children, Young People and Families

2   Child-Based Practice Development for Children in Areas of Concern: A Model for Enabling Both the Child's and the Teachers' Perspectives *Mariane Hedegaard*   21

3   Common Knowledge between Mothers and Children in Problematic Transitions: How Professionals Make Children's Motives Available as a Resource *Nick Hopwood and Teena Clerke*   43

4   Changing Practices in the Highlands of Vietnam: Transitioning from Subjects of Research to Agents of Change *Marilyn Fleer, Freya Fleer-Stout, Helen Hedges and Hanh Le Thi Bich*   67

5   Radical-Local Screening of Preschool Children's Social Situations of Development: From Abilities to Activities *Mariane Hedegaard and Naussúnguaq Lyberth*   91

Part Two   Enabling Families as Supporters of Children's and Young People's Transitions

6   Easing Transitions into School for Children from Socially Excluded 'Hard to Reach' Families: From Risk and Resilience to Agency and Demand *Anne Edwards and Maria Evangelou*   115

7   Relational Approaches to Supporting Transitions into School: Families and Early Childhood Educators Working Together in Regional Chile *Christine Woodrow and Kerry Staples*   131

8 The Transition of Roma Children into School: Working Relationally Across Cultural Boundaries in Spain *José Luis Lalueza, Virginia Martínez-Lozano and Beatriz Macías-Gomez-Estern* 153

9 Small Children's Movements across Residential Care and Day Care: How Professionals Build Common Knowledge and Practice That Matter for Children *Ida Schwartz* 175

10 Helping Children in Cross-Cultural Post-Disaster settings: Creating Relational Pathways to Resilience *Pernille Hansen* 195

Part Three   Supporting the Agency of Children and Young People in Transitions

11 When Young Adulthood Presents a Double Challenge: Mental Illness, Disconnected Activities and Relational Agency *Sofie Pedersen* 221

12 Children with Disabilities Growing Up and Becoming Adults: Sociocultural Challenges around the Transition to Adulthood *Louise Bøttcher* 241

13 Supporting the Transitions to Work of Autistic Young People: Building and Using Common Knowledge *Anne Edwards and Yvette Fay* 262

Index 279

Contributors

Hanh Le Thi Bich currently manages Plan Vietnam's Quality Education and Parenting Community Engagement programmes. She has actively engaged in the development of Plan Vietnam's Early Childhood Care and Development (ECCD) country programmes, including the Gia Lai ECCD project. Her research interest lies in how the ECCD holistic framework is applied and sustained with culturally appropriate approaches in ethnic minority areas.

Louise Bøttcher is Associate Professor at the Department of Education at the University of Aarhus, Denmark. Her research focuses on the interplay between neurobiological, social and cultural conditions for development. Her research takes as its point of departure Vygotsky's idea about disability as an incongruence between the natural and the cultural line of development and is aimed at the investigation and further theoretical understanding of children with disabilities and neurobiologically based impairment. A key publication is Bøttcher and Dammeyer, *Development and Learning of Young Children with Disabilities: A Vygotskian Perspective* (2016).

Teena Clerke has been conducting educational research since 2006, through engagement in a wide range of projects, including her PhD about women rewriting design scholarship as they move from professional to academic practices. Her research interests include how people learn in professional practices, utilizing cultural-historical theories, feminist research approaches and visual methodologies, reflecting her visual communication design background.

Anne Edwards is Professor Emerita at the Department of Education at the University of Oxford, where she held posts as Head of Department and Director of Research. She is a former president of the British Educational Research Association and has doctorates *honoris causa* from the Universities of Helsinki and Oslo. She has written extensively on inter-professional collaboration, professional learning and cultural-historical approaches to learning.

Maria Evangelou has recently returned to Greece to take up the post of Academic and Pedagogical Director at a primary school in Thessalonica. She is also an honorary research fellow in the Department of Education at the University of Oxford, where until the end of April 2018 she was an associate professor. Her research focuses on the evaluation of early childhood interventions; the development of children at risk of educational underachievement; language and literacy development in the early years; parental engagement in children's learning; parenting education and support; the home learning environment and quality learning environments; early years professional development; and evidence-based practices in education.

Yvette Fay is Assistant Headteacher at the Iffley Academy, a special school in Oxford. Among her responsibilities is liaising with local employers to create and support work placements for the school's students.

Marilyn Fleer, Laureate Professor, holds the Foundation Chair of Early Childhood Education and Development at Monash University, Australia. She was awarded the 2018 Kathleen Fitzpatrick Laureate Fellowship by the Australian Research Council and was a former President of the International Society of Cultural-historical Activity Research (ISCAR). Additionally, she holds the positions of an honorary Research Fellow in the Department of Education at the University of Oxford, and a second professor position in the KINDKNOW Centre at the Western Norway University of Applied Sciences.

Freya Fleer-Stout is a recent graduate from Monash University, Australia, in the School of Nursing and Midwifery, and volunteers for Plan International Australia. Her research interests span the areas of health and midwifery, with a special focus on the importance of nutrition and breastfeeding for young children's development in a range of cultural communities.

Pernille Hansen has worked with mental health and psychosocial support in the humanitarian field since 2005 in Africa, Europe, Asia and the Caribbean. She has conducted research on psychosocial interventions and cultural adaptation and is the author of multiple reference books and training manuals.

Mariane Hedegaard is Professor Emerita in Developmental Psychology at the University of Copenhagen, Denmark. She is doctorate honoris causa at the University of Pablo Olavide in Seville, Spain, and holds a senior research fellowship in the Department of Education at the University of Oxford, UK. Mariane has authored and co-edited 25 books. These include *Radical-local Teaching and Learning; Vygotsky and Special Needs Education; Motives in Children's Development; Learning, Play and Children's Development;* and *Children, Childhood and Everyday Life.* She has also written a number of articles in journals such as *Mind, Culture and Activity; Outlines: Critical Social Studies; Culture and Psychology;* and *Learning, Culture and Social Interaction.*

Helen Hedges is Professor at the University of Auckland, New Zealand. Her research interests are in the areas of children's learning and development in the contexts of families and communities, teacher knowledge and professional learning, and early childhood curriculum and pedagogy.

Nick Hopwood is Associate Professor at the University of Technology, Sydney, and Extraordinary Professor at the University of Stellenbosch. He has a long-standing interest in cultural-historical theory. Since 2010, he has been researching support and early intervention services for parents of children at risk. His research raises questions of emerging collaborative practices and associated shifts in the forms of expertise and knowledge work involved in these contexts. Nick has published widely on these issues, including *Professional Practice and Learning* (2016).

José Luis Lalueza is Professor in the Department of Educational Psychology at the Autonomous University of Barcelona. His research focuses on minority development, socialization processes in Roma communities and educational inclusion in environments at risk of social exclusion. For twenty years, he has coordinated the design, implementation and analysis of communities of practices for intercultural education, based on a cultural-historical approach.

Naussúnguaq Lyberth is Director at the Center for Early Childhood Education, Department of Education, Government of Greenland.

Beatriz Macías-Gómez-Estern works as Associate Professor in the Department of Social Anthropology, Basic Psychology and Public Health at the Universidad Pablo de Olavide, Sevilla, Spain. She has worked as Visiting Scholar at the University of California San Diego and King's College London. Her main research interest lies in the impact of 'otherness' experiences in the discursive construction of identity. She has analysed these processes of alterity-identity in different multicultural settings, as migration, multicultural schools and service learning in higher education programmes. Some of her key publications are Macías, B. and de la Mata M., 'Narratives of migration: Emotions and the interweaving of personal and cultural identity through narrative', *Culture and Psychology,* 19 (3), 348–68 (2013); Sánchez, J. A., Macías, B. and Martínez, V., 'The value positions of school staff and parents in immigrant families and their implications for children's transitions between home and school in multicultural schools in Andalusia', *Learning, Culture and Social Interaction,* 3, 217–23 (2014).

Virginia Martínez-Lozano is Associate Professor in the Faculty of Social Sciences at Pablo de Olavide University, Seville, Spain. Her research is oriented to the area of sociocultural studies and is focused now in teaching and learning processes through service-learning methodologies. Her collaboration with schools in marginal areas permits her to investigate different issues related to development and educative innovation.

Sofie Pedersen is Assistant Professor in Psychology in the Department of People and Technology at Roskilde University, Denmark. Her research mainly revolves around youth development in relation to specific institutional settings, and she is specifically interested in the developmental possibilities and constraints that are offered and/or created in the environment, for example, in high schools or social-psychiatric institutions. Her work is grounded in the intersection of ecological psychology, cultural-historical activity theory and critical psychology, and she has, in the past ten years, combined research with developmental work in practice.

Ida Schwartz is reader at the Centre for Applied Welfare Research at University College Lillebaelt, Denmark. Drawing on a critical psychological perspective, her research focuses on children's perspectives on their daily life in and across different welfare state institutions. She gives special attention to children and young people in difficult life situations and the issue of how children in care are included in children's communities in different institutions through their childhood. From this perspective follows a special interest in how professionals put the child's perspective at the centre of their cooperation.

Kerry Staples is a lecturer in early childhood education at Western Sydney University, NSW, Australia. Her research and teaching focus on enhancing inclusion of children with disabilities, collaboration, family-centred practices and the role of early childhood educators as community leaders. She was a member of the Futuro Infantil Hoy research team from 2009.

Christine Woodrow is Associate Professor at Western Sydney University. Her research activity is strongly focused on early education in high-poverty contexts, early childhood leadership identities and parent engagement in challenging contexts. She has been the leader of the Futuro Infantil Hoy research project in Chile and continues to undertake research with colleagues in Chile.

Series Editors' Foreword

In this book series we have chosen to focus on transitions through the lens of cultural-historical theory. Specifically, transition is conceptualized to encompass the changes in daily activity settings, the changes in everyday moves between different institutional practices and the changes on entering new practice through life course trajectories, such as going to school, leaving school, entering the work force or entering into parenthood. Through transition into new practices, children and young people meet new challenges and demands that may give them possibility for development.

Important for a cultural-historical conception of transition is the person's agency or intentions, which can be used as analytical tools for gaining the person's perspective during microgenetic transitions between activity settings within an institution, such as indoor play, lunch and outdoor activities in kindergarten, in daily moves between home and kindergarten, school or work, and during macro-transitions that involve new practices. As the person or people take forward their intention within the daily transitions or the new institutions that they attend, a dynamic interplay between the person and the institution can be observed. Cultural-historical studies of transitions across a range of contexts and countries are brought together in this book series, where they can make an important contribution to better understanding transitions globally.

1

Rethinking Professional Support for Challenging Transitions: Enabling the Agency of Children, Young People and Their Families

Anne Edwards and Mariane Hedegaard

What the book is about

This book is about how professionals can work with children and young people and their families when children and young people are undergoing particularly challenging transitions into new environments. We see these troubling transitions as *zones of concern*, where well-targeted and often intensive support for the transition is needed. The twelve chapters that follow show how professionals work together, and with families, to enable the insights and resources of all participants to be brought into play to support children and young people as they orient themselves to the demands of new activities or new practices. Between them the chapters offer fresh ways of thinking about how professionals can work relationally to give this help. Working relationally is not a new idea in most professions, but there is more to it than simply getting on well with some people. In this book we offer some practical examples of relational cooperation and concepts that can explain how zones of concern can become transformed into successful transitions through relational work.

All the discussions in the chapters focus on particularly challenging transitions. These challenges range from the difficulties experienced by young people with cerebral palsy as they enter adulthood in Denmark, to the entry into day care and formal schooling of children from communities based on hunting and fishing in Greenland. These discussions also focus on children separated from their families after the 2010 Haitian earthquake and young people with autistic spectrum conditions (ASC) entering the workplace in the UK. In these, and all the other chapters, the authors point to how professionals can help create conditions in which children's and young people's agency can unfold to enable them to propel themselves forward with confidence and dignity as learners and citizens.

A key concept for us when thinking about children and young people, therefore, is *agency*, that is, how their purposeful actions unfold in activities. The chapters, in different ways, show how professionals need to and can support the unfolding of the agency of children and young people, and how their families can be seen as partners in this support. But we are not suggesting that the goal of professional work is to create an independent and potentially isolated actor who needs to take sole responsibility for their life trajectories: such a view leads rapidly to victim blaming. Instead, we emphasize how children, young people and their families are helped to develop the kind of interdependency that gives them control, but also allows them to give and receive support.

To explain how professionals can accomplish these tasks we bring together ideas that we have separately developed in our own research. We outline them very briefly here and in more depth in relation to specific examples later in the chapter. The first explanatory concepts are *motive orientation* and *demands* (Hedegaard, 2012, 2014). When a child or young person enters a new practice, such as preschool or the workplace, they need to be able to recognize the demands that the new practice is making on them; these demands lie in the traditions in the different activity settings. In a school classroom it may be 'listen to the teacher' or 'don't leave the classroom without asking', at the workplace it may be 'wear a safety helmet' when you are in this part of the building or 'apprentices don't take the journeymen's seats at the lunch table'. These are demands that relate to immediate activity settings but they are also elements in more powerful demands in institutional practices such as 'students should learn' and 'people need to act carefully, responsibly and respectfully in the workplace'. A person's motive orientation is therefore crucial, giving direction to how she or he engages agentically with demands in the practice. In this book, we combine our focus on motive orientation and demands with Vygotsky's idea of *social situation of development* (Vygotsky, 1998). The social situation of development is created by the child or young person as they respond to demands and reposition themselves in a practice; but it also consists of the support available to them as they move forward as learners. A child's social situation of development is created when their agency unfolds as they engage across different practices. In line with Vygotsky (1998) and Elkonin (1999) we argue that children's social situations of development are characterized by age periods. One consequence of this stance is that we recognize that transitions into new practices, for example, from home to day care or from day care to school, are key to development.

> We must admit that at the beginning of each age period, there develops a completely original, exclusive, single and unique relation, specific to the given age, between the child and reality, mainly the social reality, that surrounds him. We call this relation *the social situation of development* of a given age. The social situation of development represents the initial moments for all the dynamic changes that occur in development during the given period. (Vygotsky, 1998, p. 198, emphasis in original)

Children's development can be seen as a trajectory through different practices, as we shall see in Figure 1.1. Children usually participate in more than one practice, so transition from home to day care does not mean that activities in the home practice are no longer important. We emphasize the social situation of development because it points to the importance of all the relations a child enters into. In particular it calls attention to how professionals need to be aware of a child's multiple relations to help children and young people become agentic and responsible learners.

Making a transition from one practice to another is often difficult for many of us. When we enter a new-to-us practice our actions may be based on the

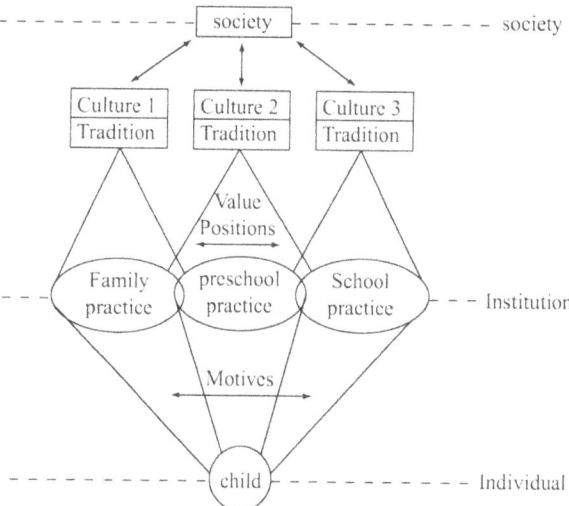

Figure 1.1 Relations between society, practice and persons.

motive orientations which have served us well in the past; but these may not serve us so well in the new practice. When the transitions are accompanied by emotional concerns, 'I don't speak the language and my family are not here', or comprehension difficulties, 'I can't explain that I sometimes need to be able to go somewhere quiet in order to calm down', the challenges of developing a new motive orientation and engaging with new social situations can be considerable. The contributions all refer to distinct challenges for children and young people in different age groups, but they all offer ways forward that have implications for how professionals work relationally, both across practice boundaries and with families.

These ways forward draw on three related concepts: *relational expertise*, *common knowledge* and *relational agency* (Edwards, 2010, 2012, 2017). In brief, the chapters in this book show how practitioners found ways of supporting transitions by working with others. The professionals exercised relational expertise by eliciting what was important, what mattered, for potential collaborators, which includes children, young people and their families, and they were explicit about what mattered for them in their work. The 'what matters' or motives of each potential collaborator combined to become common knowledge. This common knowledge, a mutual understanding of what matters in each practice, became a resource that mediated the unfolding of their relational agency when they collaborated to support the transitions of children and young people.

The concept of practice is, therefore, also fundamental to our discussion of transitions. We see practices as 'knowledge laden, imbued with cultural values, and emotionally freighted by the motives of those who act in them' (Edwards, 2010, p. 5). From this perspective, practices are usually historically formed and sustain relatively stable identities for the people who inhabit them; although there is also a dynamic between person and practice, people are both shaped by the practices they enter and may shape them through their actions in them. When we think of professional work we can see that the values and motives that are carried in institutional practices, such as teaching or residential-care work, bind practitioners together within specific practices and create their professional identities. These identities shape how they interpret the needs and strengths of clients and respond to these interpretations.

Attention to the different motives in different practices has long been at the core of Hedegaard's work and underpins her interest in transitions and the challenges they can present. Figure 1.1 (Hedegaard, 2008) helps us recognize how different institutional motives become embedded in the purposes found in the activities within the institutional practices and give direction to actions taken by people in them. Of course this embeddedness explains the importance of motive orientations and a capacity to attend to what matters in a practice.

Figure 1.1 also indicates how challenging cross-practice collaborations can be. The attention to motivated actions in activities within practice cultures in Figure 1.1 alerts us to the discrete nature of institutional practices. Teachers and parents undertake very different actions for often quite different reasons: the teacher primarily promotes pupil learning and the parent focuses primarily on the physical well-being of the same child. What they do is compatible, but each can remain ignorant of what is important for the other and why. One outcome is that the child making the transition from home to school has to do all the work, including creating a new motive orientation without the support of those who recognize where the child is coming from and therefore what strengths and needs they present in the new practice.

The book is therefore aimed at professionals working with children, young people and their families, but the focus is on the child or the young person and how the best resources can be made available to support their agency and motive orientation while they make these challenging transitions. These resources include the families as well as the other professionals with a stake in the child's or young person's trajectory. The approach therefore calls for ways of creating opportunities for mutual respect to be developed between professionals and families and between the different professionals.

We are therefore suggesting that we need to move on from images of heroic practitioners or informed parents, who can negotiate the system to support a child or young person's move through a troubling transition. Instead what is needed is what Hedegaard has termed a *wholistic approach* (Hedegaard, 2009, 2012). To explain this approach she has built on Figure 1.1 to model the relationship between people's actions, the activities they take part in, the practices in which the activities are located and the sociopolitical conditions which shape the practices and to which they respond (see Table 1.1). This development presents these as different analytic planes, or dialectically connected entry points, for the researcher who is studying these phenomena.

Importantly, Table 1.1 alerts us to the potential role of institutions, as well as the national or regional policies that shape them, in enabling successful transitions. As we shall see, this wholistic approach is captured in varying emphases across the chapters.

Table 1.1 Planes of analysis

Structure	Process	Dynamic
Society	Tradition	Societal conditions and demands
Institution	Practice	Value motive/objectives
Activity setting	Social situation (potential social situation of development)	Motivation/engagement/demands
Person	Actions in an activity	Motive orientations and demands

Identifying the pressing problems in transitions

In this section we give examples of some of the difficulties that made transitions zones of concern. We discuss how the problems were identified through attention to the closely interlinked concepts: *motive orientation, social situation of development* and *agency*. In the section that follows we give some examples of how authors used the similarly interlinked concepts of *relational expertise, common knowledge* and *relational agency*. All these ideas were used to lesser or greater degrees across all the chapters. We simply think that it may be helpful to illustrate the concepts as they are being used in the chapters, while we explain them in more depth.

First, we explain the interlinking between motive orientation, social situation of development and agency. All the chapters take the idea of motive orientation to analyse how a specific transition is particularly challenging. Hedegaard has described the development of motive orientation in the following way: 'Motive development can then be seen as a movement initiated by the learner's emotional experience related to the activity setting' (Hedegaard, 2012, p. 21). It gives direction to how people recognize, interpret and take actions to respond to the demands in a practice and is a personal response, which involves people's sense of their own competence in the field of action. Here we can connect motive orientation with the unfolding of a person's agency as they take purposeful actions in the activity settings that comprise the practices they inhabit. When a child moves from one set of practices, such as the home, to another, such as the preschool, the preschool practitioners need to enable the child to engage purposefully with the demands of being a preschool child, for example taking advantage of the opportunities for learning within a play environment.

At this point we link a child's motive orientation and agency with his or her social situation of development when discussing the learning of young children.

The social situation of development is not simply an array of resources, both human and material, that are available to support the learning and development of the child. Rather, the social situation of development is always potential and needs to be created by the child, or indeed the adult, learner. The learner creates the social situation of development by recognizing and responding to demands by drawing on the relevant available support, together with their own conceptual resources. In brief, they propel themselves forward as learners in response to what they see as the demands they need to address in different practices. This outline of the social situation of development shows how crucial a motive orientation that recognizes key demands is for the preschool child or the young person entering the work place. It also indicates how important it is for professionals who are working with children to be aware of how a child's motive orientation indicates what Vygotsky termed the 'original, exclusive, single and unique relation, specific to the given age, between the child and reality' (Vygotsky, 1998, p. 198).

The pressing problem identified by Bøttcher in Chapter 12 is the transition into adulthood of young people with cerebral palsy in Denmark. Societal expectations are that at 18 young people are ready to be treated as adults, consequently the support that is available to those with severe physical disabilities changes and does not take into account their specific social situation of development that may involve developmental delays in relation to what is expected of an 18-year-old person. The pressure to be regarded as an adult, to be able to live with carers other than their parents, is therefore often inappropriate for them. Taking the perspective of the young people, Bøttcher's argument is that the positive motive orientations they had developed up to the age of 18 become much more difficult to sustain. The particular problems she identifies are a lack of clear role models and anticipation of diminishing social and developmental opportunities.

Edwards and Evangelou are also concerned with motive orientation and the agency of children. In Chapter 6, they draw on these ideas to examine how an early intervention programme tried to ease the transition of children from socially marginalized families into school in the UK. They critique how some early intervention programmes with these 'hard to reach' families have employed partial understandings of resilience as rationales for easing transitions to school, by making the home similar to school. They argue that a risk and resilience framing of early intervention programmes would be usefully augmented by an approach to learning based in understandings of children's social situation of development. Such an approach values both home and school and focuses on how children are enabled to develop motive orientations as agentic learners in both settings. They suggest that interventions need to recognize that interactions in each setting contribute in different ways at different times to the development of a child as learner.

The potential role of families in supporting these transitions features in almost all the contributions. In every case, the argument is that they are an underused resource. In Bøttcher's chapter, the part played by parents in the support system is not factored into plans for the young people's futures. Edwards and Evangelou in their discussion of marginalized families argue that families' roles are different from those of schools in supporting children in their social situations as learners, but are nonetheless valuable in helping the child develop a motive orientation as an agentic learner, which will serve them well in school.

Schwartz, in Chapter 9, picks up on the potential that parents have for supporting their children, even when the child is in residential care. She describes the challenges shaping the transitions made by vulnerable children as they move between residential care and school in Denmark. Despite the children being in care, they spend time with their parents at weekends. The transitions from care to school are problematic because of the school's lack of collaboration with the residential-care workers. The school sees itself as the one constant in the children's lives, ignoring the ways in which parents, with their strong emotional ties with the children, might be encouraged to work with their children. Schwartz indicates how parents could be seen as part of the support system that helps the child develop as an agentic learner with motive orientations towards meeting the learning demands of schools.

The role of family support is also tackled by Hansen in Chapter 10. Here the challenging transition arises from the displacement of children as a consequence of the 2010 earthquake in Haiti. In one case study, we see how a child is taken from Haiti to the neighbouring territory of San Domingo where he does not speak the language and is at a loss without his family. Hansen shows what happens in a crisis situation when a child and his family are faced with new demands and the need for a new motive orientation, in new conditions without familiar support. She argues that professionals should not only focus on the child but also on the conditions for development, the institutional practices, and the interactions and relations the child participates in with others. In her chapter, Hansen points to how psychologists, working in the shelters established for the Haitian families, worked at building common knowledge which would enable the creation of conditions where the agency of the Haitian families could come into play.

We have already described agency as unfolding in purposeful actions in response to demands; but agency is more than simply fitting in with what practices demand. Taylor's definition of agency is one we consistently return to: 'We think of the agent as not only partly responsible for what he [sic] does, for the degree to which he acts in line with those evaluations, but also as responsible in some sense for those evaluations' (Taylor, 1977, p. 118). This understanding of agency calls for professionals to encourage joint, culturally sensitive goal setting and self-assessment when working with clients. It also calls for professionals to develop their own agency through informed self-evaluation against the goals they set for themselves. Two chapters in the present collection demonstrated these ideas in relation to how researchers from powerful cultures worked in culturally sensitive ways to develop the agency of local practitioners by collaborating with them in both goal setting and self-evaluation.

Fleer et al., working with community members and local professionals, addressed the problem of how a non-government organization (NGO) in Vietnam could evidence what was good quality in early childhood education in a relatively isolated Western Highland community. The transitions the team focused on were how children's entry into school was supported by local early years practitioners and how these local practitioners learnt to work with both the traditions of their rural communities and the demands of supporting young children as learners who can also deal with societal changes. Their solution, discussed in Chapter 4, was to enable the practitioners to create the criteria against which their work would be evaluated by the NGO and to be agents of change in relation to early education practice development. In brief, the practitioners were helped to create motive orientations as knowledgeable early educators able to help develop the motive orientations of young children. Importantly, and echoing Taylor's 1977 point, the agency of the practitioners unfolded as they set goals for their work and were able to evaluate whether they had met them.

The pressing problem of societal transition was also evident in Chapter 5, authored by Hedegaard and Lyberth. Here the setting was a national initiative in Greenland to support children's social situation of development in early childhood by evaluating whether the activities they participated in gave them the competences they needed to prepare themselves for transition to school. The rationale for the initiative was to ensure that all children had access to a pedagogical approach, based on shared productive activity, which combined generalizable knowledge with familiar local activities. Its aim was to value the principles underpinning the traditions of hunting and fishing that had characterized their communities for generations and at the same time orient children to the new life forms that characterize modern society. Like Fleer et al., Hedegaard and Lyberth was concerned with the assessment of early education, both children's learning and how practitioners enabled them to create a social situation of development within the changes set in motion by the initiative. Hedegaard and Lyberth, together with a national task force group, designed a screening tool that assessed the educational activities that the preschool children participated in as well as children's participation. The screening tool was to be used by the educators as a way of self-evaluating the pedagogical activities they set up for the children as well as to evaluate the children's competences. The practitioners' assessment of the children's development helped them develop motive orientations as educators and also find ways to create new social situations to support children who were in zones of concern to enter a zone of development as they made the transition into school.

Working together on the problems arising in challenging transitions

Having identified zones of concern where creating new motive orientations are difficult, the authors offer ways forward. These strategies, in various ways, involve strengthening support through collaborations around the trajectory of the child or young person. The collaborations were sometimes difficult to accomplish, as we will see in Chapter 9 authored by Schwartz, where the school practitioners were unwilling to collaborate with the practitioners from the residential-care institution. In many of the potential collaborations, there were also explicit and implicit professional hierarchies or times when parents were seen as part of the problem and not the solution, all of which impeded the support needed for the challenging transition. But there were also many examples of careful collaboration where mutual respect had been built and potential differences between people from different practices were overcome.

We, therefore, now focus on how successful collaborations across practices were accomplished to help children and young people in challenging transitions. We do this by exemplifying how relational expertise was exercised, common knowledge built and relational agency demonstrated (Edwards, 2010, 2012, 2017). The key concept in this collection of chapters is common knowledge, which consists of the motives of all the collaborating participants, including parents, and, as we said earlier, can become a resource that people draw on to aid their collaborations. Common knowledge is built through the exercise of relational expertise. This expertise is in addition to one's specialist expertise as, for example, a psychologist, therapist or social worker. It includes the ability to elicit the motives, or what matters, for people who inhabit other practices and being able to articulate and make clear one's own motives in relation to the problem being tackled. Relational agency is a label for the unfolding of joint purposeful work that practitioners may carry out together or may undertake with parents, while drawing on common knowledge. The unfolding of relational agency is seen when people collaborate to diagnose the problem to be addressed so that it can be understood as fully as possible and then carefully and respectfully calibrate a joint response to the expanded interpretation of the problem. Relational agency therefore involves interdependence and mutuality.

Key to exercising relational expertise and building common knowledge is the opportunity to meet and elicit what matters for each other. Edwards has described these meeting points as *sites of intersecting practices* (Edwards, 2010). These are spaces where people from different practices meet and where listening is as important as talking. They are also places where people may learn to become explicit about what matters for them in ways that have not been previously allowed: they are places of mutual respect.

This approach is the background for Chapter 2, also authored by Hedegaard. Here she puts forward a theoretically based procedure for a relational psychological professionalism when working with children and young people in zones of concern in day care and school. The premise is that the psychologist is a partner with other professionals in a consulting-oriented approach. Consequently building common knowledge between the psychologist, other professionals and the children about the child's social situation of development is crucial. The analysis undertaken by a psychologist may use action-based observation in the activity settings to analyse the motive orientations of the involved partners in the practice where a child has been located in a zone of concern. The common knowledge may be seen as an analytical tool to identify shared goals of success for intervention in the practice that change a zone of concern into a zone of development.

Pedersen in Chapter 11, in the same vein, shows how she exercised relational expertise in order to build common knowledge with young adults in a residential social-psychiatric facility in Denmark. Instead of taking the usual therapeutic line of helping people manage their symptoms by taking medication and so on, Pederson offers examples of how she focused on building common knowledge with patients during shared activities in places of mutual respect where hierarchies were eroded, such as while baking or running. This common knowledge, of what matters for them and for living in the world, enabled the unfolding of the clients' agency alongside Pederson as they talked during the activities. By working relationally in actions in activities in everyday life, Pederson was able to help these young adults to identify and articulate what mattered to them and to develop meaningful motives for their transition into and engagement with the world.

The transition into the wider world is also the focus of Chapter 13 from the UK, authored by Edwards and Fay. They discuss how young people with ASC can be helped with the transition into the workplace by using a smartphone app. The app has been designed to hold, and make visible, common knowledge. The common knowledge consists of what matters for a young person and what matters for employers and workplace colleagues. It is to be used to mediate how these young people engage with the demands of the workplace. This knowledge of what matters allows colleagues to respond relationally to the needs of the young person and for the young person to be helped to read cues in the workplace environment and recognize what they need to orient to while there. Importantly, the app is controlled by the young person. This control allows them to identify and respond to the demands of the workplace and to ask for aspects of the workplace to be adjusted to accommodate their needs, such as headphones to block noise or the opportunity for time out. The app also has the potential to involve parents, who can have a role in checking and updating it. In this way they can keep themselves informed about how their child is interpreting and responding to the demands of working life and give them support at home.

Hopwood and Clerke, in Chapter 3, also draw on common knowledge when discussing the work of Australian professionals who were working with parents to help them overcome their own anxieties and develop new parenting competences. The authors offer detailed analyses of how the practitioners built common knowledge with the parents and drew on it to shift the parents' interpretations of problems, such as a child who is not feeding. Their aim was to help them create strong parent-child relationships. Hopwood and Clerke argue that common knowledge 'was crucial, but not sufficient in securing the positive changes' and what was key was linking it to actions taken by the parents with the child. The professionals helped the parents see the problem in terms of what they could do to support the child relationally by providing a safe environment and responding to cues. The transition that was managed by the professionals was for the parents to no longer see the child as troublesome, but instead to understand the child as an active agent with whom they could build common knowledge and negotiate.

Two chapters consider how children from socially marginalized groups are helped to make the transition into school. In both cases, considerable efforts are made to build common knowledge between the children's communities and the schools. Woodrow and Staples's study is based in a large early education initiative located in a remote area of Chile. There they focused on two transitions: those of local children moving into school and changes in the practices of the educators who work with them. In Chapter 7, they reveal that key features linking both transitions were the Literacy Cafés. These were sites of intersecting practices in the communities, where parents and educators could meet without interfering hierarchies. Here common knowledge could be built through the educators' exercise of relational expertise. As a result they achieved insights into the lives of families and children, which changed how they worked in their classrooms. Importantly they were able to regard parents as collaborators in the children's transitions into school, by working in new relational ways with them.

In Chapter 8 Lalueza, Martínez-Lozano and Macías-Gomez-Estern describe two projects aimed at assisting the transition of children from Roma communities into school in Spain. Their premise is that the challenges facing schools and Roma students are the appropriation of motives that give meaning to participation in school practices and which facilitate their incorporation within the students' identity; the acquisition of cultural tools that enable participation in the school's institutional practices; and the construction of narratives for sharing meanings and establishing common goals. The two projects, one an after-school club in Barcelona and the other a rethinking of school practices in Seville, built common knowledge between the communities and the school, producing a site of intersecting practices or a 'microculture' from which shared narratives and new goals could emerge.

Building networks of support in the zone of concern

The use, or neglect, of networks of support around the transition for a child, young person or educator is a common thread across many of the chapters. These networks can help the person making the transition connect the motive orientations that worked in an earlier practice with those in the new practice and so help them move forward in developing their orientation to new demands. The networks can, therefore, ensure that the child or young person is not cast adrift in the way that Hansen described one case-study child in her Haitian study or

Bøttcher revealed in her examples of young people with cerebral palsy turning 18 and entering adulthood in Denmark. A number of studies, for example, by Bøttcher, Edwards and Fay, Hansen, and Woodrow and Staples recognized the importance of including parents in the networks of support, seeing them as valuable resources in the transition and beyond. Other studies focused more on the power of sustained support from individual practitioners. Here the chapters by Pedersen, based in the Danish residential social-psychiatric facility, and by Hopwood and Clerke on the parenting support work done in Australia particularly standout.

These networks of support, and the one-on-one relationships, were built by the efforts made by the practitioners. These efforts were sometimes supported by national initiatives, as was the case in the Greenland example given by Hedegaard and Lyberth, or they arose through the efforts of a larger organization, as we see in the chapter on the NGO work in Vietnam by Fleer et al. and in the early education initiative in Chile described by Woodrow and Staples. But more often than not they depended on insightful practitioners working sensitively across practices, sometimes without clear institutional support.

The difficulties in establishing and sustaining inter-professional networks (Edwards, Daniels, Gallagher, Leadbetter and Warmington, 2009) reveal how challenging institutions find it to offer mutual respect to each other, a point illustrated very clearly in Schwartz's discussion of the relationship between a school and a residential-care home. Much of these difficulties can be attributed to the strength of professional identities. If that is the case, it is perhaps incumbent on institutions such as schools or social-work systems to enable the development of networks and relationships that focus on helping a child or young person accomplish a difficult transition. This is a long-standing problem: a UK report which assessed the success of inter-professional working in children's services noted that it often occurred, despite the institutional conditions in which it arose. Successful support of children 'too often depends on the commitment of individual staff and sometimes this happens despite, rather than because of, the organisational arrangements. This must be addressed by senior management in every service' (Lord Laming, 2009, p. 11).

One lesson from across the studies, and evident in the framework presented earlier in Table 1.1, is the need for policies at national or regional level to respond sensitively to some of the challenges revealed in this collection and to enable responses. Examples include how the problem faced by the young people in Bøttcher's study arose from unsympathetic legislation; Edwards and Evangelou pointed to how policies rested on inadequate interpretations of the literature on resilience; while Hedegaard's chapter shows how policy changes can provide opportunities for fundamentally rethinking practices, but the process presents its own challenges.

Table 1.1 therefore gives a way to consider the challenges and how they might be addressed by institutions, but also by the policies that shape institutional practices. Interestingly in the three studies that were located within wider initiatives, with strong connections to the upper row of Table 1.1 – Fleer et al., Hedegaard and Lyberth, and Woodrow and Staples – there was a dual focus on the transitions of children and on how practitioners were supported in finding new ways of working and developing new motive orientations themselves. We therefore have to ask ourselves the question: *what kinds of professionals do we want for what kinds of future citizens?* The answer for us is: practitioners who value interdependence as well as independence and demonstrate it both in their own work with each other and families and in what they hope to engender in the children and young people they are supporting.

How the book is structured

So far in this chapter, we have discussed the chapters that follow in relation to the concepts that bring coherence to the collection, but they can also be seen to be addressing specific areas of concern. We have therefore grouped the chapters in three sections to reflect these concerns: (i) a fresh look at professional work with children, young people and families; (ii) enabling families as supporters of children's and young people's transitions; and (iii) supporting the agency of children and young people in transitions. All offer insights into the work of professionals, while keeping the gaze very clearly on the troubling trajectories of the children and young people in the zone of concern.

A fresh look at professional work with children, young people and families

This section opens with Hedegaard's account, in Chapter 2, of the development of a practical model for bringing together the perspectives of children, teachers and other educational professionals when supporting the developmental trajectories and transitions of children who are giving cause for concern. In Chapter 3, Hopwood and Clerke draw on their research on how troubled parents in New South Wales are helped to recognize and work with the emergent agency of their infants, building common knowledge with the child to enable their responsive reactions as parents who can support children's developmental transitions. In Chapter 4, Fleer and her colleagues report on how an intervention alongside early years practitioners in rural Vietnam enabled the development of the professional agency of the practitioners and their transitions as professionals who can support the transitions of children into education. Finally, in Chapter 5, Hedegaard and Lyberth gives a detailed account of the development of a Vygotsky-based assessment protocol in Greenland. The key point in this chapter is that it is possible to find ways to evaluate children's general situations of development that are oriented to children's perspectives and anchored in children's actual situations in their activities in daily everyday life. Such an approach to assessment ensures that educators are sensitive to the child's perspectives in the transitions they experience.

Enabling families as supporters of children's and young people's transitions

This section opens with Chapter 6 by Edwards and Evangelou. They argue that a deeper understanding of resilience than is evident in most government policies aimed at easing transitions in to school for children from 'hard to reach' families (i) would lead to valuing the emotional contributions made by parents, and (ii) would call for building common knowledge between schools and families. This viewpoint is taken into action by Woodrow and Staples in Chapter 7, who report on an initiative in rural Chile, which successfully built common knowledge between parents and schools to ease the transitions into school of the community's children. Similar successes are reported by Lalueza, Martínez-Lozano and Macías-Gomez-Estern in Chapter 8, with their account of two projects in Spain where schools worked with Roma parents to build mutual understandings of what mattered in each community to aid children's transitions in and out of school. Schwartz's chapter is, in contrast, set in Denmark. In Chapter 9, she observes the difficulties that arise when practitioners in different practices can't collaborate to ease the transitions of children between practice settings and points to the evidence of the potential that engaging parents as supporters of children's transitions can offer. This section closes, in Chapter 10, with an account of the isolation of a child who was sent away from his home environment after the 2010 earthquake in Haiti. Hansen reports the strategies used to support him and the ultimate importance of focusing on the family unit, the common knowledge that sustains them in cases of such dramatic transitions and the efforts to be made by the practitioners to work with the family.

Supporting the agency of children and young people in transitions

The final section focuses on the agency of those who are inhabiting a zone of concern when making transitions, but does not see agency in terms of the isolated actor, rather as someone able to connect with the resources, including other people, that enable them in their transitions. In Chapter 11 Pedersen draws on the concepts of common knowledge and relational agency to explain how she helped young adults with mental health problems develop the capacity to re-enter society after some time in residential care. Bøttcher in Chapter 12 details the challenges faced by young people with cerebral palsy once they legally become adults and need to make a transition that does not reflect their physical capabilities. Her focus is on how their continuing agency needs to be creatively supported. The agency of young people with specific support needs is also the central topic of Chapter 13 authored by Edwards and Fay. Here an account is given of the design of a smartphone app that holds the common knowledge that can mediate the young person's transition into the workplace and their coping with changes in task demands while at work, enabling them to work relationally and agentically with others.

References

Edwards, A. (2010). *Being an expert professional practitioner: The relational turn in expertise*. Dordrecht, Springer.
Edwards, A. (2012). The role of common knowledge in achieving collaboration across practices. *Learning, Culture and Social Interaction, 1*(1), 22–32.
Edwards, A. (Ed.) (2017). *Working relationally in and across practices: A cultural-historical approach to collaboration*. New York: Cambridge University Press.
Edwards, A., Daniels, H., Gallagher, T., Leadbetter, J., and Warmington, P. (2009). *Improving inter-professional collaborations*. London: Routledge.
Elkonin, D. B. (1999). Towards the problem of stages in the mental development of children. *Journal of Russian and East European Psychology, 37*(6), 11–30.
Hedegaard, M. (2008). A cultural-historical theory of children's development. In M. Hedegaard and M. Fleer (Eds), *Studying children: A cultural-historical approach* (pp. 11–29). Maidenhead: Open University Press.

Hedegaard, M. (2009). Children's development from a cultural-historical approach: Children's activity in everyday local settings as foundation for their development. *Mind Culture and Activity, 15,* 64–81.

Hedegaard, M. (2012). Analyzing children's learning and development in everyday settings from a cultural-historical wholeness approach. *Mind Culture and Activity, 19,* 127–38.

Hedegaard, M. (2014). The significance of demands and motives across practices in children's learning and development: An analysis of learning in home and school. *Learning, Social Interaction and Culture, 3,* 188–94.

Lord Laming. (2009). *The protection of children in England: A progress report.* London: The Stationery Office.

Taylor, C. (1977). What is human agency? In T. Mischel (Ed.), *The self* (pp. 103–35). Oxford: Basil Blackwell.

Vygotsky, L. S. (1998). *The collected works of L.S. Vygotsky, Vol 5 Child psychology,* ed. R. W. Reiber. New York: Plenum.

Part One

A Fresh Look at Professional Work with Children, Young People and Families

2

Child-Based Practice Development for Children in Areas of Concern: A Model for Enabling Both the Child's and the Teachers' Perspectives

Mariane Hedegaard

Introduction

This chapter presents a new way of working relationally with vulnerable children or children who are in a zone of concern. The zone of concern is chosen to indicate that the problems children present are not characteristic of the child itself, but are related to societal expectations of how children have to act in different institutional practices. Therefore, it is in these contexts that someone has a concern about a child or children. In the Danish system of social services for children, a change started in the 1980s and is still underway. This change can be characterized as 'the relational turn' (Edwards, 2010) where professionals in psychology and pedagogy instead of working as sole experts came to work relationally in cooperation with other professionals in day care and schools to analyse problems with children. Through the cooperation, common knowledge in relation to the problems – that is, knowledge of the professional motives, what matters professionally, for each collaborating professional (see Chapter 1 for an extended explanation of common knowledge) – may be created. Working relationally does not mean that the psychologists or the teachers lose their specialist expertise, but instead calls for an additional form of relational expertise. Edwards has formulated this kind of collaboration in the following way:

> The relational turn in expertise is not about *depending on* relationships and is not about ignoring the importance of structures. It is about knowing how to engage in fluid working relations in activities where actions are coordinated to provide

enriched responses to complex problems: these activities need structuring conditions which allow people to develop expertise in working with resources that are available to them. (Edwards, 2010: 41)

The change, from pedagogical psychologists being experts working with children separately from teachers to becoming facilitators for changes in school practice, started when school psychology service for school children in Denmark was reconfigured to become a service for all children from 0 to 18 years. But the relational turn did not happen overnight – it has been a long process and is not finished yet. This chapter aims at contributing to support this change. It also uses the Danish system to theorize how the relational turn in pedagogical psychological practice for creating common knowledge among collaborating professionals still has areas to be developed. For example, what matters for the children in focus has also to be included in this new approach (see Vassing, 2011b). In this chapter, the focus will be on how to include the teachers' and carers' views on what matters for them, as well as the child's perspective. I shall argue that by taking this stance the professionals are well placed to help in changing a child or children's social situations from a zone of concern to a zone of development and to support children in the transition from one institutional practice to a new one (i.e. home, nursery, kindergarten, school).

From school psychologist to pedagogical psychological consultant

When the former school psychological practice dominated, the psychologist was requested primarily to investigate behavioural or learning problems in the individual child or to locate cognitive, social or emotional deviancy. The psychologist, using various research methods and conversations with the child, was expected to diagnose the child's difficulties as well as suggest which pedagogical measures and special assistance, if any, are needed to be put in place (Szulevicz and Tanggaard, 2017). The approach was deemed serviceable because the institution or school was served relative to its immediate needs. However, this form of service has been criticized for assuming that behavioural or learning problems have to be found in the individual child. Critics have pointed out that the conditions for children's social interactions in everyday life have to be considered (Hedegaard, 1984, 2013 [1992]; Hedegaard and Chaiklin, 2011; Højholt, 2011a, b; Højholt and Szulevicz, 2017). The serviceable approach was built on the then-dominant child psychology, primarily Piagetian and Freudian psychology. Simultaneously, with the advancing critique of this version of school psychology, the dominant child psychology was criticized for not locating the child in her everyday life (James, Jenks and Prout, 1998; Corsaro, 1997) and for holding a conception of children that was not seen as historically anchored (Wartofsky, 1983). Burman (1994), for example, criticized the dominant child psychology for being too far removed from the child's everyday life and argued that a child psychology was needed to support practice with children who were in, what I am terming, 'zones of concern'.

In Denmark, this critique, together with new demands for school psychologists to work with not only school children but all children in zones of concern, led to new forms of school psychology. At the same time, there was a new way of organizing the institutional practices into pedagogical psychological centres, placing them in relation to a municipality's administration and as no longer directly connected to schools. These changes gave rise to new conditions and challenges for educational psychology practice, including the introduction of counselling and preventive methods. Inspiration for new approaches to working with vulnerable children came from Sweden between the 1980s and 1990s. There, ideas from how Caplan (1970) helped resolve the problem of the increase in numbers of children who needed help because of the wars in Israel became transformed into a systemic approach of consultation (Carlberg, Guvå and Teurnell, 1984; Hansson, 1995). This approach informed the relational turn for the Danish school psychology. Systemic consultation as a psychological method implies that psychologists, instead of giving advice, should see themselves as partners with other professionals and that solutions exist in the institutional practice. But one danger is that it may end up focusing on the teacher's problem and not taking the child's perspective into consideration.

Edwards's (2010, 2017) ideas that experts solving complex problems should work relationally, creating and using common knowledge, are very important. This chapter takes these ideas as points of departure to present a theoretical model for psychologists as consultants, enabling them to enter into a new psychological professionalism around children and young people in zones of concern in day care and school. The psychologist-consultant in the Danish system is located in a pedagogical psychology centre (PPC) under the municipality to which the school and day care belong. Teachers from a day care or school who are concerned about a child or children and who contact the PPC shall be called consultee. The premise is that the psychologist is a partner with the teacher who asks for help, in a consulting-oriented approach. In this approach, parents and other teachers can be involved, but it is central to the approach that, the perspectives of the child or children who are located in a zone of concern are sought when the professionals are working on practice change. I call this a *child psychological practice development* approach. The problems that are met in this approach are connected to a child or to children who are seen to be in a zone of concern, where the psychologist guides the joint analyses towards changing the child's social situation of development from a zone of concern to a zone of development. In this approach, I advocate that action observation of the participating child in her everyday life in school, in most cases, will be a useful strategy (Hedegaard, 2009).

By using interaction observation, it becomes possible to strengthen the psychologist's professionalism and engage in dialogue with the consultee about interpretations of the specific observed situations (Hedegaard and Chaiklin, 2011; Vassing, 2011a, b; Højholt and Szulevicz, 2013). The question is, therefore, how the psychology consultant can develop his or her cooperation to create a joint reflection space with the consultee, using interaction observations as a shared tool for analysing the zone of concern identified by the consultee.

From the very first meeting it is therefore important that the consultant and the consultee see each other as partners who both have to contribute to the solution of the problem that the consultee brings. How they work together as partners will be different in the different phases of the problem-solving process. The psychology consultant has the major responsibility for the theoretical analysis and for creating common knowledge by offering their motives and eliciting those of the consultee; the consultee has her major task in planning and realizing the intervention. But importantly, in all phases, a relationship must be maintained between them so that a successful intervention can lead to a change in a child or children's zone of concern.

Pedagogical psychology practice development for children in zones of concern

The systems approach (Carlsberg, Guvå and Teunell, 1984; Hansson, 1995; Lambert, Hylander and Sandoval, 2004) has encouraged psychologists' orientation towards interaction with other people in the concrete practice where a child's zone of concern is located. Therefore, in the systemic approach to consultation, children are not seen as having a problem, but seen as being in difficulty, which necessitates an analysis of practice. The practice development approach to consultation has its origins in psychology and is in some ways different from the systems approach. It also sees the child as being in difficulty, but differs from the systems-oriented consultant approach by taking into consideration the different perspectives of the people in the zone of concern. This *child-based practice development* approach requires both insight into and understanding of children's motive orientation related to developmental periods (the child's perspective) (Hedegaard, 2014; Chapter 1, this volume), as well as knowledge of the institutional daily practices of day care or school and home that the child participates in (the institutions' objectives and the teachers' and carers' perspectives).

To address the child's perspective, one has to conceptualize the child's social situation of development (Vygotsky, 1998; Chapter 1, this volume). But only by looking at the child's social situation of development from the perspectives of the child, the caregivers and the society, do we recognize the normative expectations which are the reasons for a child being in a zone of concern (Hedegaard, 2009). It is important that the psychologist is aware of how these norms contribute to locating a child in a zone of concern. The child's social situations in the different settings the child participates in together create her social situation of development. It is therefore only when we look at what the child is engaged in and oriented towards across settings, and see this in connection with the expectations and demands that the child has to meet, that a specific child's social situation of development becomes clear.

I have at times been presented with cases where *clarification of what is important (what matters) for the participants* has not been worked through. I will give an example from research about a consultation where the psychologist counsellor takes the expert role without explicating her developmental reasoning for this (Stæhr, 2018).

A case

A teacher has contacted a PPC for help, having problems with a boy in the third grade. The teacher describes the boy as having reading problems and concentration difficulties. A pedagogical psychologist from the centre has agreed to observe the boy in math and reading/writing lessons. She takes notes on her pad, but does not make a fully written observation. The psychologist has agreed to be observed and interviewed as part of a research project. After the psychologist has observed the child in the math lesson and the beginning of the reading/writing lesson, the psychologist makes a sign to the teacher and leaves the classroom. Outside she announces. There is nothing wrong with this boy. Then, after lunch, the psychologist has a shared meeting with the teacher who led the reading/writing class and the math and sports teachers. The school's vice director leads the meeting. The psychologist repeats her statement and gives examples from the math lesson to argue that the boy Mads takes initiative and solves the math tasks very creatively and that he does not seem to have concentration problems. The teacher then says that after the psychologist had left she asked Mads to find his reading book, but instead he started to walk around in the classroom. The teacher emphasized that the psychologist was not in the class when there were problems and did not observe what the problem was. The sports teacher remarked that perhaps the boy Mads had a problem with being accepted by his classmates. The vice director stops their discussion and says that they have to continue with the schemes for measurement and rewards they have constructed for home-school cooperation around Mads. Then the vice director asks the psychologist, since she does not think there is any problem with Mads, if they should do some pedagogical follow-up when Mads did not behave properly. The psychologist becomes uneasy because she is now expected to give a solution on what to do with Mads. Instead she suggests that she should have a talk with Mads, perhaps it could help her to get his point of view on what was going on, to find a solution.

Reviewing this case, we can see that the teacher consultee was frustrated because for her it seemed that the psychologist did not take her problem seriously. The psychologist tried to use observation to change the conceptual framework, bringing forward the child's perspective with her description of positive examples of how the child mastered the math lesson, which led to a confrontation. The more the psychologist focused on the positive stories, the more the teacher emphasized the problems. What the psychologist did not realize was that she had put herself in the expert position with her statement about Mads, and had not taken seriously the teacher's concern with Mads. It was therefore difficult for the psychologist to establish the meeting as a shared reflective space where they could work together to find common knowledge and a common solution. Furthermore, the observation was not a shared tool but only based on the psychologist's impressions and was used as a way for her to get information. Because the vice director wanted to have a solution to their problem, so they could move on to other matters, he also positioned the psychologist in the expert position without giving an opportunity to find a shared solution to the concern with Mads in school. This then became the sole responsibility of the psychologist.

This case illustrates the importance of building common knowledge (in this case, knowledge of what matters professionally to each practitioner) that could have expanded how the psychologist and teacher (consultee) interpreted the problem of Mads's learning. Doing so would have allowed the problem to become anchored by the relational expertise of the psychologist and teacher (Edwards, 2017).

Let us rethink the process using the strategy of the *child psychological practice development*. First, I will describe the three ideal phases in the strategy: (1) problem expansion through child development and practice analyses; (2) identification of goals of success and plan for intervention; and (3) intervention and evaluation of the success. Although the phases are sketched as a sequence, one can switch back and forth between the phases if that is necessary for the intervention to succeed. I briefly illustrate phase 1 in relation to the Mads example. Energies in phase 1 should have been directed at expanding the problem so both the child's and the institutions' perspectives could be included. The psychologist should have accepted that the teacher had a problem with the boy. It was relevant to include the boy's perspective, but the psychologist should have explained about what is important for children in early school age and given the teacher reasons for her suggestions so that she, together with the teacher consultee, could have used this as a starting point to analyse the concrete practice in the math and reading/writing lessons. Such an analysis would draw on the teacher's knowledge by including the goals in teaching a particular subject matter and the relations between the children. Such a sequence takes more time than what the vice director had allowed, but this could be one of the conditions that the psychologist has to demand in relation to being a consultant. One could then hope that the extended analyses could be the foundation for formulating the second phase: the goals of success and plans for intervention.

A case exemplifying the interaction observation and the challenges of child psychological practice development

In the example that follows, I show how interaction observation (Hedegaard, 2008), focusing on children in a zone of concern, can provide a basis for creating common knowledge and planning for activities and interactions for the involved persons and in doing so indicate areas where there are challenges for the work of the psychologist.

The project started as a collaboration between myself and a third grade class (class A) and their teacher on designing teaching. A second class, class B, from the same school also joined the project. Class A participated for three years finishing at fifth grade, while class B participated only in the fourth grade for one year. The project explored *the double move* in the teaching (Hedegaard, 2002). This teaching concept has been used in several projects.[1] The double move in teaching is characterized by the teacher guiding the children through the content and concepts of teaching by formulating tasks while the teacher always takes the children's understanding of the area as her departure. The process of class A's participation is described in Hedegaard (2002).

From analysing the protocols of activity observation and talking to the class teacher, I realized some months into the project that several children in class B were in a zone of concern. The teacher pointed to a group of children whom she was particularly worried about. At that point, I assumed the role of psychologist-consultant, while also remaining the researcher in the teaching project. As the psychologist-consultant, my task became to find solutions to the problems over the next three to four months. I will use this example to show how a *child psychological practice development* analysis can support a teacher in creating interventions for students in a zone of concern and what can go wrong.

The consultation task

The consultation task was divided into three periods. A first period referred to the analysis of the area of concern. In this analysis, a common understanding of children's development was formulated, so that common knowledge between the teacher, the researcher and student researchers could be built. This was followed by a practice analysis where the teacher's lessons were observed through the use of interaction observation in three teaching sessions. The second period was targeted at the formulation of success goals and an action plan. The third period was aimed at the realization of the action plan, where the teacher tried to accomplish the jointly formulated interventions of the teaching, which was, again, followed by interaction observation.

The double move in teaching: Class A and B's shared teaching project

Class B's teaching was based on the same ideas as class A, which was the double move in the teaching. Classes A and B collaborated in planning fourth grade teaching within the study of biology, history and geography. The teaching was oriented towards the origin of humans and the historical change of societies. The concepts in focus were how people's relation to nature, tools for production and division of labour created living conditions and different types of communities. In the experimental teaching, joint activities were developed for the two classes.

Two student-observers made action observations in both classes in each session of experimental teaching (three hours each week). Each week, I met with the two teachers and the student-observers to discuss the teaching using the observation protocols and to plan for the following week. Since it was a research project the teachers had some free time to participate in the planning.

The history of class B

I soon discovered that there were big differences between classes A and B with respect to student engagement. According to their head teacher, class B had a particularly unsettled history that started in kindergarten. In first grade, the teacher therefore gave up the traditional classroom education and divided the class into two groups: one with the troubled children, where the children had individual help, and the other which was oriented towards learning. In second grade, the teacher took maternity leave.[2] During this period, several students left the class and new students arrived. When the head teacher returned in third grade, another teacher connected with the class, the maths teacher, went on maternity leave, and the children had difficulties with the temporary maths teacher. At the end of the third grade, the head teacher nonetheless claimed that the class had become quite functional and she therefore enrolled in the teaching experiment. Class B was now only 15 students in fourth grade (12 girls and 3 boys). I, as a researcher, had not been informed about the problems when class B was introduced into the project. Later, class B's head teacher admitted that one of the reasons she wanted to participate in the project was that she thought it might help her to solve some of the problems she still experienced in her class. When the problems became clear to me, I decided to take on the parallel role in class B as consultant. One of the student-observers was allowed to undertake her thesis about the process (Røikjær, 1995).

When the 15 students in class B started fourth grade, they were divided into four groups. The double move in teaching is based on a division of work between the four groups and among the members in each group. Two of the children, Lise and Annie, in one of these groups with four students seemed especially to be in a zone of concern. These two girls struggled to concentrate on the teaching and most of the time played together and teased each other and the boy in the group (Mikkel), because they did not understand what they were supposed to do. This group became the focus for the consultant's task, which was to reformulate the teacher's zone of concern into a zone of development in order to change the interaction among the students and create learning. The group was observed for three periods of three hours each, over five weeks (the gaps were due to a museum visit and a winter holiday). In addition, there was special attention to one of the girls, Lise, who became the focus child for Røikjær's thesis.

Application of observation protocols from class B to formulate action plans

When the double move project meetings finished, the researcher, now working as a psychology consultant, the teacher, and Røikjær as a student-observer in class B continued with discussions about the children in the zone of concern. The observation protocols formed the basis for these discussions, where the teacher could comment both on the inaccuracies she found in the description and what she saw as the problems in the children's and/or her own actions. As the psychology consultant, I tried to orient the dialogue towards the following questions: What tasks and requirements do the children meet in the teaching? What was the children's motive orientation directed at? Which problems occurred during the teaching process?

The teaching content and tasks

The children had been working on the Stone Age and the Iron Age in the first half of the year. When the consultation started, the task was to finish a poster with an overview of 'what we know' and 'what we do not know' about human development in these periods. A pattern had been settled where the teacher oriented the students to the current teaching process by writing an agenda on the board in each session and explaining the different tasks.

The children's orientation towards the teaching tasks and their problems
Understanding of the assignments was missing

In the first session, the teacher's overview on the board was intended to form the basis for the children's assignments, preparing them for visits to a museum, and to formulate their own questions about the living conditions and use of tools that they would research at the museum. In the first hour in the first session after the initial instruction, nobody in Lise's group was aware of what to do.

Lise only listened partially, but the other three who listened attentively did not understand what to do and why. In the second hour of this period, the teacher went to their table, but her help was not enough. She did not explain the content they should work with, and the children still did not understand what to do. This was repeated again when the teacher returned and tried to get them started on the task, but they still did not know what to do. In the third hour, the student-observer helped them get started without children's understanding of the task becoming particularly clear.

The children's understanding of the task was missing in all the three analysed sessions. The observations showed that the teacher reviewed the task of the day and gave questions to the students. She demanded that the children themselves concretize the content of their assignment, but her questions did not make it clear for the children what to work with at the general level – that they should study how the people lived – so they did not succeed in concretizing the content.

In the first session, Annie answered the teacher's question of who 'the first people' were that it was Adam and Eve. Lise replied that it was God. The teacher perceived it as a provocation from the group, and did not understand that it was because the girls had no insight into what 'the first people' referred to.

Annie's and Lise's responses that the first people were Adam and Eve, and God, respectively, were repeated later. The general problem in all the three sessions was that the teacher did not go sufficiently into the content in her explanation. The problem became very clear when the teacher asked the class to answer if they had been adequately prepared for the museum visit and a girl from another group responded: 'My group could not understand what we should do, though we really listened.' Following this, the teacher asked the children to present their posters on 'What we know and do not know about the living conditions of humans in the Iron Age' without the concepts they used becoming clear, so they could not follow each other's presentation. The *group work* in Lise's group did not function. There was a constant conflict between Mikkel, who would like to work, and Lise and Annie, who were joking and teasing, and the fourth girl was just passive.

Lise's intentions and problems

Lise's activities in all the three observed sessions were interpreted as being oriented towards the children's community. She appeared to have problems with the content of teaching because it seemed that she was afraid she was not able to handle it. She had difficulty controlling her own activity in relation to the teaching objectives, and was therefore unable to formulate her own goals in relation to the assignment and meet the teacher's requirement of working independently. Her self-assessment seemed to be very low, so instead of working on the assignments, she tried to sidetrack the group's work by joking so that nobody could see that she could not work out what to do.

Success goals seen in connection with the general research project

The teacher and the consultant decided to initiate an intervention that was directed specifically at (1) the reorganizing of the student groups; (2) the teacher's instruction of the students; and (3) Lise's understanding of the tasks.

1) Cessation of an inappropriate group interaction:

    To support the focal group's orientation towards the content of the teaching, we decided to reorganize all groups so that the playful interactions between Annie and Lise and their teasing of Mikkel was stopped.

2) Change of the teacher's task instructions:

    The teacher would try to be clearer about the content. We agreed that the initial instruction was of great importance to improve the students' ability to engage, work purposefully and independently with the various tasks. We assumed that it would help the understanding of the tasks for all students in the class if the teacher went more into the content of the subject area (which requires a balance between telling enough about the tasks and still giving the students the possibility for exploration).

    The teacher also had to clarify the individual goals in each group based on an understanding of where the different children were in the process and to support how each one may contribute to the shared goal (e.g. to support the division of work in the groups).

3) Support Lise to understand the tasks and to get a better self-assessment:

    When Lise could not get started at a task, the teacher would ask her to repeat the task with her own words.

    The teacher should set close goals for her in the group work and then return to see how far she had come in solving the tasks.

    The teacher would remind her of how her work is part of the group's work as a whole.

The intervention

The intervention in class B was aimed at the class as a whole, at Lise's group and at Lise as a person. The intervention in relation to the class was aimed at clarifying the aspects that were specific to the experimental project.

Reorganizing the working groups

This process was started especially for the target children (Lise and Annie) to become oriented towards the tasks instead of teasing other children.

Change of the teacher's instruction in relation to the whole class

The content of the teaching in the three following periods was aimed at the Viking era. The teacher was to instruct the students in the next three sessions again on the concepts of nature, production of tools and creation of living conditions and community in the Viking Age. The students, after visiting a Viking exhibition, criticized the exhibition for having too few scenarios of how people lived in the Viking Age; therefore, the teacher decided that the children during the first intervention session should work on the production of miniature models. In the following two intervention sessions, the students continued to work on these clay models.

The teacher was able to associate her summary of previous teaching at the beginning of each session with the tasks for the day. Through questions, she got the students to formulate at the start of a session what they now knew about the Viking Age and what they did not know. The teacher structured the students' comments in relation to the three main concepts: nature, use of tools and way of life. At the last intervention session, however, the tasks were barely oriented towards a historical understanding of the Viking Age, but were nearer to being merely play with clay, which was only very superficially connected to a way of life or the use of tools.

Lise's change

Already, in the first intervention session, Lise took part in solving the tasks in her new group and made relevant suggestions for what she could contribute; she also engaged in the subsequent teaching session in a discussion of the task of how to model life forms. When the teacher asked the children to draw ideas before starting the model-building process, Lise drew a dinosaur, indicating that she still had an erroneous perception of prehistoric periods and very little understanding of the teaching content. But a change had started which could be seen in the second intervention session during which she took several books, from the book collection, and studied the pictures from the Viking Age, and later engaged in the teacher's reading of a novel from *The Golden Dragonhead* that was used to give the children insights into the ways of life and community in the Viking Age. During the third intervention session, Lise concentrated most of her time contributing to the modelling of a Viking settlement.

Evaluation

We can see that the teacher, by forming new groups, succeeded in moving Lise from a zone of concern to a development zone. A process was initiated. Lise began to orient herself towards the teacher's explanations of the tasks, probably because she would not be left outside of her new group's activity with the tasks. This meant that she also began to orient herself towards the content of teaching. At first sight, this appears to be a success. But if we look at the bigger picture, which is the teaching and the class activity as a whole, there was also a step back.

Instead of working with the historical concepts for building a holistic understanding of historical periods, the teacher's orientation towards the children's wishes meant that her management of the class in relation to the subject area became inadequate; so the class ended up working with an activity that was more relevant for learning in first grade than in fourth grade. The children worked on shaping scenarios in clay for almost three teaching sessions (nine lessons). Also, the head teacher in class B barely followed up on the planned activities in the joint meetings with the project group which included class A, and started to be absent at some of these meetings. Likewise, she did not follow the decisions on clarification of tasks for Lise's group or for Lise.

I, as the researcher/consultant, did not tackle this because it was difficult to both manage the double move project and create a space for joint reflection in the consultation process. The challenge here was to create shared agency with the teacher, building and sustaining common knowledge while keeping the problem of children's misconceptions in focus and to take Lise's perspective.

This experience made me wonder how a PPC consultant may participate in the process of formulating common knowledge and goals of success. The problem for a consultant is how to participate in achieving common decisions, which result in agreed activities. Although a PPC consultant and teacher may create a shared space for reflection, the PPC consultant has the responsibility to hold on to the goals of success as common goals. Sometimes, the retention of common goals can be a demanding task for the psychology consultant. Hopwood (2016) highlights this point in his analysis of counselling practice, where parents with infants in areas of concern can come for a week's stay with their infants to solve problems with sleep, diet or crying problems and the counsellor needs to hold firm on the desired outcomes.

It is a challenge to create a shared space for reflection and assume the role of consultant while still being both non-critical and sharing agency with the consultee so that the latter can take forward the intervention. Therefore, the relationship is imbued with problems of power and questions about whose knowledge counts for most, when the PPR consultant has more theoretical knowledge than the consultee and therefore, when necessary, may feel they need to assume the role of supervisor. However, it is still always a consultee who must be the one who takes forward and realizes the common action plans. The difficulties I encountered with class B led to a considerable amount of reflection on how it might have worked better as the problems were not entirely due to the dual role I inhabited. These reflections have produced the three-phase framework for enacting the role of psychologist-consultant within a practice-developing approach to collaboration between psychologists and other professionals, which I now discuss.

Phases in a child psychological practice development approach to consultation

Phase I: Problem expansion by analysing child development and practice

Problem expansion consists of three parts: (a) clarification of what is important for the participants, (b) alignment of understanding of child development that provides the tool for (c) analysing the concrete practice in which the concern is located.

Clarification of the problem of concern

The first task for the psychology consultant is to clarify for the consultee that they are partners in trying to solve the consultee's problem. Therefore, the first task is to create a common reflective space where the consultee can feel that their problem is accepted and that together with the consultant they can analyse and elaborate on the problem. In the case of Mads discussed earlier, where the psychologist stated that the boy did not have any problem, this may be experienced by the teacher that the psychologist denied that she needed to have any concern about the boy's way of acting in her lessons. This became a difficult situation for the psychologist, because she wanted to have an unbiased look at the child in the classroom. But I would have advised the psychologist to have a conversation with the teacher about what the teacher's concern was and together they should have clarified the teacher's area of concern. In order to expand the understanding of the problem, so the child's perspective should be included, it is necessary that the psychologist as a consultant explains her understanding of development and therefore her professional motives, and tries to find a shared agreement with the teacher consultee about what could be common knowledge for this case. 'Common knowledge, a respectful understanding of different professional motives, can then become a resource, which can mediate responsive collaborations on complex problems' (Edwards, 2017: 9). I therefore point to the need to explicate the psychological view of what is important for the child's age period worked with. It is important to recognize that the psychologist understands the intersection of practices of consultation and teaching: 'recognising similar long-term open goals, such as children's wellbeing, revealing professional values and motives in discussions, by legitimizing asking for and giving reasons for interpretations and suggestions; and listening to, recognising and engaging with the values and motives of others' (Edwards, 2017, p. 10).

Values connected to children's development

An understanding of children's development must be related to general assumptions about a good life for children in different age periods. What a good life is for a four-year-old child in preschool is different from what is a good life for a nine-year-old child in third grade. This can be seen both from children's perspectives and from the society's perspective. A good life course in a Danish context is primarily related to the family, day care, school and leisure-time institutions. The good life for children in day care is related to their possibility for play and close relations to other children and adults outside home and school, as well as getting experience about everyday life in their community. In school, the good life for children is that children participate in the learning activities and manage the demands for learning, as well as having a good interaction with other children and the teacher. The idea of a *child developmental psychological practice approach* to intervention is therefore to allow the psychology consultant together with the consultee to analyse what the child is oriented towards, what demands the child meets and whether they accept and can manage the demands in interaction with the other children and adults, or if the demands create any difficulties.

Analyses of practice

A practice analysis takes place through an informative conversation between the psychology consultant and the teacher consultee as well as other teachers who are connected with a child in a zone of concern (Hansson, 1995); through gaining knowledge of the institutional practices in which they participate in order to understand the teacher's problem; and through observing the child in different class settings, as in the case of Mads. In school, the focus may be on how a child participates in different activity settings, such as math or reading/writing lessons, how the interactions are taking place and whether there are misalignments and conflicts between the child's motive orientation and the demands. Participant observation is a key method for a *child psychological practice development* approach. Participant observation enables one to investigate the interaction between people in different activity settings that have been designated as sites of zones of concern so as to avoid locating the problem with in a child.

Interaction observation as a method of analysis

I have been focusing on a definitive version of participant observation method, described as interaction observation, which results in a written protocol (Hedegaard, 2009, 2013 [1992]). Interaction observations support a common reflective space for the psychology consultant and the consultee, where a joint discussion of an observation protocol gives opportunities for analysing the interaction between participants in a zone of concern. A key aspect of the use of interaction observation is that, because it follows children's activities in the zone of concern, it can provide clues for how to intervene and change practices that may support children's learning and bring them into a zone of development.

The starting point for interaction observation is the observer's presence in the specific situation. In this context, the observer is usually the psychology consultant, but it could be another person, for example a research assistant or a support teacher. The observer writes quickly and spontaneously, describing what she or he experiences as significant in the situation. In order to get the child's perspective, the method is based on the interaction between the child and the other participants in the setting. Only through active participation in the situation does the observer get an opportunity to understand what the child is oriented towards and what is required of the child (what demands the child meets). This approach enables the observer to gain insights into how the child realizes his or her intentions or is prevented from doing so, and how the child reacts to requirements and how others react to the child's demands. The activities the children participate in and the setting being observed must be interpreted in order to explicate (1) the child's intentions and concerns; (2) environmental demands that are reflected in the child's participation in activities and interaction; (3) the child's interpersonal and conflictual relations with other people; and from this conclude about (4) the child's motive orientation, competences and areas of concern. Though this interpretation is the psychologist's own, and although it may guide his or her interaction with the consultee, the consultee also has to read the observation protocol and make his or her own suggestions.

In the cases that I draw on here, it is the practice in school that comes into focus for children in a zone of concern. This does not mean that family practice is irrelevant, but that, as Hansson (1995) very rightly points out, the psychologist working with a teacher team about a problem should only involve the parents through the teacher's invitation because the psychologist-consultant needs to be loyal to the person who has asked for help. This does not mean that parents cannot participate in joint meetings about their child in school settings. But if the psychologist-consultant considers that a child's zone of concern is centrally rooted in family practice, in a degree that surpasses the school's capacity for contact, she must take steps to involve another psychologist or social worker who can work with the family.

Phase II: Changing a zone of concern to a development zone through the formulation of success goals and an action plan

Setting success goals requires a holistic analysis to take into account all the involved partners. In this context, the task of the psychology consultant is to help balance the various success goals so that the child's and the teacher's success goals are also included; the parent's goals should also be included if they had been involved by the teacher. The outcome is then a common formulation of the development zone that an action plan is aimed at. The observation protocol that a psychology consultant shares with a consultee teacher can be seen as a mirror for the teacher's activities together with the child or children. This mirror can, through the teacher's comments and the psychologist's questions, become an interpretation of the activities where both the teacher's and the child's intentions and wishes can be seen in connection with the demands that they put on each other. If the observation has to be used in meetings where others are involved in the debate, the teacher has to accept this. The observation together with debates where other teachers or parents also participate may enable different perspectives to be seen and the formulation of goals of success from these perspectives. The joint analysis of the consultant's observation of the interaction in the different activity settings in school practice should not only provide the basis for formulating the development zone, directing towards the goals of success, but also give ideas for intervention.

Phase III: Realization of the action plan

It is the teacher and other responsible adults who have the opportunity to change conditions so that the child can move from being located in a zone of concern to being seen in a development zone. It is important that the psychology consultant, when the zone of concern for a child or group of children has been formulated as a development zone, helps the consultee teacher/team to see that the way forward is not to start training the child or the children through direct instruction.

The realization of an action plan formulated jointly by the psychology consultant and the consultee becomes ultimately the consultee's task, as it is in the concrete practice where the problem and concern are located and where intervention has to be made. The example above with Lise shows how success goals resulting from such an analysis can be formulated as action plans that are intended to be realized through planned interventions. Action plans often need to be renegotiated and revised, but working with the everyday practice where the problem exists allows for changes for the child or children who have been located in a zone of concern. New problems may then become visible, as the example shows, and will be discussed in the conclusion.

Conclusion

The aim of this chapter has been to support changing the role of psychologists from isolated experts to collaborators with other professionals and change their way of seeing children as problems to see them in zones of concerns, where collaboration between professionals may change this to a zone of development. There are several different models for how to be a consultant. This chapter is based on a cultural-historical understanding of children's development as formulated in interaction observation (Hedegaard, 1984), and later developed further in Hedegaard (2009, 2012), Hedegaard and Chaiklin (2011) and Vassing (2011a, b). This approach is aimed at a developmental psychological practice analysis through dialogue in a shared reflective space between the consultant and the consultee, using observation of the everyday practice where the consultee anchors her problems. In this chapter, I have argued that, from this model, it is possible to create a common space for cooperation between the consultee and the psychology consultant. This does not conflict with the systemic psychology consultant approaches (Hansson, 1995). However, there are decisive differences in *the child psychological practice developmental approach* the consultant is expected to contribute to a change, both from the perspective of the children and from the perspective of practice.

If a shared space for reflection is to be successful, it should be aimed at changes in practice that are in line with the institution's goals as well as the development goals for the children. It is the consultant's task to evaluate this. If the consultant is too friendly it can be difficult to create change. In the teaching experiment that led to the reflections behind the three-phase approach, the psychology consultant was not strong enough to point out that the construction of scenarios with clay became a play activity and not a process of education, where the children might acquire key concepts that could support their exploration of historical periods. At the same time the psychologist-consultant should not take refuge in their high-status expertise; instead they need to exercise relational expertise and build a mutual understanding of what matters for the other stakeholders as well as being explicit about what matters for them as a psychologist. To be able to make such demands probably means that, as Hansson (1995) points out, a written contract has to be established that mutually commits the psychology consultant and the teacher consultee to proceed to find an acceptable shared solution.

In summary, the psychology consultant's task is to build common knowledge and use it as a resource to challenge the consultee, so that a process of change can take place within a child's or children's zone of concern directed at their zone of development.

Notes

1 Hedegaard (1988 [1995]), Hedegaard and Sigersted (1992), Hedegaard and Chaiklin (2005).
2 In the Danish system maternity leave is one year.

References

Burman, E. (1994). *Deconstructing developmental psychology*. London: Routledge.
Caplan, G. (1970). *The theory and practice of mental health consultation*. New York: Basic Books.
Carlberg, M., Guvå, G., and Teurnell, L. (1984). *Konsulentarbejde i daginstitutioner*. Copenhagen: Dansk Psykologisk Forlag.
Corsaro, W. A. (1997). *The sociology of childhood*. Thousand Oaks, CA: Pine Forge.

Edwards, A. (2010). *Being and expert professional practitioner*. Dordrecht: Springer.
Edwards, A. (Ed.). (2017). *Working relationally in and across practices. A cultural-historical approach and collaboration* (pp. 1–24). New York: Cambridge University Press.
Hansson, U. (1995). *Konsultation som psykologisk metode i skolen*. Copenhagen: Dansk Psykologisk Forlag.
Hedegaard, M. (1984). Interaktionsbaseret beskrivelse af småbørn og børnehaveklassebørn i deres dagligdag. *Psykologisk Skriftserie Aarhus*, 9(4), 1–75.
Hedegaard, M. (1988). *Skolebørns personlighedsudvikling set gennem orienteringsfagene*. Aarhus: Aarhus University Press.
Hedegaard, M. (1998 [1995]). *Udvikling af tænkning og motivation i skolealderen*. Aarhus: Aarhus University Press.
Hedegaard, M. (2002). *Learning and child development*. Aarhus: Aarhus University Press.
Hedegaard, M. (2008). Developing a dialectic approach to studying children's development. In M. Hedegaard and M. Fleer (Eds), *Studying children. A cultural-historical approach* (pp. 10–64). New York: Open University Press.
Hedegaard, M. (2009). Child development from a cultural-historical approach: Children's activity in everyday local settings as foundation for their development. *Mind Culture and Activity*, 16, 64–81.
Hedegaard, M. (2012). Analyzing children's learning and development in everyday settings from a cultural-historical wholeness approach. *Mind Culture and Activity*, 19, 127–38.
Hedegaard, M. (2013 [1992]). *Beskrivelse af småbørn*. Aarhus: Aarhus University Press.
Hedegaard, M. (2014). The significance of demands and motives across practices in children's learning and development: An analysis of learning in home and school. *Learning, Social Interaction and Culture*, 3, 188–94.
Hedegaard, M., and Chaiklin, S. (2005). *Radical-local teaching and learning*. Aarhus: Aarhus University Press.
Hedegaard, M., and Chaiklin, S. (2011). Supporting children and schools: A developmental and practice-centered approach for professional practice and research. In H. Daniels and M. Hedegaard (Eds), *Vygotsky and special needs education* (pp. 86–108). London: Bloomsbury.
Hedegaard, M., and Sigersted, G. (1992). *Undervisning i samfundshistorie*. Aarhus: Aarhus University Press.
Hopwood, N. (2016). Professional pedagogies of parenting that build resilience through partnership with families at risk: A cultural-historical approach, *Pedagogy, Culture and Society*, 24, 599–615.
Højholt, C. (Ed.). (2011a). *Børn i vanskeligheder*. Copenhagen: Dansk Psykologisk Forlag.
Højholt, C. (2011b). Communities of children and learning in schools. In H. Daniels and M. Hedegaard (Eds), *Vygotsky and special needs education* (pp. 67–85). London: Bloomsbury.

Højholt, C., and Szulevicz, T. (2013). Observation som konsultativ praksisform. *Pædagogisk Psykologisk Tidsskrift*, 5, 36–47.

James, A., Jenks, C., and Prout, A. (1998). *Theorizing childhood*. Southern Oaks, CA: Polity Press.

Lambert, N. M., Hylander, I., and Sandoval, J. H. (2004). *Consultee-centered consultation: Improving the quality of professional services in schools and community organizations*. London: Erlbaum.

Røikjer, A. (1995). Forholdet mellem selvbevidstheden og faglige præstationer. Kandidatspeciale, Department of Psychology, Aarhus University.

Stæhr, H. (2018). Psykologens konsultative arbejde med observationer I PPR – med fokus på barnets perspektiv. Kandidatspeciale, Department of Psychology, Copenhagen University.

Szhulevicz, T., and Tanggaard, L. (2017). *Educational psychology practice*. Dordrecht: Springer.

Vassing, C. (2011a). Developing educational consultative practice in school framed with cultural-historical theory of child development. In H. Daniels and M. Hedegaard (Eds), *Vygotsky and special needs education* (pp. 109–27). London: Bloomsbury.

Vassing, C. (2011b). Developing the practice of educational psychology consultation in schools to become supportive to the development of children in difficulties. PhD thesis, Department of Psychology, Copenhagen University.

Vygotsky, L. S. (1998). *The collected works of L. S. Vygotsky: Vol. 5. Child psychology*. New York: Plenum.

Wartofsky, M. (1983). The child's construction of the world and the world's construction of the child. From historical epistemology to historical psychology. In F. S. Kessel and A. W. Siegel (Eds), *The child and other cultural innovation* (pp. 188–215). New York: Praeger.

3

Common Knowledge between Mothers and Children in Problematic Transitions: How Professionals Make Children's Motives Available as a Resource

Nick Hopwood and Teena Clerke

Introduction

Children's learning and development are interconnected with why and how they take part in practices in institutions (Hedegaard, 2008; Hedegaard and Edwards, 2014; Hedegaard, Edwards and Fleer, 2012). The family is one such institution, comprising everyday settings that can be studied to understand the social situation of children's development (Hedegaard, Fleer, Bang and Hvid, 2008). Our interest is in how professionals help parents construct a social situation of development with the child.

We examine three cases where transitions in the everyday practices of a family became a zone of concern and help was sought from professionals. This help was provided in institutional settings of a day-stay clinic, a parent education course and a toddler clinic. The potential of cultural-historical concepts in understanding interventions that straddle home and professional early intervention institutions is not yet fully realized. We explore how specialist expertise is taken up in collaborative work with parents so that parent–child interactions change in response to problematic transitions. This addresses Hedegaard et al.'s (2008) call for studies of how others contribute to children's intentional activities and interactions. We show how professionals enable parents to support children's transitions through actions informed by specialist expertise and an understanding of a child's perspective. Approaching the issue of children's transitions from a different angle, the chapter extends the cultural-historical literature on forms of expertise in the ways adults work together around children at risk.

The focus on change orients the analysis to revealing how possibility – *what can be* – emerges (Chaiklin, 2012). The cases illustrate commonly occurring problems that arise in children's everyday activities (Hedegaard, 2008). The concerns discussed are a newborn infant learning to breast feed, a seven-month-old transitioning from breast milk to solid foods and a toddler adjusting to joint play with his younger sibling. These are middle-level transitions within the family institution, spanning weeks and months in their accomplishment. They are between what Keisanen, Rauniomaa and Siitonen (2017) describe as macro (e.g. between day care and school) and micro (e.g. between play and getting ready for bed) levels. This chapter connects with and builds on prior work investigating changes within families through such a middle-level analysis (e.g. Hopwood, 2017; Hopwood and Edwards, 2017; Hopwood and Gottschalk, 2017; Hopwood, Clerke and Nguyen, 2018).

Development arises in ongoing social interactions rather than 'under the skull' (Stetsenko and Arievitch, 2004). At issue in interactions between parents, children and professionals are questions of how people create meaning in collaboration (Kaptelinin, Vadeboncoeur, Gajdamaschko and Nardi, 2017). How does professional expertise create new meaning in interactions between parents and children? Folding questions of professional expertise into understandings of collaboration around children's development leads us to work with a novel combination of cultural-historical concepts. These include the social situation of development (Vygotsky, 1998; Hedegaard, 2012, 2018), common knowledge (Edwards, 2017) and the space of reasons (Derry, 2014).

The children we focus on range in age from nine weeks to three and a half years. A motive-focused approach, taking up contemporary readings of Vygotsky, Leontiev and Elkonin, can be applied across our three cases. Children start to orient themselves intentionally to the world in interaction with others *from the moment they are born* (Hedegaard, 2018). The dynamic of children's development springs from this intentional orientation (Hedegaard, 2008, referring to Bruner, 1968). Zinchenko suggests that 'the infant is far from being indifferent to the language atmosphere that surrounds it' (2012, p. 70) and that voice and word are meaningful in a baby's life from birth. A child's intentional orientation is a relation between motives in activity and the demands of institutional practice (Hedegaard, 2008). Development involves qualitative change in the child's motive and competence, connected to a change in her social situation (Hedegaard and Chaiklin, 2011).

Motives, demands and the social situation of development

> In order to understand children we must be cognisant of the social, cultural and historical practices in which they live and learn. That is, we need to be aware of the social situation of children's development. (Hedegaard et al., 2008, p. 1)

The social situation of development became a focus in Vygotsky's later life (Daniels, 2012); so contemporary work often draws on his collaborators, including Leontiev and Elkonin. Leontiev (1978, 1981) understood the social situation of development as a system of relations between a developing subject and her surroundings, as well as demands and expectations imposed by the social environment (Karabanova, 2010; Hedegaard and Chaiklin, 2011). Examining a child's social situation requires understanding the child's perspective, interpreting her motive orientation in specific activity settings in institutional practices and observing how she meets the demands placed on her (Hedegaard, 2018). Hedegaard (2018) frames such demands in Lewinian terms that address the dialectic of child-environment relations – as forces from the world and from the child. This proposes the active or agentic position of a child in developing self-milieu relations (Karabanova, 2010; Stetsenko and Ho, 2015).

The child is thus conceived as an active agent who can co-create conditions for her own learning and development. Others, especially adults, play a crucial role in shaping these conditions (Hedegaard et al., 2012); children are far from passive recipients of support offered by those around them (Zinchenko, 2012). Vygotsky's great insight – that all intrasubjective processes first originate as intersubjective ones – is maintained (Stetsenko and Arievitch, 2004).

Relations in a child's social situation of development are created by the coordination of activities around the child (Hedegaard and Chaiklin, 2011). We focus on how professional expertise enables parents to adjust this coordination. Demands from caregivers and the possibility of children realizing their own intentional activity within a social situation lead to development (Hedegaard, 2008). Motives are created as children experience and participate in activities, what Elkonin regarded as a dialectic between competence and motive in child development. The agentic child meets demands from others and puts demands on others. Transitions are jointly accomplished achievements, shaped by participants' moment-to-moment contributions (Keisanen et al., 2017).

> The dynamic tension between the agency of the child and the demands and affordances of an activity setting, as played out in each activity, is where learning occurs. ... This analytic emphasis on demands calls for attention to both how children act in relation to the demands in the practices and activities they move

between; and how experienced participants in those practices and activities mediate the demands that are placed on children as learners. (Hedegaard and Edwards, 2014, p. 186)

The cultural-historical researcher is thus concerned with the demands that practices put on children and how possibilities for children to respond to these are generated. We explore how professional expertise can be used to make such demands and the children's motive orientation explicit.

Common knowledge

Focusing on practices necessitates analytical attention to motives, as practices are 'knowledge-laden, imbued with cultural values, and emotionally freighted by the motives of those who already act in them' (Edwards, 2010, p. 5). A cultural-historical notion of motive adopts a relational logic (Chaiklin, 2012). Motives are not understood as properties of people (adults or children). Rather, they are conceived *outside* the individual (Fleer, 2012; Stetsenko and Arievitch, 2004), arising as a dynamic relation between person and practice. Leontiev (1978) connects motive with problems people are working on – activities and what matters in those activities (see Hedegaard et al., 2012; Edwards, 2017). Motives give activities a determined direction and bring the person and object into a dialectical relationship. Motives make actions meaningful in social situations (Daniels, 2012).

Common knowledge concerns understanding what matters to others (Edwards, 2011, 2012a, b, 2017), and is related to concepts of relational agency and relational expertise (Edwards, 2017). Focusing on relational forms of practice, these concepts shift analytical attention from individual action to action with others. Common knowledge was suggested as a mediator of relational agency at sites of intersecting practices (Edwards, 2011). Rai (2017) and Hopwood and Edwards (2017) broadened this to consider how professionals and parents work together. The latter pointed to a key aspect of intervention relating to shifting parents' understanding of and response to children's needs. We pick up where that analysis left off, showing how common knowledge is crucial in changing interactions between parents and children.

Common knowledge consists of the motives that participants bring to working on a problem (Edwards, 2017), that is, what matters. It can be conceived as a second stimulus – a cultural resource or tool used to work on a problem (Vygotsky, 1997 [1960]; Edwards, 2017). The point is not that what matters has to be the same for each party, but that efforts are needed to make what matters explicit and align actions to the motives of others.

Space of reasons

Knowledge of what matters to others can help understand their reasons for acting in particular ways (Derry, 2014). Humans, including young children, can respond not just to causes, but to reasons and the environment is 'second nature' – made meaningful through the significance given to it in social practices (Derry, 2007). Derry quotes Vygotsky to argue that concepts feature in children's learning not as representations of the world, but as bases for inferences:

> According to our hypothesis, we must seek the psychological equivalent of the concept not in general representations … we must seek it in a system of judgments in which the concept is disclosed. (Vygotsky, 1998, p. 55)

The space of reasons refers to this system of judgements. The fact that the child may not explicitly articulate reasons does not mean reasons are not in play. Interpreting these reasons, entering the space of reasons from the child's perspective, forms a key focus of professional work with parents, which simultaneously changes parents' own space of reasons and the inferences they make in relation to their children.

Study details

We focus on three families who participated in the longitudinal phase of a larger study (see Hopwood and Edwards, 2017; Hopwood et al., 2018). Data collection began with observation of interactions between professionals, parents and children in a range of services. Parents (in these instances, mothers) were interviewed while their participation in each service was ongoing, shortly after it was completed, and once or twice more several months later. The professionals working with the families were also interviewed during and immediately after their work with the families. Table 3.1 summarizes the three cases and data collected in relation to them. These examples correspond to three generally occurring problems (Hedegaard, 2008): problems between mother and child in relation to breastfeeding, those in relation to weaning from breast milk, and difficulties when children are expected to share during play. These were taken up as zones of concern between the triad of professional, parent and child.

Table 3.1 Overview of data collection

Parent and child	Child age[1]	Service	Transition	Problem	Final interview[2]
Mary and Siân	9 weeks	Day stay	From passive feeding in the womb to breastfeeding	Breastfeeding nutrition concerns, maternal anxiety	8 months later
Ching and Fia	7 months	Circle of Security[3]	From breastfeeding to eating solids	Maternal and child distress at mealtimes	4 months later
Marlie and George	3.5 years	Toddler clinic	From playing alone to (shared) play with his younger brother	George's physical aggression and tantrums	5 months later

[1] At time of first appointment with service.
[2] Months elapsed between conclusion of work with service and final interview with parent.
[3] See Powell et al. (2016).

Transition from passive feeding in the womb to breastfeeding

Mary was referred to a day-stay service due to difficulties in feeding the nine-week-old Siân (see Table 3.1). Day-stay services involve parents visiting specialist centres two or three times, for several hours each time (see Hopwood and Edwards, 2017). Siân's significant weight loss in the days and weeks after birth raised concerns about nutrition. Breastfeeding was a major zone of concern for Mary, who was constantly either trying to feed Siân or expressing milk and trying to boost supply while Siân slept. The day prior to her first appointment, she didn't leave the bedroom all day. She explains:

> Last night she was pulling off a lot. She'll suck for a little while and fall asleep after getting herself in such a state. She works herself into a frenzy and literally goes rigid and then knocks herself out. … I'm worried if I don't have enough milk, how much is she actually getting? How do I tell if she's getting enough?

Her later reflection on these early weeks conveys how difficult things had become:

> I was doing 10 minutes, 10 minutes, trying to take a break, giving her a bottle, trying to go back again because I was worried about the supply. It was just a nightmare, so I was on the edge.

Three-hour attempts to feed in the day left Mary exhausted, anxious and frustrated. She felt at least part of the problem lay with Siân, remarking 'Oh what's the matter? What's the matter with you?' during the first feed at the day stay. What was going on for Siân seemed confusing: she fussed at the breast, protested when taken off, but then took from a bottle; her feeds throughout the day and from day to night were inconsistent. Figure 3.1 conceptualizes this initial situation.

Early on, Hilary, the nurse working with Siân, explained how feeding at this age can be understood in terms of a transition from the womb:

> You go back to the nine months of utero, gulping the amniotic fluid. Everything's provided on tap and then suddenly I'm here. They must feel quite strange and vulnerable. ... So they can give us a lot of mixed messages, so it's trying to discern what's happening.

Hilary framed the transition from passive feeding to practices in which Siân has to be an active co-participant as both physically and emotionally challenging for the infant. This provided a foundation for exploring what matters to Siân. Hilary explained that Siân needs help regulating her emotions and that frequent feeding and being in arms can be a 'survival tactic' especially later in the day when very young infants find emotional regulation harder and so tend to cluster feed (feed several times in close succession). Hilary's suggestion that feeding and sleeping are closely linked at this age gave reasons for apparently confusing messages about whether the child is hungry, in pain or tired.

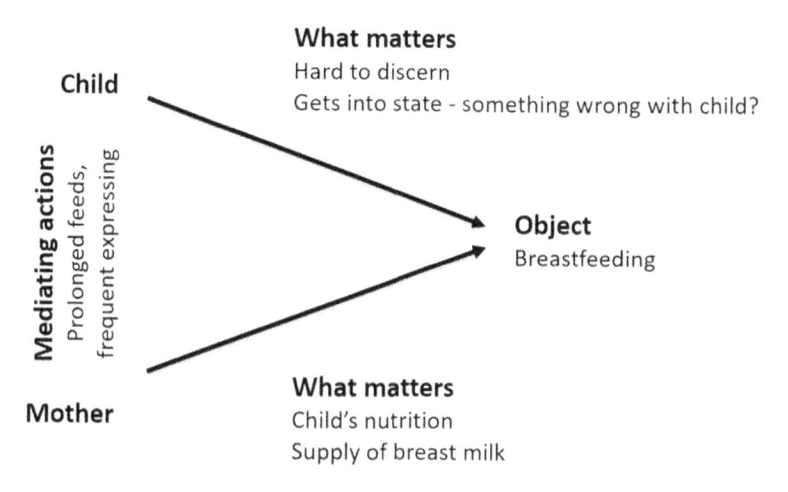

Figure 3.1 Mary and Siân prior to the day stay.

Hilary suggested offering the breast before the bottle as a means to support the child's learning to feed from the breast, given this was such a concern for Mary:

> We always say go for the breast first so at least they learn that's what they do first, versus if the bottle comes in a lot more on the first instance, that's what they might start to prefer because they don't have to work so hard.

Hilary explained the importance of Siân having a positive experience of breastfeeding. This meant both mother and child should be relaxed and that Siân should have a 'say' as to what she needs and wants in the process. A time limit was put on the breastfeed, after which the bottle would be offered. Hilary made the period *between* feeds significant as a means to interpret what Siân's needs might be, particularly because hungry and tired cries are difficult to distinguish at this early age. The nurse explained how to use other information as 'clues to what Siân needs' – building up a space of reasons that connects the mother and child.

> The only way we can work things out is thinking, well, what are the weight gains like? What are her wet nappies, poos like? What was that last feed like? How long ago was it? Well, it was three hours ago. It was a good feed but she must be hungry. It was two hours ago. You barely had anything, so maybe you are hungry. So it's a lot of that logical thought to help discern what's going on, because how do you tell the difference between a hungry cry, tired cry, pain cry?

Hilary also showed how visual and aural cues during a breastfeed can be used to tell what is happening and infer what Siân needs.

> Hilary: Because I can see the jaw line and her temple move. It's just getting the right position.
> Mary: She goes off a lot. Her grasp is quite shallow.
> Hilary: Okay. I can hear her swallowing a little bit there.
> ...
> Hilary: We can see she's actually doing the action. Rather than just going on and doing a little bit of comfort suction, she's trying to do that good suck. So all we can do is go by her.

Giving the child a break during the feed, and Mary prompting and supporting Siân to persist, were tested as ways to maintain feeding as relaxed and positive for the child. Hilary suggested Mary verbalize what is happening, balancing taking charge herself with following Siân's lead.

If she looks a bit sleepy, I'll wake you up, take you off, remind you 'now come on, you've got some more work to do here', and see what she does. We'll give her a break, a bit of breathing space. We don't want it to become frustrating for her or for you. ... If she's getting a bit too sleepy and half-hearted about it, well, no, we're not going to tolerate that. ... So we'll just remind her this is feed time. I can give you a break, reoffer. That's fine. The more you do that, the more she'll realize this is when the shop is open, so to speak, this is when I need to do everything I need to do. Otherwise once it closes, that's it until next time.

Hilary also addressed what mattered to Mary. The mother's motives expanded in ways that aligned with new understandings of Siân. A positive experience of feeding was equally important to Mary. The time-limited feed was redefined to include a short time for her to express breast milk, also a means to promote milk supply:

If you are feeding every two hours and trying to express halfway between that for an hour or more, your body doesn't get time to build the supply back up. That's why I want to, as much as possible, consolidate the feed, get you expressing straight after the feed, so you have a couple of hours break.

Hilary connected these ideas with Mary's self-care:

Rather than all I seem to be doing all day is feeding you, if we can make it a little bit more reasonable for you, how can we cut back on the workload there? We're moving on, because it's distressing for you, distressing for her ... you still need time for you. You need to get out, you need sanity, to get out of these four walls. ... How can we consolidate it all to make it reasonable for all of you?

Feeding was thus reinterpreted as about a positive, relaxed relationship between parent and child. The quotes below come from follow-up interviews, concluding when Siân was 10 months old, when these ideas and actions had become embedded in institutional practices of the family.

I don't get as frustrated whereas before I would have persisted for at least half an hour with trying to get her on, taken the bottle out, she'd scream, try and latch her on. It was quite distressing for both me and Siân. Now if she starts to get stressed I just stop. I don't persist with it because it's not fair on her.

If I'm not patient with her, I'm going to get frustrated and it's going to rub off on Siân. That's why that's really important to keep it calm for her. I want her to have the best start that she can have, calm and easy-going as possible.

I'm happier because I get a little break as well throughout the day.

Child

What matters
Being supported by parent
Having messages understood
Having a say
Enjoying feeding

Mediating actions
Consolidated feeds, time out, verbalising

Object
Breastfeeding

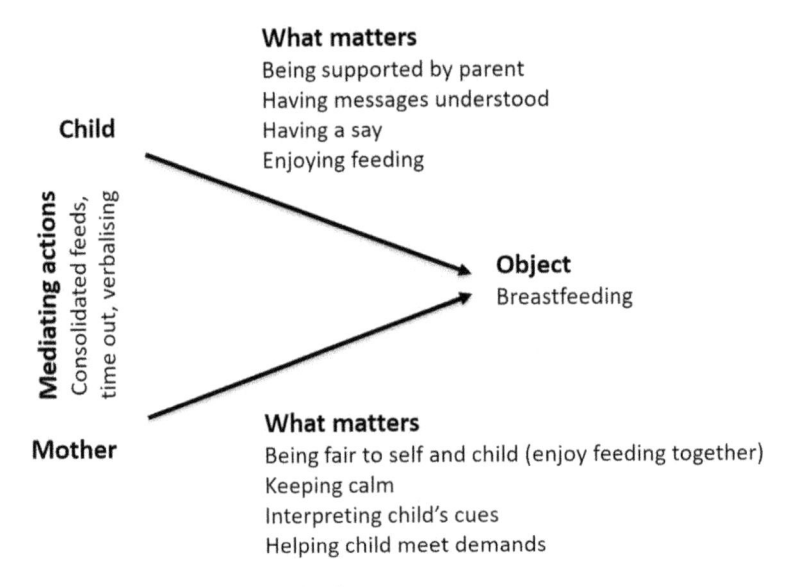

Mother

What matters
Being fair to self and child (enjoy feeding together)
Keeping calm
Interpreting child's cues
Helping child meet demands

Figure 3.2 Mary and Siân after the day stay.

These quotes convey the significant breakthrough in the zone of concern for Mary, and how Siân was supported in the transition from the womb to the world. Mary's comment shows attunement to Siân and a flexible balance between following her cues, giving her a 'say' and stepping in when needed. A new space of reasons is clearly expressed in Mary's comments. Figure 3.2 conceptualizes this new scenario, in which Mary supports Siân as an agentic learner in a social situation of development, responding to what matters to the child in a new space of reasons.

Transition from breastfeeding to eating solids

Ching completed a parenting course called Circle of Security-parenting (Powell, Cooper, Hoffman and Marvin, 2016). Her zone of concern was her daughter Fia's transition to solid foods, which Ching had introduced two months prior. At the time the course started, Fia was seven months old. Ching had experienced depression and anxiety since Fia's birth, describing her own parents as unsupportive and emotionally unavailable. Circle of Security involves a two-hour class every week for eight weeks, for parents of children from a few months to several years old. Each class involves watching a DVD that introduces key ideas, and taking part in a group discussion facilitated in this case by two child and family health nurses. The facilitating nurses helped parents link generic ideas from the DVD to concrete instances concerning what matters to them. Ching described feeding Fia as problematic for both her and her daughter prior to the course:

> When she's refusing I'm upset and I always try to push her to eat. I force her to accept the food. Even then she's turning away, and even when she's screaming, she opens her mouth, right? I try to put food into her mouth, then she screams harder. It's like 'Ah, I don't want this, how come you do this to me again?'

Ching found the mess associated with trying to feed Fia hard to cope with – one of several aspects where she felt she was losing control in life. Concerns that Fia wasn't eating enough were amplified when she refused food, eroding Ching's confidence in herself as a parent. Figure 3.3 conceptualizes this initial situation.

The course suggests that children's behaviour can be understood as a form of communication. This means not seeing the child as the problem and seeking to change the child's behaviour, but to 'hear and respond to the message'. The message may not always be clear – for example, what seems like a 'being difficult' cry can mean 'I'm lost, I need you'. Ching expressed this on her own terms:

> You have to see through the behaviour. There's nothing wrong with the behaviour because they don't know what is right and wrong. Their behaviour is usually saying their needs. You have to try to figure out what's their needs.

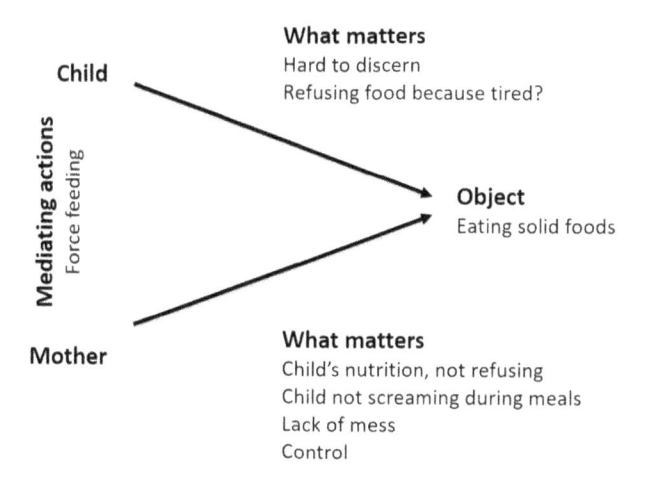

Figure 3.3 Ching and Fia prior to Circle of Security.

The facilitators used this idea to open up new reasons why Fia might refuse food and scream, and underpinned Ching's understanding that, at these moments, what Fia needs is a connection with her parents and for her parents to help her. This was referred to as an 'organize my feelings' moment for the child, where the parent responds by being with the child, naming their emotions. The facilitators explained that the transition to solids involved new tastes and textures, and demands the infant learn to regulate the pace and volume of eating. Ching realized that transitioning to solid food was hard for Fia and that refusal reflected in this struggle.

Ching particularly embraced the course mantra 'being bigger, stronger, wiser and kind' as a means to cope when Fia found things difficult. What mattered to the mother was to become close to Fia and help her understand what she was experiencing by taking the child through the process:

> The most important theory was you have to recognize the emotion instead of ignoring them. Try to help children name it. … As long as you are being there with her, and keep talking and help them to realize what is happening. … Let her know that she's not alone.

Associated with this was a suggested balance between trusting the child and the need for parents to step in. The idea of behaviour as communication helped Ching to see Fia as a little person with her own thoughts, desires and needs. It also helped her identify moments when Fia relied on others. Several months after the course, she said:

> So that's why the being strong, bigger, wiser and kind thing is always in my head now. You have to see the child's need and understand what is the need. Then whenever necessary you have to take charge.

Following the translation of the general ideas of the course to Ching's specific context, Fia was given more say at feeding time, with the facilitators helping Ching read and follow the child's cues. Ching came to see trusting Fia as a way to help the child learn to regulate her appetite and consumption – rather than this risking her becoming under-nourished. This was a big change from force-feeding:

> Before I was thinking she just didn't want it any more. Now I realize she wants a break. It's like as an adult, you won't go straight eating, eating, eating and finish it.

Common Knowledge between Mothers and Children 55

> You would talk, look around. Social eating, it's not just for fuelling your stomach. So you have to realize that with baby as well.

Ching explained how she found 'being kind' hard because kindness was not something she experienced from her parents as a child. The course concept of 'shark music' – a metaphor for recognizing stressful moments – helped her in this regard. Shark music expands the principle of thinking less about the child as the problem and more about how the parent responds. Ching realized her shark music played when Fia refused food and they both became distressed during mealtimes.

> I start to realize you have to separate the baby from your emotions, when we talk about shark music. ... It helps me to see that we as parents [are] afraid of certain emotions.

The facilitators helped Ching identify actions she could use at such times. One that Ching was still using months later was slow breathing. It worked as a time out for her so she could come back and be available to the child. Figure 3.4 represents the new scenario, with Ching responding to what matters to Fia, supporting her learning in the transition to solid food.

Child

What matters
Having needs met / getting help when needed
Connection with parent
Having (some) control / say in feeding

Mediating actions
Slow breathing, labelling emotions, pause

Object
Eating solid foods

Mother

What matters
Understanding, responding to behavioural messages
Noticing shark music
Be available to support child
Judging when to trust the child, when to take charge
Being bigger, stronger, wiser and kind

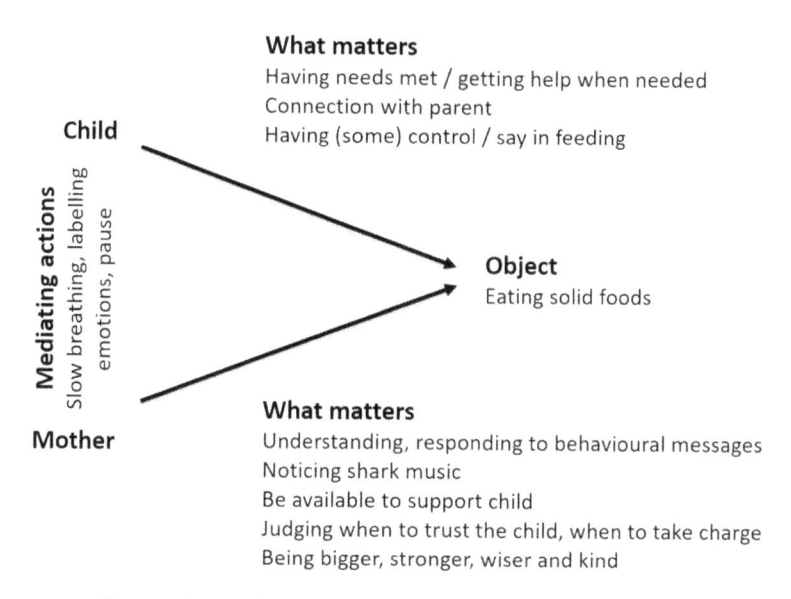

Figure 3.4 Ching and Fia after Circle of Security.

Transition from playing alone to playing with others

Marlie was referred to a specialist toddler clinic offering parent–child interaction therapy (PCIT; Hembree-Kigin and McNeil, 1995) over a 12-week programme. The programme focuses initially on relationship enhancing and promoting positive behaviour in toddlers through 'special play'. Sessions run for an hour each week, beginning with five minutes of parent–child play observed by a practitioner who assesses the frequency of the parent's PRIDE actions (praise, reflection, imitation, description and showing enjoyment). The practitioner then coaches the parent, watching through a one-way mirror. After several weeks, the programme moves on to dealing with challenging behaviour, while maintaining the same visit format.

Marlie's zone of concern arose after the arrival of her second child (Paolo, 17 months), which created a disruption for George (aged three and a half). She sought help from nurse Klara with sibling rivalry, George's challenging behaviour, physical violence and refusal to share toys. George was struggling to cope with the transition from playing alone or just with his parent(s) to play activity in which his sibling was included. George's behaviours were creating conflict not just between the siblings, but with his mother too. Marlie had been punched in the face by George and had been pushed so hard she fell over. She was reluctant to leave the house for fear of George's meltdowns, rating her confidence in coping with his behaviour as three out of ten:

> My biggest concern is I feel like I just scream and shout from morning to night. I can't control his behaviour. George lashes out, not listening, I start to repeat myself, then scream. ... He hits me.
>
> We're a cranky house, I don't enjoy the boys. I want a happy home. ... I'm very concerned his behaviour is affecting our relationship. I don't want him to think I'm always shouting, I don't want to be that mum.

Marlie reflected on what might be behind some of these issues for George:

> Jealousy that he's no longer the centre of attention, he has to have everything first. It's difficult to manage, I don't know how to explain, or if he understands that it's not all about him.

Figure 3.5 conceptualizes this initial situation.

Klara built on Marlie's taking George's point of view, helping her understand that this was a demanding period of transition for the boy. Klara helped Marlie recognize demands associated with adjustment to the presence of his younger

Figure 3.5

Child — **What matters**
- Hard to discern
- Attention from parents
- Having toys to self

Mediating actions: Raising voices (Absence of options)

Object: Sibling and parent-child relationships

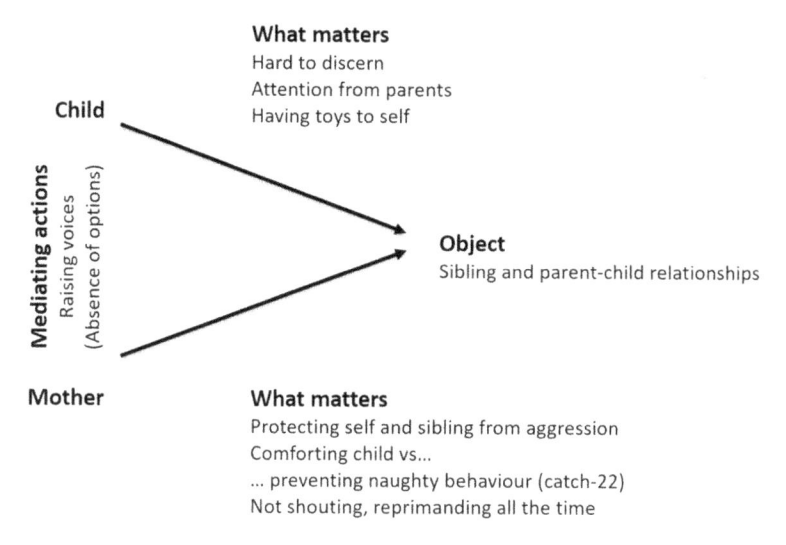

Mother — **What matters**
- Protecting self and sibling from aggression
- Comforting child vs...
- ... preventing naughty behaviour (catch-22)
- Not shouting, reprimanding all the time

Figure 3.5 Marlie and George prior to PCIT toddler clinic.

sibling, perceptions of reduced parental attention, expectations of sharing toys over which he previously had complete ownership, controlling his aggression, using language rather than physical responses and complying with instructions from parents.

Klara's early focus was on developing Marlie's PRIDE skills and avoiding commands, questions and criticism during play. Praise and description (the P and D of PRIDE) proved especially significant for Marlie. Klara explained the importance of labelling praise so George knows what he is being praised for:

> So when he touches you gently, 'I love it when you touch my hand gently'. When he cuddles you, that's where he's got to get the attention when he's doing that beautiful gentle cuddling. When he's talking to you in a really nice voice, when he's using his manners, all those sort of things I want you to really praise him.

Klara explained and modelled descriptions as a 'running commentary on everything he is doing with his hands'. Giving words for George's actions was suggested as helping him concentrate, and promoting language development, which in turn offers George a verbal response to frustrating situations.

The PRIDE approach was explained in relation to it being important for the child to feel special, take the lead in play, know their parents think they have good ideas and enjoy being with them, and have their messages understood. This assumed George's preference for warm relationships with his parents, even when his behaviours suggest otherwise. What mattered to Marlie in play shifted from responding to bad behaviour to establishing a special relationship and atmosphere in which George feels supported and positively valued and supporting language development through play.

Klara gave Marlie homework of five minutes PRIDE-based 'special play' with George each day, which Marlie accomplished consistently. Klara's coaching began with more correction and prompting, shifting to more confirmation and affirmation, as shown in the excerpts below (Klara was watching from another room, speaking to Marlie through an earpiece):

> Marlie: Shall we put that on the race track?
> Klara: Just try and work with what he is doing. You've got two cars, they go really fast.
> Marlie: Ooh you've got two cars! They go really fast!
> …
> Marlie: That was very clever when you got that unstuck!
> Klara: Oh fantastic praise, you're really using that labelled praise very effectively. He's looking at you because labelled praise helps him to know when you like what he's doing okay. That makes him feel happy about what he's doing.

A few weeks into the programme, Marlie described PRIDE actions as feeling a bit awkward, but recognized that 'from George's point of view he probably thinks it's fantastic. He thinks I think he is just the best thing ever.' Even by then, Marlie had started to 'use those tools just in my day-to-day conversations with him'. Several months later, they were a feature of general institutional practices of this family:

> It was something I got into the habit of doing, because you have the homework sheets that you need to fill in every week, it's great because it gets you into the habit of doing those things every day. And I found that I was doing them without having even thinking about having to fill in the homework, so in terms of a big change, that is something that has carried on from the clinic days and it's just something that's part of our day now, which is great.

Two months later still, praise and descriptive commentary had become 'something I use every day' including with Paolo, as he got older and the two boys played together more. Marlie's understanding of why this was so important in reducing George's problematic behaviour was closely linked to her appreciation of what matters to George:

> I don't shout as much any more. Focusing more on his positive behaviour definitely helped me be a lot calmer in my approach to him. It's also helped him because he doesn't feel like he's constantly being criticized for things.

Child

What matters
Warm relationships with parents
Taking the lead in play
Feeling proud, good at things
Help when things are hard

Object
Sibling and parent-child relationships

Mediating actions
Labelled praise and behavioural descriptions

Mother

What matters
Helping child concentrate and enjoy play
Promoting language development
Establishing warm relationships through play

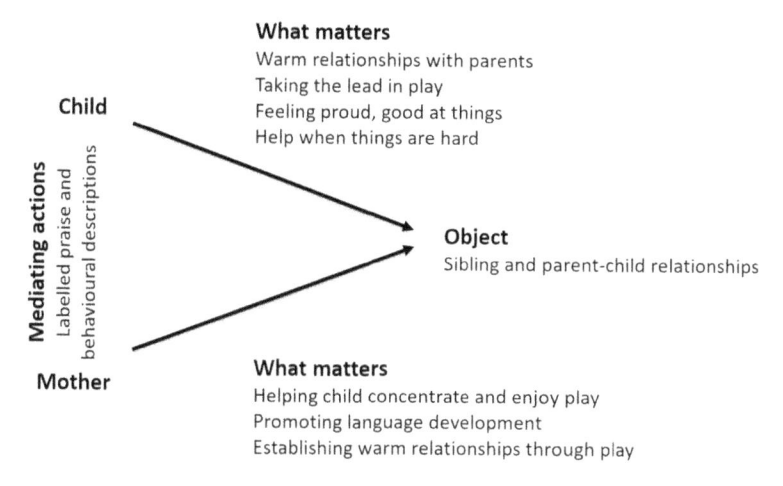

Figure 3.6 Marlie and George after PCIT toddler clinic.

> You can see his whole face light up and he gets a sense of pride that 'Oh mummy's noticed that I've done that.' … If he's being too rough then I'll go up there and I'll say 'I'm going to put that down gently' and then he will copy what I am doing and be really happy that he could do it just like mummy.
>
> I'm just not the shouty mum any more.

The new situation is represented in Figure 3.6.

Discussion

We now reconsider the three cases together, identifying common features that can be taken to form a conceptual understanding of how professional intervention and expertise works to support parents and children through problematic transitions. The different zones of concern around transitions, child ages, family institutions and professional services strengthen the argument that this analysis discerns more general principles rather than aspects that are tied to particular cases.

Over time, the professionals built up a set of tools around the object. These acted as second stimuli, changing the relationship between the parent and child, and between them and the problem they were working on together. Common knowledge came to serve this mediating function. Previous work on the concept of common knowledge has tended to describe what matters as stable, with effort focused on aligning responses to what matters to others. In these cases, what matters to the child remained stable, but became available as a resource to support joint work on a problematic transition. However, what matters to the parents *expanded* through each intervention. The initial motives involving nutrition and safety remained in place, but these became more complex. This happened by bringing parents into a new space of reasons – new inferences became available based on common knowledge, which in turn helped to define new motives. This shift is not a purely symbolic one, nor does it originate in some 'under the skull' change for the parent: it emerges through professional expertise guiding the parent's interpretation of and response to the object.

Common knowledge was crucial, but not sufficient in securing the positive changes described. Its potential as a second stimulus was secured by anchoring it to embodied actions, which included sequencing and timing actions in breastfeeding, various kinds of pause or time out, breathing, and diverse uses of parent verbalizations. Verbalizations are particularly striking as they connect with the centrality of language and Zinchenko's (2012) argument that even the youngest infants are not indifferent to spoken words. These actions replace others that perpetuated or escalated the problems. They function in a way similar to that described by Sannino (2014) in relation to double stimulation: as kedges – anchors thrown into water to help move a sailboat during calm or against a wind – directing the parents' attention to concrete actions. These actions are part of a space of reasons and are identified through forms of reasoning. They mediate not as universal imperatives, but as actions tied to if/then reasoning based on parents' interpretations of children's cues, discernment of patterns relating to the child, and common knowledge.

There is not only a shift in inference but a linked change from task orientation to a child-in-relation orientation. The task orientation foregrounded the problem (ingestion of milk or solid foods, controlling the child's behaviour, etc.), while the relational orientation foregrounds the means to address the problem: relaxed, supportive and warm connections, understanding and responding to cues, balancing the child's say with the parent taking charge. This change is from a functional focus to one occupied with diagnosing problems in the child's social situation of development, with a view to identifying and enacting institutional practices that construct a different social situation (Hedegaard, 2018). Expressed more concretely, the shift is from the refusing or troublesome child to what the parent can do to help the child meet the demands of the situation.

In all three cases, the child is understood and supported as an active agent, as co-authors of themselves and their world (Stetsenko and Ho, 2015). This was expressed in terms of 'having a say' or 'following their lead'. Two special conditions surround the development of the child as agentic in this way. The first is that it does not simply spring independently from the child. The parent plays a crucial role in shaping conditions (the social situation of development) in which the child can express her agency. The parent who does not notice and attend to the child's cues does not create a situation in which the child's agency is legitimized and fostered. Secondly, this agency develops within a dynamic balance between the child and parent as co-leaders of joint activity. Parents were positioned as having a responsibility, to foster the agency of the child, to take charge when needed, and to enter a space of reasons that supports their judgements in this regard. This shows how intervention sets up a contradiction between (child) agency and (parent) control – a contradiction that has been described in relation to children's participation in classroom activity (Rajala, Kumpulainen, Rainio, Hilppö and Lipponen, 2016) and outdoor family interaction (Keisanen et al., 2017). Professional expertise made available through diverse services helps parents resolve this contradiction through dynamic, situated inference mediated by common knowledge and anchored to bodily actions.

The professionals all addressed the child's emotional experience as inseparable from their developing competence and motives. This included the importance of relaxed, positive experiences of breastfeeding or meal times, as well as the child's sense of parents' enjoyment and pride in them during play. Thus, the documented changes functionally addressed a unity of affect and intellect (Zinchenko, 2012). Common knowledge was not just a question of affectively neutral understandings, but helped to establish a shared emotional experience between the parent and child (Karabanova, 2010). This is important, as the influence that the social situation has on a child is not detached from their affective experience (Vygotsky, 1994).[1]

Thus a set of common principles can explain how professionals supported parents and children through different problematic transitions. The forms of expertise involved in enacting these principles varied, shaping the institutional practices of the intervention itself. In the day stay, common knowledge became available through the nurses' commentary on what she was seeing and hearing while the child was feeding. In the Circle of Security, the facilitators' expertise involved connecting generic ideas to parents' particular situations, while in the toddler clinic, role modelling and in-the-moment coaching were especially important. While further discussion is beyond our present scope, this analysis has nonetheless shown how concepts of common knowledge, the space of reasons, and social situation of development can help to specify forms and pathways of professional expertise in early intervention work.

Conclusion

This chapter extends the study and conceptualization of children's transitions and their relationship to motives and learning (Hedegaard and Edwards, 2014). It does so by approaching this from a distinctive angle, focusing on support from professionals who intervene in the institution of the family and by bringing three concepts together in a novel analysis. We have shown how professional expertise constructs the agentic child by understanding what matters to the child and expanding parent motives, promoting interactions that create conditions for the child's new social situation of development. The child's competence and motives arise dialectically in this situation, which is shaped by parents resolving a dynamic contradiction between agency and control. The function of common knowledge as a resource depends on particular forms of reasoning and is supported by anchoring parents' own motives and understanding of the motives of their children to concrete, bodily actions.

This chapter has addressed Edwards's (2012a, p. 177) argument that 'too little attention has been paid to the production of mediating artefacts in practices and the relationships which obtain between these mediators and what is being worked on in activities in practices'. It has done this by extending the application of common knowledge to address for the first time its functions in mediating parent–child relationships. Specifically, we have traced its origins in institutional practices of professional early intervention, how it becomes embedded in the institutional practices of families and its significance in overcoming problematic transitions in children's development.

Acknowledgements

We wish to thank staff and clients of Karitane, Tresillian and Northern Sydney Local Health District for their support. The study was funded by the Australian Research Council, Project Number DE150100365, approved by South Western

Sydney Local Health District Research and Ethics Office (HREC/15/LPOOL/77) and ratified by the University of Technology Sydney Human Research Ethics Expedited Review Committee (2015000284).

Note

1 The (difficult to translate) concept of *perezhivanie*, which relates to lived experience (Fleer, Gonzalez Rey and Veresov, 2017), would be useful to further explore this aspect of early intervention work.

References

Bruner, J. (1968). *Processes of cognitive growth: Infancy*. Heinz Werner Lecture Series, Wouster, MA: Clark University Press.

Chaiklin, S. (2012). A conceptual perspective for investigating motive in cultural-historical theory. In M. Hedegaard, A. Edwards and M. Fleer (Eds), *Motives in children's development: Cultural-historical approaches* (pp. 209–24). Cambridge: Cambridge University Press.

Daniels, H. (2012). Changing situations and motives. In M. Hedegaard, A. Edwards and M. Fleer (Eds), *Motives in children's development: Cultural-historical approaches* (pp. 191–208). Cambridge: Cambridge University Press.

Derry, J. (2007). What is it to be a human knower? *Philosophy Now*, 63, 10–11.

Derry, J. (2014). Abstract rationality in education: From Vygotsky to Brandom. In M. Young and J. Muller (Eds), *Knowledge, expertise and the professions* (pp. 33–46). Abingdon: Routledge.

Edwards, A. (2010). *Being an expert practitioner: The relational turn in expertise*. Dordrecht: Springer.

Edwards, A. (2011). Building common knowledge at the boundaries between professional practices: Relational agency and relational expertise in systems of distributed expertise. *International Journal of Educational Research*, 50(1), 33–9. doi:10.1016/j.ijer.2011.04.007.

Edwards, A. (2012a). Expertise in the children's workforce: Knowledge and motivation in engagement with children. In M. Hedegaard, A. Edwards and M. Fleer (Eds), *Motives in children's development: Cultural-historical approaches* (pp. 173–90). Cambridge: Cambridge University Press.

Edwards, A. (2012b). The role of common knowledge in achieving collaboration across practices. *Learning, Culture and Social Interaction*, 1, 22–32. doi:10.1016/j.lcsi.2012.03.003.

Edwards, A. (2017). Revealing relational work. In A. Edwards (Ed.), *Working relationally in and across practices: Cultural-historical approaches to collaboration* (pp. 1–21). Cambridge: Cambridge University Press.

Fleer, M. (2012). The development of motives in children's play. In M. Hedegaard, A. Edwards and M. Fleer (Eds), *Motives in children's development: Cultural-historical approaches* (pp. 79–96). Cambridge: Cambridge University Press.

Fleer, M., Gonzalez Rey, F., and Veresov, N. (Eds). (2017). *Perezhivanie, emotions and subjectivity*. Dordrecht: Springer.

Hedegaard, M. (2008). A cultural-historical theory of children's development. In M. Hedegaard and M. Fleer (Eds), *Studying children: A cultural-historical approach* (pp. 10–29). New York: Open University Press.

Hedegaard, M. (2012). The dynamic aspects between children's learning and development. In M. Hedegaard, A. Edwards and M. Fleer (Eds), *Motives in children's development: Cultural-historical approaches* (pp. 9–27). Cambridge: Cambridge University Press.

Hedegaard, M. (2018). Children's perspectives and institutional practices as keys in a wholeness approach to children's social situations of development. *Learning, Culture and Social Interaction*. doi:10.1016/j.lcsi.2018.04.008.

Hedegaard, M., and Chaiklin, S. (2011). Supporting children and schools: A development and practice-centred approach for professional practice research. In H. Daniels and M. Hedegaard (Eds), *Vygotsky and special needs education: Rethinking support for children and schools* (pp. 86–108). London: Continuum.

Hedegaard, M., Edwards, A., and Fleer, M. (2012). Introduction: Cultural-historical understandings of motives and children's development. In M. Hedegaard, A. Edwards and M. Fleer (Eds), *Motives in children's development: Cultural-historical approaches* (pp. 1–6). Cambridge: Cambridge University Press.

Hedegaard, M., and Edwards, A. (2014). Transitions and children's learning. *Learning, Culture and Social Interaction*, 3(3), 185–7. doi:10.1016/j.lcsi.2014.02.007

Hedegaard, M., Fleer, M., Bang, J., and Hviid, P. (2008). Researching child development – An introduction. In M. Hedegaard and M. Fleer (Eds), *Studying children: A cultural-historical approach* (pp. 1–9). New York: Open University Press.

Hembree-Kigin, T. L., and McNeil, C. B. (1995). *Parent–child interaction therapy*. New York: Plenum Press.

Hopwood, N. (2017). Expertise, learning, and agency in partnership practices in services for families with young children. In A. Edwards (Ed.), *Working relationally in and across practices: Cultural-historical approaches to collaboration* (pp. 25–42). Cambridge: Cambridge University Press.

Hopwood, N., Clerke, T., and Nguyen, A. (2018). A pedagogical framework for facilitating parents' learning in nurse–parent partnership. *Nursing Inquiry*, 25(2), e12220. doi: 10.1111/nin.12220.

Hopwood, N., and Edwards, A. (2017). How common knowledge is constructed and why it matters in collaboration between professionals and clients. *International Journal of Educational Research*, 83, 107–19. doi:10.1016/j.ijer.2017.02.007.

Hopwood, N., and Gottschalk, B. (2017). Double stimulation 'in the wild': Services for families with children at risk. *Learning, Culture and Social Interaction*, 13, 23–37. doi:10.1016/j.lcsi.2017.01.003.

Kaptelinin, V., Vadeboncoeur, J. A., Gajdamaschko, N., and Nardi, B. (2017). Negotiating motives, power and embodiment: Studies of creating and sharing meaning in social context. *Mind, Culture and Activity*, 24(1), 1–2. doi:10.1080/10749039.2016.1267227.

Karabanova, O. A. (2010). Social situation of child's development: The key concept in modern developmental psychology. *Psychology in Russia: State of the Art*, 3, 130–53.

Keisanen, T., Rauniomaa, M., and Siitonen, P. (2017). Transitions as sites of socialization in family interaction outdoors. *Learning, Culture and Social Interaction*, 14, 24–37. doi:10.1016/j.lcsi.2017.05.001.

Leontiev, A. N. (1978). *Activity, consciousness, and personality*. Englewood Cliffs, NJ: Prentice-Hall Inc.

Leontiev, A. N. (1981). The concept of activity in psychology. In J. Wertsch (Ed.), *The concept of activity in Soviet psychology* (pp. 121–45). Armonk, NY: ME Sharpe.

Powell, B., Cooper, G., Hoffman, K., and Marvin, R. S. (2016). *The Circle of Security intervention: Enhancing attachment in early parent–child relationships*. London: The Guildford Press.

Rai, P. (2017). Building and using common knowledge for building school-community links. In A. Edwards (Ed.), *Working relationally in and across practices: Cultural-historical approaches to collaboration* (pp. 99–112). Cambridge: Cambridge University Press.

Rajala, A., Kumpulainen, K., Rainio, A. P., Hilppö, J., and Lipponen, L. (2016). Dealing with the contradiction of agency and control during dialogic teaching. *Learning, Culture and Social Interaction*, 10, 17–26. doi:10.1016/j.lcsi.2016.02.005.

Sannino, A. (2014, 23–27 June). Double stimulation as anchoring forward: The unity of conceptualization and agentive action. Paper presented at the International Conference of the Learning Sciences, Boulder.

Stetsenko, A., and Arievitch, I. (2004). The self in cultural-historical activity theory: Reclaiming the unity of social and individual dimensions of human development. *Theory and Psychology*, 14(4), 475–503. doi:10.1177/0959354304044921.

Stetsenko, A., and Ho, P.-C. G. (2015). The serious joy and the joyful work of play: Children becoming agentive actors in co-authoring themselves and their world through play. *International Journal of Early Childhood*, 47(2), 221–34. doi:10.1007/s13158-015-0141-1.

Vygotksy, L. S. (1994). The socialist alteration of man. In R. van der Veer and J. Valsiner (Eds), *The Vygotsky Reader* (pp. 175–84). Oxford: Basil Blackwell.

Vygotsky, L. S. (1997 [1960]). The history of the development of higher mental functions, Chapter 12: Self-control. In R. Rieber and J. Wollock (Eds), *The collected works of L. S. Vygotsky, Vol. 4: The history of the development of higher mental functions* (pp. 207–19). London: Plenum Press.

Vygotksy, L. S. (1998). Chapter 2: Development of thinking and formation of concepts in the adolescent. In R. Rieber (Ed.), *The collected works of L. S. Vygotsky, Vol. 5: Child Psychology* (pp. 29–81). London: Kluwer Academic / Plenum Publishers.

Zinchenko, V. P. (2012). Early stages in children's cultural development. In M. Hedegaard, A. Edwards and M. Fleer (Eds), *Motives in children's development: Cultural-historical approaches* (pp. 63–76). Cambridge: Cambridge University Press.

4

Changing Practices in the Highlands of Vietnam: Transitioning from Subjects of Research to Agents of Change

Marilyn Fleer, Freya Fleer-Stout, Helen Hedges and Hanh Le Thi Bich

Introduction

This chapter is concerned with the question of how professionals from different professional practices, working together with parents and other community members, with the common goal of improving the life conditions of Bah'nar children in the highlands of Vietnam (Baulch, Chuyen, Haughton and Haughton, 2007), transitioned from being subjects of research to agents of change during the process of developing a locally relevant evaluation tool. To answer this question, we drew upon Edwards's (2016) concepts of common knowledge, relational expertise and relational agency to study the process of tool development. Hedegaard's (2014) concepts of motives and demands guided how we came to understand the way local professionals negotiated their expertise and built common knowledge of what mattered to them during the process of developing the evaluation tool.

In many countries, agencies are charged with creating better conditions for children's learning and development. Through international funding, both human and material resources are provided to support local initiatives in schools and early childhood and family-based settings. But with this philanthropic funding comes the need for external evaluations to determine if and how best to further develop these programmes. Most NGOs contract international researchers to undertake these evaluations, where a range of ways of evaluating programmes feature and a range of ways of conceptualizing practices emerge. But how local and indigenous knowledge, practices and agency in resource-poor contexts are evaluated continues to be problematic

(Fenech, Sweller and Harrison, 2010). Emerging from these contexts is the need for localized ways of developing research tools that capture what matters for the participants of these programmes, rather than being externally evaluated on criteria that could be irrelevant to local needs, values and motives (Gregory and Ruby, 2011).

Central to this chapter is an NGO established in 1993 with the brief to work in partnership with local people, including educational organizations and the different government bodies responsible for the education and health of Vietnamese children. Like many other NGOs, the overall goal was to improve the educational experience of all children, especially the Bah'nar children. The target was *education for all* by setting up and implementing an early childhood care and development project between 2012 and 2017 in the province of Gia Lai (Le Thi Bich and Nguyen, 2013). The project, known locally as the 4 Cornerstone Education and Care Program, focused specifically on increasing access to schooling, improving the educational experience of children in preschool and in the first year of school, and supporting families and educators through increased child-development knowledge. A summary of the programme is shown further below. As with other established and piloted programmes, the NGO faced the challenge of evaluating their programme by bringing in external evaluators new to the programme and new to the collaborating participants and children and their families. *The central problem for the NGO* was how best to evaluate their 4 Cornerstone Program, which was being implemented in a province where there were sensitivities in relation to outsiders due to past conflicts. For example, foreigners had not been previously allowed to visit, and even the Vietnamese professionals at the centre of the initiative had to seek local Bah'nar community members' approval in order to engage with them. *The central problem for the external researchers* was how to do this in a way that reflected what mattered for the local peoples of the highlands of Vietnam.

Achieving the twin goals meant developing in partnership the evaluation tool to meet specific local needs, values and motives of the participants and the NGO. This chapter is concerned with these twin goals, with a specific focus on understanding the transition process of the local participants:

- Creating a new evaluation scale directed at the local Bah'nar people living in the highlands of Vietnam;
- Developing the evaluation scale into a tool to show the impact of the 4 Cornerstone Program that was developed by the NGO;
- Negotiating with each other to effect change and create new conditions for Bah'nar children.

To achieve the goal of understanding the transition of participants from subjects of research to agents of change during the process of developing a locally relevant evaluation tool, we begin this chapter by presenting an example of one of the features of the evaluation scale and an overview of the study itself. This is followed by a case study of the development of the evaluation tool and a discussion of what was learnt. The chapter concludes with a discussion of the transition practices evident in the case study. The central findings of this study are theorized as *double researcher subjectivity, multiple interagency contradictions* and *agents of practice change*.

Unless stated otherwise, the term 'collaborating participants' captures the parents from the communities, local community leaders, the NGO staff, principals, early childhood teachers, primary teachers, an independent local quantitative research company, and international cultural-historical researchers (first three authors). We specifically focus our analysis on the interagency professionals, including the local community leaders, the NGO staff, principals, early childhood teachers and primary teachers.

Creating a new evaluation scale directed at the local Bah'nar people living in the highlands of Vietnam

The evaluation tool named in English as the 'Vietnamese Quality Rating Scale' was developed in partnership with local participants and international researchers and was named locally as Thang đo chất lượng giáo dục tại Gia Lai <Tên>. The term '<Tên>' is a space for naming the tool in relation to the local context of a particular commune. This reflects the importance of localizing at the commune level what matters and what constitutes evidence for them. Figure 4.1 shows one page of the digital scale for Indicator 2 of what mattered at that level for the adaptation of teaching methods in the local communes. The text in the scale is a list of possible criteria that participants said were indicators of evidence of adapting teaching methods. One of the pillars in the 4 Cornerstone Program was concerned with supporting local teachers in modifying the dominant textbook-based approach and in focusing on using local resources and engaging in meaningful curriculum content by incorporating local content. In a scale of 1 to 5 levels, the text and images together shown in Figure 4.1 are examples of indicators at the second level in the scale for the adaptation of teaching methods.

The space for inserting a video or photograph was included in the scale to allow the users of the scale to capture commune-specific images or videos. That

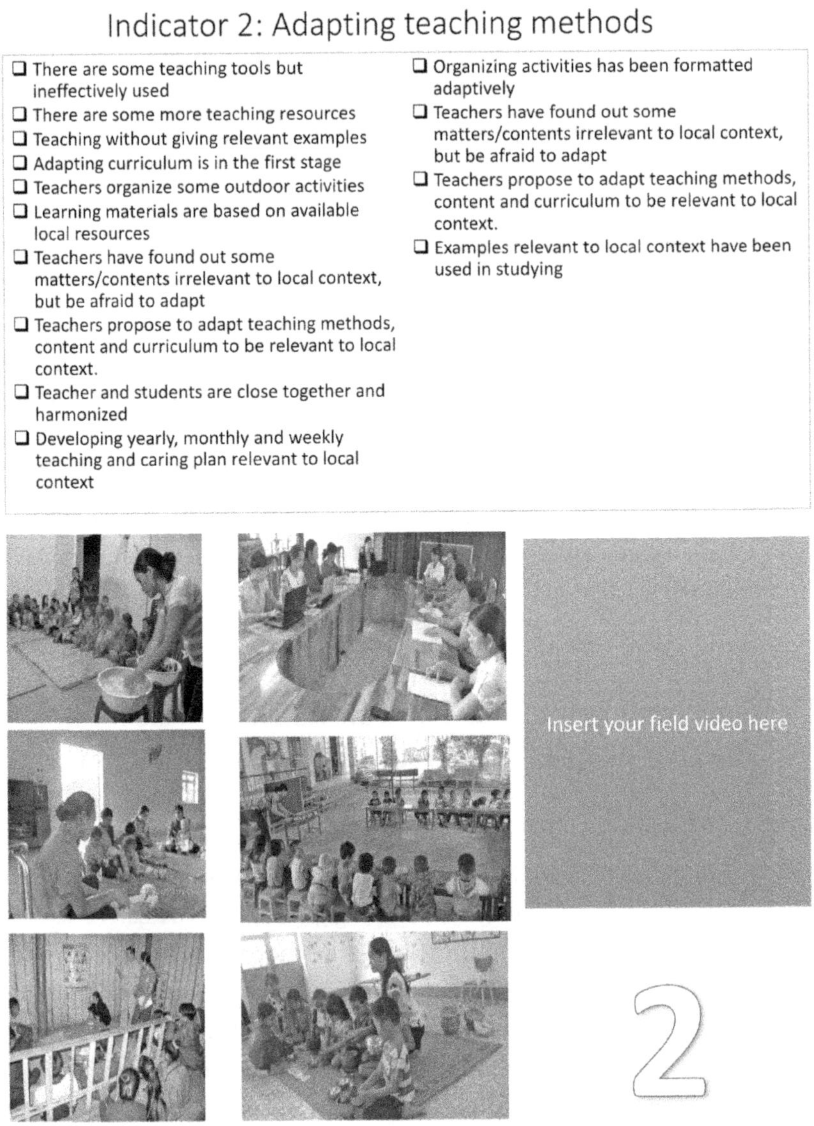

Indicator 2: Adapting teaching methods

- ❏ There are some teaching tools but ineffectively used
- ❏ There are some more teaching resources
- ❏ Teaching without giving relevant examples
- ❏ Adapting curriculum is in the first stage
- ❏ Teachers organize some outdoor activities
- ❏ Learning materials are based on available local resources
- ❏ Teachers have found out some matters/contents irrelevant to local context, but be afraid to adapt
- ❏ Teachers propose to adapt teaching methods, content and curriculum to be relevant to local context.
- ❏ Teacher and students are close together and harmonized
- ❏ Developing yearly, monthly and weekly teaching and caring plan relevant to local context

- ❏ Organizing activities has been formatted adaptively
- ❏ Teachers have found out some matters/contents irrelevant to local context, but be afraid to adapt
- ❏ Teachers propose to adapt teaching methods, content and curriculum to be relevant to local context.
- ❏ Examples relevant to local context have been used in studying

Figure 4.1 English translation of Tool 2 – digital quality environmental rating scales.

is, the tool could be used for evaluation by local researchers as they went from commune to commune to document the practices of the local teachers, or it could be used by the local teachers to capture their own images and to place them within the scale. The latter was a form of self-reflection by the teachers and the former acted as a tool for a general evaluation of the impact of the 4 Cornerstone Program over time for the NGO.

The digital evaluation tool was designed to be suitable for any digital device that used PowerPoint and could be used in the field to upload captured images of practices as is shown in Figure 4.1. All the participants had computers and most communes used smartphones regularly. Overall, there were five separate scales with five levels that were developed. They mirrored the pillars in the 4 Cornerstone Program, but the tool also included an additional scale to capture partnerships with families more explicitly.

Scale 1: The nature and quality of the reading and language environments
Scale 2: The extent to which teaching and learning environments are child friendly
Scale 3: The extent to which teaching and learning environments are child centred
Scale 4: The extent to which teachers are adapting teaching methods to be responsive to Scales 2 and 3
Scale 5: The ways teachers are implementing partnerships with families

The digital tool that was developed and used was not an externally imposed scale; but, rather, what was produced was done in partnership to reflect what mattered to the NGO and the local participants who had participated in professional learning about the 4 Cornerstone Program and who had been implementing the programme in their communes for 18 months to 24 months (at the time of developing the evaluation tool). The tool was to be used each year for a period of three years in order to assess the impact of the implementation and change over time of the conditions for learning in the communes. To understand how the local participants transitioned from being subjects of research to agents of change during the process of developing this locally relevant evaluation tool, we used Edwards's (2016) concepts of common knowledge, relational expertise and relational agency to study the process of tool development and Hedegaard's (2014) concepts of motives and demands to understand how the local participants negotiated their expertise with each other and how they built common knowledge about what content should be in the tool and how this should be represented as scales. Figure 4.1 is a representative example of what mattered to the locals about what should be viewed as evidence for level 2 in the scale on adapting teaching resources.

Focus of the research

The programme to be evaluated was being implemented and supported by the NGO and consisted of 4 cornerstones. It is viewed as a holistic intervention for the seven communes that make up the Gai Lai province in which the NGO worked. Designed as an intervention model, it was originally developed by a group of collaborating local professionals made up of a consultative group with Plan Vietnam for implementation in the Bah'nar communities. The programme is summarized below.

Cornerstone 1

- Starting at the beginning (prenatal to three years of age);
- Supporting the development of early childhood knowledge and practices of parents/caregivers;
- Increasing community-based support for improving practices of parents/caregivers in early childhood education and care; and
- Undertaking a pilot for early stimulation initiatives in community-based settings for seven communes.

Cornerstone 2

- Providing opportunities for learning and discovery (between three and five years of age);
- Enhancing preschool infrastructure for Bah'nar families living in the seven respective communes; and
- Building capacity of preschool teachers and school principals to develop child-centred preschool programmes for Bah'nar children.

Cornerstone 3

- Making schools ready for children (six to eight years of age);
- Implementing child-friendly initiatives; and
- Building capacity of teachers and school principals to adapted materials and develop appropriate teaching approaches for children in the early years of school for Bah'nar children.

Cornerstone 4

- Developing policies for early childhood;
- Improving awareness of early childhood education and care, and the importance of integrated initiatives for policy writers; and
- Providing an evidence base in support of early childhood education and care through research, monitoring and evaluation, and documentation.

The objective of the activity was to develop an evaluation tool for measuring quality in the local communes in the highlands of Vietnam where Bah'nar families live and where the 4 Cornerstone Program was being implemented. In this chapter, the focus is on how local collaborating participants transitioned from being subjects of research to agents of change when building the evaluation tool that was to be used for measuring evidence of quality. Specifically, what is reported in this chapter is concerned with the process of developing the tool in relation to the following questions:

- What were the iterative practices that supported the development of common knowledge (including cultural understandings) between international researchers and local interagency professionals being positioned as researchers in pursuit of a common problem?
- How do local interagency professionals deal with contradiction about what constituted evidence by different interagency professionals?
- How did local interagency professionals negotiate what mattered to them?
- How did relational agency develop for the local interagency professionals?

We digitally recorded key moments during the three days of workshopping, much of the field trip, and made extensive notes of all the meetings, interviews and interactions in the field. Post-workshop reflections by key members among the interagency professionals were also documented, some of which were based on their own discussions with others. These different data were taken over five full days and evenings.

Inclusive of the interagency professionals are the international researchers. How the international researchers transitioned their methodological practices has been reported elsewhere (Fleer, Hedges, Fleer-Stout and Le Thi Bich, 2018) and, hence, not discussed in detail in this chapter.

The complexity of the context of this research required powerful concepts for understanding how the participants transitioned. We now turn to an expansive discussion of the concepts that helped us better understand what took place during the process of developing the overall tool (five scales, each with five levels).

Analysis

The interwoven concepts of common knowledge, relational expertise and relational agency, as introduced by Edwards (2016), capture the capacity of collaborating professionals to 'recognise, respect and work with the professional motives' of others (p. 7) when working on a shared yet complex problem across professional boundaries. In this chapter, the collaboration extends beyond professionals and the shared problem was determining concretely what quality early education looked like locally and what counted as evidence of quality early childhood education for children. This local evidence was to be the foundation of the content for developing the evaluation tool.

Relational expertise is the capacity of someone to work relationally with another person or with team members to elicit what matters to others and be explicit with others about what matters to oneself in order to expand understandings of the problem being worked on and sensitively make a joint response (Edwards, 2016). Therefore, when the focus is on a complex problem, professionals need to jointly interpret the problem and develop a joint response to it. This means learning, knowing about, understanding and respecting the expertise of others, as well as being able to decide upon the kinds of expertise required to jointly resolve the common problem. In our study, we were interested to know about how this was realized during the five days (two field days and three workshop days) when the participants came together to design the evaluation tool for making judgements about the quality of early childhood education practices. The work of Edwards (2016), and those that have used her concepts (e.g. Hopwood, 2016; Rai, 2016; Montecinos, Leiva, Campos, Ahumada and Galdames, 2016), has shown that it becomes important to create the right conditions for sharing expertise so that an understanding and a solution to the problem can emerge jointly in the context of tuning into the relevant expertise. In our study, this meant building into the workshop and field trip opportunities for participants to recognize the standpoints and motives of others, as well as being able to align their own motives when interpreting problems and responding with possible solutions and expert knowledge from their own practice. Relational expertise is different from the specialist expertise that one has as an educator or community leader. It is an additional form of expertise revealed in knowing how to work relationally with others and is obviously valuable when bringing participants from different practices together to work on a joint problem, such as an evaluation tool for evaluating the cornerstone programme.

As the editors discuss in Chapter 1, common knowledge, consisting of the motives or what matters in collaborating practices, is both built through the exercise of relational expertise and contributes to sustaining it. In the study discussed here, *the what matters* that emerged and contributed to the common knowledge that informed the evaluation tool included knowing that for community members what mattered was, for example, that the teachers of their children could speak and write in the Bah'nar language. An example of what mattered for the NGOs is evidence of pedagogical practices in the classroom where words and familiar cultural objects from the Bah'nar-speaking community were being drawn upon in support of literacy and other curriculum outcomes.

Edwards (2016) has argued, 'Common knowledge does not arise spontaneously; attention needs to be paid to the conditions in which it is built' (p. 10). Specifically, her research has shown that in sites of intersecting practices, such as the five-day meeting (including field trip with participants) we have mentioned, common knowledge can arise if there is a recognition of the long-term goals that everyone is working towards; of the fact that space is created to allow for sharing of values and motives in each participating practice; and that people actively listen and engage with what is being shared. In our analysis, this meant looking for evidence over the five days for whether, and how, ground rules were established and protocols for reasoning were being promoted, including opportunities for asking questions about the reasons for why something matters. Through this kind of analysis, it becomes possible to determine if participants were gaining insights and building a common knowledge base for their negotiations. Through this, we could examine if relational expertise was being developed or used in the process of learning about each other's practices and motives.

Relational agency captures the idea of how individuals work together on a common problem, drawing on the common knowledge they have built to expand the problem and calibrate their informed responses to it. Therefore, through active listening and by gaining insights into each other's expertise and motives, it becomes possible for deeper insights and an expansion of the common problem to emerge. In our study, we thought the concept of relational agency could potentially give insights into the transitioning of the local collaborating participants as they moved from being subjects of research to agents of change, as they worked together on developing the evaluation tool. Consequently, a close study of the actions that took place during the development of the evaluation tool, as well as following how participants negotiated what mattered to them, gave us a context for better understanding the transition of participants from being subjects of research to agents of change.

Transition is a key concept in the work of Hedegaard (2014) and for those who have drawn upon this concept, because it makes visible in research critical moments in everyday practices that act as a positive source of a person's development. Practice traditions emerge in institutions, and different institutions have different practice traditions based on what a particular society values and expects. How people transition between these institutions has been a focus of Hedegaard's research. She argues that there are different demands in different institutions, for example, as on entering school, children are expected to participate in learning activities, whereas, at home, play and everyday life support activities dominate. How a person transitions into new practice traditions will always be associated with the kinds of demands that are made of the person, as well as the person's motive orientation and how they shape the activity setting in which they are participating. For instance, a child with a motive for play, on entering into formal schooling will encounter activity settings which focus on learning, and this will place new demands upon the child to become oriented to learning. Children through their participation in the different activity settings in the classroom will also shape the practices because of the demands they place on the teacher and classroom community when learning new things. In line with Vygotsky (1998), Hedegaard (2012) argues that new demands placed upon children as they transition into a new institution act as critical moments in their development. Societal values, differing institutional practices and the demands and motives of the person participating in the different activity settings within institutions (Hedegaard, 2012) give a holistic perspective that usefully informs our research on how collaborating participants negotiate values and motives with each other in the process of developing an evaluation tool.

Hedegaard (2016) has used Edwards's concepts in her own intervention study of professional pedagogues transitioning children from kindergarten to school, where she seeks to respectfully support kindergarten pedagogues and school teachers to make visible what matters for them during the transition process of children. She specifically draws out the 'alignment of values through discussion' (p. 249) as a key point for going beyond a social position (Bozhovich, 2009) about what matters to capturing how professional negotiations make visible professional expertise of others as well as the expert practice of the individual professional.

Studying how collaborating participants work together in the development of an evaluation tool in Vietnam can be better understood when the practices are examined in light of motives and institutional practices (Hedegaard, 2014), alongside the concepts Edwards (2016) has developed and deployed. That is, we examined the societal expectations and values, the practice traditions of the relevant institutions, and the demands and motives of the collaborating participants themselves when engaged in the joint problem formulation and resolution while developing an evaluation tool for Bah'nar children in Vietnam.

With this conceptual analytical backdrop, we now present the case study of the practices of the research process for tool development through the lens of the concepts introduced in this section. We do this to illuminate how the participants transitioned from subjects of research to agents of change during the process of developing a locally relevant evaluation tool for measuring the impact of the 4 Cornerstone Program.

Case study

At the end of 2014, Australian and New Zealand researchers travelled to the central highlands of Vietnam with Plan Australia/Vietnam to begin the first stage of an evaluation study. Ravaged by war only decades ago, the central highlands is a remote part of the recovering country that is not on the tourist route and rarely visited by Vietnamese or international tourists. The Bah'nar speak their own dialect with few adults speaking Vietnamese. Their children are taught in Vietnamese at school, as it is the national language of the country. Generally, the teachers in our case study do not speak the local language; therefore, interactions, as well as instruction, are in Vietnamese. While some teachers have worked to develop their understanding of the local language, there is still a language barrier evident between the teachers and the parents.

Step 1: Two-day field trip

The study began with the NGOs organizing a field trip with local communes and officials in the Gai Lai province with the goal of orienting the international researchers to the context of the evaluation. This trip was also for the NGO field staff who had not had an opportunity to visit the province previously and other professionals such as local ministry officials. The trip involved two days in the field visiting local preschools and primary schools to observe and document local practices, while also ensuring that our presence was accepted (Fleer et al., 2018). We had to adopt communicative tools and stances appropriate for cultural exchanges at community council meetings, talking to education officials and, as we also observed, having the chief of police from one of the villages observe us from the fence line of the school. This field trip allowed us to begin to develop an understanding of the context we were in and provide local teachers with an opportunity to share their insights on teaching that were being successfully incorporated into the community, but also to share challenges that emerged in the curriculum for them, such as children learning about Ho Chi Minh City when they had never left their village.

At the same time as teachers, community members, families, children and other leaders were sharing with us their motives and strategies; we were also sharing with them what the research was about and developing new research strategies, such as dialogue through digital technology (capturing and sharing visual images of practices), community walks (where communities shared what mattered to them) and research selfies (reciprocity of researchers filming/photographing the contexts while community members filmed/photographed international researchers) (Fleer et al., 2018). Many of the professionals and community members documented our presence and ways of working. In addition, we found that many of those who were to participate in the subsequent workshop were members of the communities we visited on the field trip.

Step 2: Three-day workshop

The workshop was three full days of intensive data and knowledge sharing. In attendance were the NGOs (the Plan Australia team and Plan Vietnam team), local external quantitative researchers and a selection of professionals from the villages we had just visited. This involved a total of 38 people – principals, preschool and primary teachers, as well as community leaders and individuals who ran community education groups, such as after-school reading groups and playgroups. The local participants came from seven communes and four districts in the central highlands. All participants were asked to bring along photographs and video clips of ways of working and acting from their villages and communes. Some of the material brought to the workshop was also captured by the researchers and some of the professionals who participated in the field trip when visiting other schools and preschools.

The workshop began with the international researchers sharing examples of quality rating scales (e.g. Harms, Clifford and Cryer, 2005) that had been developed in Western contexts, as well as a digital quality rating scale that we had created during the field trip as a prototype using local images familiar to the local professionals to ensure what was presented were culturally relevant. The prototype showed the idea of a digital Likert scale, where criteria of quality were listed on one screen, followed by photographs and video clips of local practices that illustrated a particular level (e.g. 1–5), and where space was provided for professionals to add their own examples of practices. The example was developed by the local participants to be reflective of their wider range of contexts. The context of sharing began formally as an expectation of the local participants, but soon changed to the room configuration shown in Figure 4.2, where the process of collaborating participants developing their own digital rating scale had commenced. Figure 4.2 illustrates the beginning of a process by which all the participants began working on a common problem of creating their own digital quality rating scale.

Figure 4.2 Working on a common problem.

Common problem is negotiated early on in the workshop

The original prototype was translated into Vietnamese as an example of what we were trying to create with them as a digital tool which could capture the impact of the NGO's involvement in their schools, centres and communities through the 4 Cornerstone Program. In these moments of interaction about the purpose of the research, the common problem was being negotiated between the professionals and the other participants. That is, the participants expected us to provide a ready-made evaluation tool to them, and the researchers had expected they would support the different groups of participants to develop a tool of what mattered for them in making judgements about the impact of the 4 Cornerstone model. The initial differences were reflected in the field notes made after the three days of workshopping, where participants were discussing their expectations about the process, and which H, an NGO participant, reported as part of the post-workshop reflections:

> Normally at the training workshop they think it will be passive learning, not that they will be the ones with the expertise to share. (This may be why there was a slow start on day one.)

On the first day of the workshop, the local professionals were seen to be directly copying the text we had created using their own photographs, keeping the video and photographs we had taken, and writing some of their own text, or a combination of the two. The participants appeared to be hesitant to make changes to what we had suggested as an example and were also anxious about their own knowledge. This was evident by how involved we were as international researchers in guiding discussion and in our explicit mention of ranking criteria with practices captured in a Likert scale. One of the external local quantitative researchers, C, suggested ideas to us (through translators) and sought confirmation that they were on the right track, rather than discussing and debating their ideas with the rest of the group. For instance:

> Some expected that the workshop would be more instructional rather than just the development of the tool – this was more of an initial expectation.

We noticed that collaborating participants' expectations was to be informed about a tool, as opposed to developing a tool, appeared to create a double social situation for them, as participants, but also as researchers. To build more confidence in their own knowledge in this new context of developing a digital rating scale, we initially asked the local participants to work in small groups of similar institutional backgrounds (community group, primary school group, preschool group, NGO group). We encouraged all groups to look at the visual material they had brought to the workshop, to express their ideas and opinions to each other in their small groups about what constituted evidence of a quality practice, and to prepare a digital presentation of their agreed results to be shared and debated with everyone. This created common knowledge of what mattered for them, which in turn supported a positioning that they were experts of their own community-based settings, school, preschool or 4 Cornerstone Program as the following quotation from D, a commune leader, shows:

> the participants enjoyed the fact that they were treated like peers, rather than being taught. They felt empowered that they were part of the building process.

The local participants said that this initial digital process was too slow, and it was decided by the group to work in a different way. For instance, the building process that is mentioned by D above and shown in Figure 4.3 involved five large pieces of paper that were positioned around the room, where each small group was encouraged to write down practices that fitted under each of their agreed scale headings taken from the 4 Cornerstone Program, for instance 'adapting teaching approaches'. Then within each scale of levels 1 to 5, people debated what would constitute levels 1 through 5. An example from level 1 was 'examples relevant to local context that have been used in studying …'.

Figure 4.3 Negotiating practices as a whole group.

Initially the participants did not move from their own groups. Many tried to confirm with us that they were placing their cards under the correct level and were hesitant to disagree with the cards other groups had put down. Although the common problem had been negotiated, it was common on day one to stand back and not debate a particular identified practice (on card as text), suggesting some nervousness around identifying practices, labelling these practices, deciding upon levels of quality and critiquing the perspectives of other groups.

Negotiating practices and building relational expertise over the course of the third day of workshop

By the third day, the participants had iteratively worked through four of the five scales (language and literacy, child centredness, child-friendly environments, adapting teaching methods) and were now more confidently and freely debating wording, changing orders and suggesting alternatives as a whole group in the process of building relational expertise and relational agency. The change in practice was also noted through how the group took control of the group discussions in the process of negotiating practices and discussing motives. It appeared that local participants were respectful of the motives of others and were attentive in their listening to what mattered for particular groups. For instance, our video data showed moments where the researchers were organizing the discussions but then the microphone was completely taken over by the participants as they challenged each other's ideas and notions of what strategies should fall under each level. This positioning is shown in Figure 4.3.

As further evidence of the change, one of the principals, E, said later, 'The workshop allowed us to realize our own knowledge from personal experience and from what we have developed with the support of NGO' (E, Principal). Relational agency appeared to have developed over the workshop period. This was also reflected in the post-workshop comments of C, an external local quantitative researcher, who said he had not experienced or used such an approach before in the development of research tools:

> The active approach that we took was different than they expected. This active methodology is reflective of what we as a team and Plan specifically are hoping for the teachers to develop with their children. We as a team are doing what we want the teachers to be doing with their children.

The reflections during the workshop period, and those captured in the post-workshop reflections, also focused on the challenges that NGOs had when developing educational programmes in disadvantaged communities (their target groups). What was identified was that the process of developing the digital quality rating scale appeared to help align the motives of the programme developers with the motives and realities of the communities where the programmes are implemented. For instance, L from the central NGO office said:

> It is often a struggle to create a bridge between the poorer communities and educational development. This tool that we have developed as a team is helping to close the gap. In the past, the educational development disconnects before it reaches the communities that needed educational support the most. As Plan offers support in these communities this tool that has been developed will help to ensure universal support.

Developing common knowledge

Common knowledge had developed through the process of making visible what mattered for the different participants. Participants came with their own funds of knowledge about valued practices (Moll, Amanti, Neff and Gonzalez, 1992). However, to move beyond a simple sharing process, it was important to develop common knowledge of what quality looked like for the successful implementation of the 4 Cornerstone model across the settings of preschool and school. Evidence of this awareness of others' knowledge and motives emerged during the workshop on the final day, when the principals from the schools asked about using the tool for their school as part of their own continued development and development of their teams back in their village. As part of the discussions during the workshop, we suggested that, while the scale they had created only went up to level 5, in the future they could expand the scale to level 7 or even 10 as they continued to develop their work and negotiate with each other what evidence constituted quality at higher levels. To this end, we found what the teachers in the reflections at the end of the workshop expressed:

> The development of the indicators and the examples that they needed to provide helped to develop aspirations and knowledge about positive teaching. The indicators help us [who were teachers] because we can use the tool for self-development and the development of our colleagues.

There appeared to be a recognition that the motives of others who had not participated in the workshop could be made visible by further developing the digital tool to capture new practices and negotiate what matters.

Discussion

In summary, the object of the activity for the collaborating participants during the workshop was to develop an evaluation tool for measuring quality in the local communes in the highlands of Vietnam where Bah'nar families live. In line with Edwards (2016), the object of the activity had initially been viewed as fixed using pre-existing tools, such as early childhood environmental rating scale (ECERS). However, through the iterative process of negotiating quality indicators and identifying video and photographic images of concrete practices as evidence of what mattered, the participants came to view the object of the activity as provisional, rather than fixed. Indeed, the final tool was named by them to reflect this, and spaces within each tool to upload localized examples of quality practices featured, further supporting the view of provisional and adaptable to context, rather than a fixed object of the activity.

In line with the object of the activity, the collaborations between participants needed to be responsive to the needs of the group for achieving the common goal of developing a quality rating scale that was aligned with the 4 Cornerstone Program. Knowledge about what counted as evidence of quality practices had to be collectively negotiated, and understandings of the different motive orientations of the professionals needed to be understood. Negotiating motives could be achieved because the local participants – rather than the international researchers – were positioned as the people to develop the tool. In so doing, local expertise was made public. Through this common knowledge of valued strategies and quality teaching practices that were reflective of the local context, it was possible to collectively develop a tool that captured the educational needs of the Bah'nar community. This process is very different from what dominates most evaluation studies, and this particular localized approach to building tools for evaluation gives new directions to NGOs who need to have their interventions externally evaluated.

Common knowledge develops over time and is not straightforward, as this case study shows. The practitioners met many contradictions between the motives and valued practices of others, and this needed to be negotiated respectfully. Through bringing in video recordings and photographs of valued ways of working, the local participants could, in the context of aiming at the common goal, negotiate what quality practice looked like and what evidence would be needed to confidently rate what constituted a practice.

How professionals came to negotiate the value placed on strategies and motives were based on the sharing of their expertise about what mattered. But this occurred by actively listening to and negotiating with others about what they considered to be valuable and what they came to learn was valued in other practices. The iterative process of negotiating what constituted quality criteria when developing the quality rating scales gave the possibility of gradually building common knowledge. The findings show that this process was highly valued by the collaborating participants, and indeed this had been an unexpected process at the beginning of the workshop. We argue that this experience builds relational expertise because participants are not just engaging in the process of building common knowledge about what matters, but are actively building expertise in how to do this in ways that are respectful to the others. We suggest that this is also an important component of undertaking external evaluations, and time and space should be given for collaborating professionals to do this important work. It should not be rushed. We found that the iterative nature of building the tool around the 4 Cornerstone Program in relation to what constituted evidence of locally valued practices took longer the first time. But on the development of each scale, this became quicker because trust had been established and the valuing of the others' views foregrounded.

The case study reported in this chapter is an example of how the idea of boundaries between practices can be re-conceptualized as sites of intersecting practices. This study was not about how professionals physically cross professional boundaries by being in another professional's workplace, but rather it was about how professionals working on a common problem make visible what matters to each other as sites of intersecting practices. As explained by Edwards (2016), sites of intersecting practices are where people from different practices meet. The workshop was a good example of such a site. Here the local participants were successful in developing the digital quality rating scale and felt their own funds of knowledge and expertise were valued in the group and were important for contributing to and realizing their common goal. Consequently, we argue that, when undertaking external evaluations, it is important to bring different professionals with different professional practices together to work on a common problem, because the differences between practices create opportunities for really teasing out what matters, and this in turn makes conscious key practices that need to be understood in an external evaluation.

Conclusion

In this chapter, Edwards's (2016) concepts of common knowledge, relational expertise and relational agency were located within a holistic frame developed by Hedegaard (2014). In this framing the concepts of demands and motives are used and together these ideas have provided the conceptual tools needed for understanding the transition of the participants in the study from subjects of research to agents of change. Overall, the findings are in line with Edwards (2016) who has shown in her own research how professionals successfully work together through collaborations that recognize that

1. the object of the activity being considered is provisional, rather than fixed;
2. the sites of intersecting practices need to have established ground rules that comfortably allow participants to elicit each other's motives to determine what matters for them and why;
3. spaces for exploring joint interpretations and responses are needed, where it is recognized that it is possible for common knowledge to develop over time;
4. processes for supporting collaboration that are responsive to the needs of the group in achieving their common goal are important.

The case study in this chapter builds on this summary of Edwards's ideas and introduces three new concepts to explain the transition process observed for the professionals in this study.

First, the group's participation in the practices over the five days (two days in the field and three days workshopping) can be captured through the concept of a *double social situation of the local collaborating participant*. The participants were both thinking about their own professional knowledge and how to explain and show this to others from outside of their profession, while continually discussing how best to capture their negotiated knowledge of strategies in the evaluation tool being developed. That is, they were simultaneously both participants and researchers.

What appeared to be happening over time was that as participants took on the role of preparing an evaluation tool, they became more consciously aware of their own motives and what mattered to them in terms of their professional knowledge. *At the same time*, they appeared to be sensitive to what mattered for others as they showed video and photographic images of valued practices in the preschool, school and community. How they spoke about these valued practices appeared to align over time with the expert knowledge being expressed by others and where terms, criteria and images of valued professional strategies were being negotiated.

Hedegaard (2008) in analysing the role of the researcher in cultural-historically designed studies has introduced the concept of the doubleness of the researcher. In drawing upon the work of Alfred Schultz, she has argued that the researcher is a partner in the activity that is being researched. 'She enters into a social situation with other persons where she has to *understand* what is going on as a participant in everyday practice. But she is also entering the activity setting as a researcher *researching* the activities' (p. 202). Hedegaard (2008) argues that researchers have to conceptualize their role in relation to their own participation – their motives, the project and their intentions. *In our study, the participants did not originally enter into the practice of the research as researchers. Rather, they transitioned into this role through the practice of developing the research tool.* What we found over time was that as participants took on the role of preparing an evaluation tool, they became more consciously aware of their own motives and what mattered to them in terms of their professional knowledge, as well as what might constitute evidence of valued practices in support of the research goal. Consequently, they appeared to become sensitive to what mattered for others as they showed video and photographic images of valued practices in the kindergarten, school and community. How they spoke about these valued practices appeared to align over time with the expert knowledge being expressed by others, where terms, criteria and images of valued professional practices were being negotiated and which eventually informed the scales in the research tool.

In our analysis of this transition, we found that as external researchers we had also entered into the process of sensitizing ourselves into the activity setting in ways that gave voice and agency to local participants to bring forth and use their knowledge, to draw upon their values and to work with their local practices to concretely inform the development of the tool. This is in keeping with past practices for successfully engaging in localized indigenous research practices (see Fleer and Kennedy, 2002).

Second, as with the research of Hedegaard (2016), who found that twin demands on professionals by departments of education motivated the professionals to formulate their own ideas about what mattered for kindergarten practices, this study also found that there were twin demands. In this study, the twin demands of Vietnamese curriculum, which did not align well with the values, practices and resources found in the Bah'nar communes, were different from the expectation in the 4 Cornerstone model to realize *education for all* by the NGO. But what was different in this study was that there were further demands because of the international researchers bringing expert knowledge of research about quality provision in early childhood settings in differently resourced communities. This knowledge of research had to be negotiated in relation to the expert knowledge held by the local participants, and this placed additional demands upon them.

Multiple demands created multiple contradictions that participants had to resolve, and, in so doing, this created a new level of awareness about valued strategies and what was valued in their different institutional practices, as well as that ideas of quality should be negotiated and not viewed as fixed constructs as is often portrayed in quality assessment tools. This finding supported the development of participants' motive orientation towards moving away from fixed international measures of quality towards localized strategies that were culturally meaningful in the Bah'nar communes. We capture this idea through the dynamic concept of *local-global contradictions* for measuring quality.

Third, the common goal of foregrounding what were indicators of quality for the education in the communities was embraced developmentally/incrementally, and this meant that participants transitioned from subjects of research to agents of change – through the researchers organizing a process of negotiation where the assumption was that local participants had greater knowledge of the context than we did and by creating the conditions that positioned them as *agents of practice change*. The NGO staff were participants in the process of developing the tool, as were the international researchers, but all participated in ways that positioned them as one of a group of *agents of practice change* drawing on their own expert knowledge and emerging relational expertise. The methodology has been previously presented in relation to the tool development (Fleer et al., 2018), but how the development of the tool supported the development of the different professionals was not considered.

The agentic position that resulted was made visible through the conceptual tools of common knowledge, relational expertise and relational agency within a holistic research frame of analysing motives and demands of participating professionals. What we theorize through these concepts and the findings is that the transition discussed in the case study can be collectively explained through the concepts of *double social situations of the local researchers, local-global contradictions* and *agents of practice change*. These concepts contribute to the literature by capturing and explaining how the local professionals transitioned from subjects of research to agents of change for their own communities.

Acknowledgements

This project was supported by Plan Vietnam. Members of the team who worked with the researchers in Vietnam were Binh Nguyen Lang, Hau Hoang Thi Thai, Giang Thai Thu and Chau Nguyen Thi Diep. The overall research being undertaken also involves Liang Li, Hilary Monk, Gloria Quiñones and Corinne Rivalland from Monash University. Support from Nicole Rodger, programme manager (ECCD and Education) from Plan International Australia is also acknowledged. The intervention project is implemented by Plan International Vietnam with technical support from Plan International Australia. The main donor is the New Zealand Aid Program, with some match funding provided by Australian Aid. The project was reviewed and approved by Monash University's ethics committee approval number C174/1388-2014001723.

References

Baulch, B., Chuyen, T. T. K., Haughton, D., and Haughton, J. (2007). Ethnic minority development in Vietnam. *The Journal of Development Studies*, 43(7), 1151–76. doi:10.1080/02673030701526278.

Bozhovich, L. I. (2009). The social situation of child development. *Journal of Russian and East European Psychology*, 47(4), 59–86.

Edwards, A. (2016). Revealing relational work. In A. Edwards (Ed.), *Working relationally in and across practices. A cultural-historical approach to collaboration* (pp. 1–21). New York: Cambridge University Press.

Fenech, M., Sweller, N., and Harrison, L. (2010). Identifying high quality centre-based childcare using quantitative data-sets: What the numbers do and don't tell us. *International Journal of Early Years Education*, 18(4), 283–96. doi: 10.1080/09669760.2010.531615.

Fleer, M., and Williams-Kennedy, D. (2002). *Building bridges: Researching literacy development for young Indigenous children.* ACT: Australian Early Childhood Association.

Fleer, M., Hedges, H., Fleer-Stout, F., and Le Thi, B. H. (2018). Researcher intersubjectivity: A methodology for jointly building an interactive electronic early childhood quality involvement/rating scale. *International Journal of Research and Method in Education*, 41(1), 69–88. doi:10.1080/1743727X.2016.1219982.

Gregory, E., and Ruby, M. (2011). The 'insider/outsider' dilemma of ethnography: Working with young children and their families in cross-cultural contexts. *Journal of Early Childhood Research*, 9(2) 162–74. doi: 10.1177/1476718X10387899.

Harms, T., R. Clifford, and Cryer, D. (2005). *Early childhood environment rating scale.* Revised edition. New York: Teachers College Press.

Hedegaard, M. (2008). The role of the researcher. In M. Hedegaard and M. Fleer (Eds), *Studying children. A cultural-historical approach* (pp. 202–7). Berkshire: Open University Press.

Hedegaard, M. (2012). Analyzing children's learning and development in everyday settings from a cultural-historical wholeness approach. *Mind Culture and Activity*, 19(2). 127–38.

Hedegaard, M. (2014). The significance of demands and motives across practices in children's learning and development. An analysis of learning in home and school. *Learning, Culture and Social Interaction*, 3, 188–94.

Hedegaard, M. (2016). When daycare professionals' values for transitions to school do not align with the educational demands from society and school: A practice developing research project for daycare professionals' support to children's transition to school. In A. Edwards (Ed.), *Working relationally in and across practices. A cultural-historical approach to collaboration* (pp. 247–64). New York: Cambridge University Press.

Hopwood, N. (2016). Expertise, learning, and agency in partnership practices in services for families with young children. In A. Edwards (Ed.), *Working relationally in and across practices. A cultural-historical approach to collaboration* (pp. 25–42). New York: Cambridge University Press.

Le Thi Bich, H., and Nguyen, L. B. (2013). Indigenous study report on early childhood care and development knowledge and practices in Bahnar ethic minority communities. Unpublished Report. Ha Noi: Plan Vietnam.

Moll, L. C., Amanti, C., Neff, D., and Gonzalez, N. (1992). Funds of knowledge for teaching: Using a qualitative approach to connect homes and classrooms. *Theory into Practice*, *31*(2), 132–41. doi:10.1080/00405849209543534.

Montecinos, C., Leiva, M. V., Campos, F., Ahumada, L. and Galdames, S. (2016). An analysis of the use of relational expertise, relational agency, and common knowledge among newly appointed principals in Chile's public schools. In A. Edwards (Ed.), *Working relationally in and across practices. A cultural-historical approach to collaboration* (pp. 78–95). New York: Cambridge University Press.

Rai, P. C. (2016). Building and using common knowledge for developing school-community links. In A. Edwards (Ed.), *Working relationally in and across practices. A cultural-historical approach to collaboration* (pp. 96–112). New York: Cambridge University Press.

Vygotsky, L. S. (1998). *The collected works of L.S. Vygotsky: Vol. 5. Child Psychology*. Ed. L. S. Vygotsky. New York: Plenum.

Additional references

Sakai, L. M., Whitebook, M., Wishard, A., and Howes, C. C. (2003). Evaluating the Early Childhood Environment Rating Scale (ECERS): Assessing differences between the first and revised edition. *Early Childhood Research Quarterly*, *18*(4), 427–45. doi:10.1016/j.ecresq.2003.09.004.

Vermeer, H. J., van Ijzendoorn, M. H., Carcamo, R. A., and Harrison, L. J. (2016). Quality of child care using the environmental rating scales: A meta-analysis of international studies. *International Journal of Early Childhood*, *48*(1), 33–60. doi:10.1007/s13158-015-0154.

5

Radical-Local Screening of Preschool Children's Social Situations of Development: From Abilities to Activities

Mariane Hedegaard and Naussúnguaq Lyberth

Introduction

This chapter presents theoretical considerations for constructing a radical-local screening tool for preschool children in Greenland. The instrument was created to evaluate three- and five-year-old children's developmental situation and also to assess whether the latter were prepared to enter school. The material has been named UBUS 3 and UBUS 5 (Undersøgelse af Børns Udviklings Situation) – in English, *Investigation of Children's Developmental Situation – At Three and Five Years Old*. In this chapter, we discuss the background and reasons for the construction of a radical-local screening tool and illustrate how this may be done. We argue that while constructing an instrument to evaluate children's social situation of development, the focus should be on the child's activities, instead of their functions and abilities in isolation from the environment. This perspective means that both the conditions and children's competence and orientation to participate in developmental activities are assessed. Such an approach to assessment will offer insights into the possibilities for intervention in a child's actual developmental situation if it is judged to be problematic. This also has implications for identifying the kind of support needed for preparing children's transition from home or nursery to preschool and from kindergarten to school. The instrument can be seen as *radical-local* because it builds on a wholeness theory of child development that focuses on children's learning and motive orientation as cultural, anchored in local conditions and traditions (Hedegaard and Chaiklin, 2005; Hedegaard, 2012).

The background for creating a new screening tool for assessing children's development in Greenland

The creation of UBUS 3 and UBUS 5 was initiated by the government of Greenland. The government has been concerned about the quality of the home and day-care environments experienced by young children in Greenland and the impact unfortunate conditions can have on children's development.

The history of early childhood education in Greenland has to be seen in relation to the Danish colonization of the country. The preschool institutions and practices are modelled after the Danish system. When the first preschool was introduced, the teachers spoke Danish, though the children have always been allowed to speak Greenlandic. When Greenland, in 1979, got home rule, the most prevalent language among preschool teachers became Greenlandic. Today, two third of all young children attend preschool.

In 2007, the government in Greenland initiated a research project led by the Danish National Center for Social Research. This resulted in a rather depressing report about family conditions for children from birth to 14 years of age. The research method was quantitative, based on a representative selection of Greenlandic families and children. Primarily, the mothers were interviewed about their children's well-being. One conclusion from the project was that one third of all children in Greenland had troublesome developmental conditions (Christensen, Kristiansen and Baviskar, 2008). This conclusion is debatable as the validity of the telephone interview method is questionable. The questions were about sensitive areas of upbringing and could not be easily discussed in a telephone interview using an interpreter. Nonetheless, as a result of the project, the Ministry of Education in Greenland created, in 2012, the Center for Early Childhood Education (CECE) for which Naussúnguaq Lyberth became the leader. The research study also led to Government Act No 16 of 3 December 2012, § 5, that in subsection 6 stated: 'Screening of children's health and development are compulsory when a child reaches the age of three and when a child reaches the age of five.'[1]

This government act was followed by the demand for an instrument that could assess the children and guide day-care practitioners in supporting vulnerable children's development and prepare them for transition from kindergarten to school. The Ministry of Education assigned the task of creating a screening tool to the CECE. The focus was to be on three- and five-year-old children's well-being and psychological development, and CECE was to work in cooperation with a task force group with representatives from other departments in the government of Greenland that work with children. The task force group included the Ministry of Health and Infrastructure (PAN) Department of Family and Justice (IAAN) and Department of Church, Culture and Gender Equality (IKIIN), as well as the organization of pedagogical consultancies and the organization of school psychologists (PPR). The head of the ECCE, Naussúnguaq Lyberth, became the head of the task force group. The group held several meetings reviewing available screening materials for young children. These included materials already in use in Greenland as well as international materials that were useable and could be modified in relation to the screening of three- and five-year-old children in Greenland.[2]

The task group decided that materials that already were in use in Greenland did not adequately depict the health, well-being and developmental situation of children in Greenland. They similarly found that the American/British screening materials that the CECE had knowledge of were not adequate for assessing children in a Greenlandic context. They came to the conclusion that the CECE had to construct their own screening tool to be able to evaluate children's health, well-being and developmental situations in Greenland, because both the conditions and traditions were different from where the available material had been developed. This decision also had to be seen in connection with the initiative the government had taken to renew the early educational practice in Greenland. The government had supported the introduction, in 2007, of an educational programme developed by Roland Tharp in Hawaii named after Center for Research on Education, Diversity and Excellence as CREDE. The programme built on the cultural-historical traditions from Vygotsky and had been adapted to the Greenlandic context and named *Effective Pedagogic*. Staff in the different early childhood institutions (preschool and family day care) in Greenland have over the last 10 years participated in educational activities related to this programme through courses held locally by the CECE (a report of the results of this initiative is under preparation by the CECE).

The task force group invited Professor Mariane Hedegaard (Copenhagen University) to collaborate with them. Hedegaard works within the Vygotskian cultural-historical tradition and had some knowledge about the education in Greenland, being a teacher for masters students in educational psychology there. She has written about and argued for the importance of taking both cultural conditions and the child's perspective into consideration in any evaluation of children's learning and development (Hedegaard, 2008, 2012, 2018). Hedegaard and the CECE took on the task of constructing a screening tool that was sensitive to the conditions that children faced in Greenland, focusing on children's social situation as well as their development. This focus can be seen as radical-local, since the aim was to create a tool oriented towards children's general development (radical: cultural-historical) that included the concrete social conditions at the same time (local: situated and concrete) (Hedegaard and Chaiklin, 2005).

The task force group identified six areas for the assessment of a child's social situation of development. The goal was to provide care workers in day-care institutions and carers at home insights into the child's current social situation of development through their answers to questions in relation to the child's well-being and development of activities. Insights from these answers could then be used to initiate educational activities. The intention was that these new activities should draw on the principles of Effective Pedagogic, with which day-care staff in Greenland were already familiar.

The result of the task force group's work became a screening tool that reflected the activities and competences that the educational system in Greenland evaluated as important and was designed so that early childhood education staff and carers could use it as a tool to assess a child's well-being and activities that all together characterizes his or her social situation of development. By the child's social situation of development we mean both the child's activities and the conditions that pedagogues and carers provide to enable the child to take him or herself forward as a learner. The assessment was directed at six areas: the first one (1) was connected to the child's *health and well-being*. The following five were connected to how the child relates to other people participating in shared activities: (2) *social interaction and competences* (focus area: how the child relates to other people and creates contacts), (3) *communication and language competences* (focus area: how the child relates to other people through language), (4) *sensation and movement* (focus area: how the child relates to other persons by moving around and paying attention), (5) *cooperation and initiation of activities* (focus area: how the child contributes to shared frameworks and children-led activities), and (6) *knowledge of nature and culture* (focus area: how the child relates to nature and cultural activities in Greenland).

Theoretical foundation for developing a screening tool directed at children's social situations in everyday practices

All assessments and screening materials for studying children's development are based on assumptions about how children develop. Most materials today assume a relatively fixed view of development of various functions, which reflects a fixed order of stages of development. An example of such an approach, well known in Greenland, is *Kuno Beller's developmental description* (Weltzer, 1995), which has questions aimed at the institutional assessment of children's functions from which a profile is created describing the child's strong and weak functions. We will not go into detail on this approach, but would simply note that, although the screening material we have constructed to investigate three- and five-year-old children's developmental situation, UBUS 3 and UBUS 5, may at first glance look like Kuno Beller's developmental description, they are quite different. Although they require employees in preschools to answer sets of questions, the differences are crucial. Our understanding and the construction of UBUS 3 and UBUS 5 builds on the theory of Lev Vygotsky (1993, 1998) and are directed towards evaluating children's activities in everyday settings. Kuno Beller's material built on Jean Piaget and Erik Eriksson's theories – theories that conceptualize children's development in relation to psychological functions (cognitive, perceptual, motor, social or emotional) as series of stages that follow each other in a fixed order. These functional approaches do not reveal the importance of the cultural conditions children live in and the values in the social interaction that is the foundation for children's development.

Max Wartofsky, in the early 1980s, questioned Piaget's stage description of children's thinking in which he proposed that development occurred through a fixed sequence from motor actions to logical thinking. Wartofsky argues that Piaget used an essentialist ontology of childhood where the child is conceptualized as a genetically fixed and determinate entity. In opposition to this, he writes:

> What is needed instead is a radically cultural conception of *childhood*, one that acknowledge the historicity of the conception, and therefore also the extent to which the category essentially transcends the biogenetic characterization; and that also acknowledges the extent to which the biogenetic characterizations themselves mirror different cultural and historical norms. (Wartofsky, 1983, p. 192)

Erik Erikson's description of children's emotional development as progression through eight stages in a straightforward sequence has been similarly questioned. The counterposition, offered by Margaret Mead (1956) and Barbara Rogoff (2003), is that stages or periods in development have to be seen as anchored in a cultural tradition and historical time. In line with this, the child's developmental situation with its cultural activities is seen as central to UBUS 3 and UBUS 5. Ways of participating in everyday activities and relating to the world are assumed, in our designing of the screening material, to have a greater influence on a child's life course than the biological potential a child is born with (Hedegaard, 2008; Rogoff, 2003; Vygotsky, 1993, 1998). Our assumption is that only if a child's way of acting in everyday activities is included in the evaluation, is it possible to see how education has and potentially can support a child's learning and development.

A wholeness approach to children's development

Vygotsky, in his writing in the 1920s and early 1930s, argued that children should not only be seen in their context but that the contextual conditions and the child are a unit (1998, p. 198). To express this, Vygotsky formulated the concept of the child's social situation of development. Leontiev followed Vygotsky's approach and described the relation between people and the social conditions in which they are situated as united in a dynamic relationship with each other:

> Humans do not simply find external conditions to which they must adapt their activity. Rather these social conditions bear with them the motives and goals of their activity, its means and modes. (Leontiev, 1978, pp. 47–8)

A way to extend Leontiev's theory is to locate the social conditions in institutional practices, such as home or preschool, each with purposes that children are expected to orient to and acquire (Hedegaard, 2009, 2012). Focusing on institutional features allows an analysis of the conditions of a child's development in some detail. One implication of this dialectical relation between a person and their environment (life world) is that when researching human development one cannot separate a person from their life world (Barker and Wright, 1949, 1971; Brofenbrenner, 1979; Bozhovich, 2009).

This view that acting subjects and their environment are intimately related requires analytic tools that capture this dynamic relation. The dynamic can be caught when focusing on the relation between the person's motives as she engages in an activity and the demands of the practice in which the activity is located, seeing it as a mediated relation. This mediation is usually conceptualized as an educational process in which tools, artefacts and procedures in all their variations are important mediators (Hedegaard, 2012, 2014).

Interplay between biology and culture in children's development

A child's development is both biological and cultural. Biology is the foundation for the child's acquisition of cultural competences, but this is not one-dimensional and can take different forms, reflecting how the interaction in local activities takes place (Rogoff, 2003).

One of Vygotsky's (1987) most important theoretical points is that children with disabilities also have developmental processes where the community and communication are crucial for their mental development, but different forms of community and communication may be needed from those available for children without disabilities. Louise Bøttcher (2018; Bøttcher and Dammeyer, 2016) is one of the researchers who has strongly pointed out that, in relation to children with disabilities, caregivers (such as day-care staff and teachers) must be aware that the biological conditions of children with disabilities mean that their progress does not match that of children in mainstream educational provision. This does not mean that pedagogy should not support the development of disabled children in day care or in school. Rather, the development of these children must be supported by other means (tools) in order for disabled children to gain competencies so they can participate in activities that are valued in the society in which they live and that can help them lead a dignified life. Children with disabilities need both support and challenges and opportunities to play and have fun, in the same way as other children. We therefore need to look at children's activities and their developmental potential in order to offer the most developmentally conducive conditions for them.

Culture and educational requirements

A central characteristic of modern society is that there is compulsory schooling for all children for a period of at least 9 to 10 years. It gives a certain common foundation for children's personality formation because children, at the very least, learn to read, write and calculate, but hopefully also get knowledge and competences in relation to nature, history and culture of their own country and of the world in general. However, even with a common basis for schooling, there may still be major differences in the way of life and in day-care institutions within the same society. In Greenland, differences between settlements and the city and between West and East Greenland engender different living conditions. In Nuuk, the capital, you have central heating and running water, sewerage and an extensive road network. In the different settlements in the countryside, you need to collect water, take care of your own sewage and heat, and in East Greenland one might be at risk of meeting a polar bear close to one's home or school. In spite of this diversity, however, there is a common basis for children growing up through common government, language, news media (radio, television, etc.), schooling, childcare and other welfare arrangements.

When assessing the children's development situations, we need to see these in connection with the specific living conditions. While we have tried to find a middle ground, we do not, however, wish to eliminate the differences between different life forms in Greenland. We believe that activities and competences associated with modern society give children the freedom to choose their future; therefore, day care and schooling are important. The conditions for children's learning and development in early childhood must give them possibilities for learning at school. The skills children receive through schooling should then give them opportunities to be able to participate in the local community and, if they want, to move to new communities, where there are other competencies needed that extend beyond their local community.

We recognize that the children may meet different values and demands in different institutional practices (i.e. home, kindergarten and school) and these differences can present challenges that are important for children's development. Most important here is that the differences between home, day care and school in educational practice may complement, rather than contradict, each other, and the institutions accept each other's different requirements.

Despite the fact that we do not accept fixed inborn stages as characteristic of children's development, we do need to talk about periods in children's development. These periods, however, are related to the educational practice children become involved in as well as their biological growth (Elkonin, 1999). Children are in different development situations, whether they are at home, in day care, in nursery or kindergarten or at school, or when they are older, in higher education. In recognizing these changes as developmental conditions, moving from one practice to a new we concentrate on the differences in children's activities. Developmental periods in children's development reflect which institutions are leading their activities. These differences in institutional practices come to characterize different developmental periods, where the change from one dominant practice to a new one influences children's motive orientation and competences.

Play as the central way to learn in preschool age

In the Danish and Greenlandic nurseries, day-care and family traditions for infants and toddlers, children are given the freedom to explore their surroundings. In infancy and early childhood, this freedom is largely linked to meaningful imitation of actions where play as a way of exploration begins to take the form of trying out activities; play is therefore seen as significant for day-care children's learning.

Children's play is closely related to the culture they inhabit. Children's play is not always self-evident; therefore, it is important that parents and caregivers are aware of the need to create conditions for play. It is also important for children's play development that adults take time to play with children (Stern, 1985; Fleer, 2014). Play changes when a child moves from explorative play onto symbol use, such as when the child starts to use objects or actions as substitutes for other objects or activities (Vygotsky, 1967). There is a separation between the object and its meaning when a child, for example, plays with a spoon, flying it like an airplane. In this way an object becomes a symbol of another object. A spoon symbolizes an airplane, and the movement of the child waving her arms symbolizes that the plane is flying. This distinction between object and meaning, and between action and meaning, creates the basis for children learning to use symbols in their activities and communication. Through joint play activities and negotiation in play, children also get a basis for learning to control themselves, to plan activities and to come to understand narratives that are not linked to concrete experienced situations, but can arise from other children's imaginations. Through play, children begin to deal with rules for, and models of, their activities and explorations (Schousboe, 2013), and learn to manage their feelings (Winnicott, 1977; Hedegaard, 2016). Play is therefore very important in creating the foundations for schools' intellectual activities.

When children enter school, it is important to understand that play is still important for their intellectual activities. Here, play more directly may take the form of exploration and planned experimentation – a way of learning that is very important in school education (Davydov, 1990; Hedegaard, 1988, 2002; Hedegaard and Chaiklin; 2005; Tharph, Estrada, Dalton and Yamauchi, 2000). In UBUS 3 and UBUS 5, we therefore investigate children's opportunities for play and exploration and how the adults create a developmental situation that promotes children's learning through play.

Design of UBUS 3 and UBUS 5 as a radical-local tool

The task of constructing a screening tool, given to the task force group, was initiated by the government *to support children in difficulties* as early as possible. The group extended this task so that the screening instrument could also be seen as a tool for *educational support to all children* in Greenland, as well as a means of finding vulnerable children. The task force group agreed therefore to build a screening tool that took both children's development of competences to participate in activities and the local conditions for early childhood education into consideration. To accomplish this, the construction of UBUS 3 and UBUS 5 draws on the theory of development, as outlined above, as well as knowledge of the concrete traditions of the institutional practices for early childhood education in Greenland.

Although the institutional practice traditions in kindergarten in Greenland have their origin in the Danish kindergarten traditions, they have been renewed with inspiration from the CREDE initiative developed by Tharp and his colleagues in Hawaii.

The educational ideas that come from Denmark emphasized play as an important activity in early childhood. In 2004, the Danish Ministry of Family and Consumer Affairs confirmed this as a priority which was reflected in the six learning areas to be implemented in Danish early education. These six areas became the starting points for the development of the Greenland screening tools.[3] The educational practice with inspiration from CREDE started in 2007 through courses held initially by Roland Tharp, the head of CREDE (Tharp, Estrada, Dalton and Yamauchi, 2000). Tharp had been invited by the Educational Department of Greenland government to advice on how to develop education in Greenland's schools. A major concern was language diversity, stemming from a two-languages politic of using Greenlandic and Danish language in schools and from value differences manifested in Greenlandic and Danish living traditions. Both features of school life made it difficult for children to learn and for teachers to teach.

Lyberth, as head of the task force group, played a central role in creating UBUS 3 and UBUS 5, drawing on her knowledge of the practice traditions in early childhood education and how it had evolved in Greenland. She had a Danish Pedagogue's education and was quite familiar with the CREDE standards. She reformulated the CREDE standards to principles for preschool education in Greenland and, since 2008, together with the staff from the CECE, held courses for staff in Greenland's kindergarten to mediate these reformulated CREDE standards as Effective Pedagogic.[4]

The task force group took departure from the Danish learning areas for early childhood education and the standards of Effective Pedagogic stemming from CREDE when formulating the questions in UBUS 3 and UBUS 5. This resulted, as we have seen, in six areas for assessment. While the first centred on children's health and well-being, the other five areas focused on children's competences to participate in activities.[5] Together these areas are seen as tools for evaluation the social situation of development for a specific child, which also has to be seen as the child's pedagogical situation. An early year's worker has to fill out an evaluation form for each focus area with three questions when a child turns three and when she or he turns five. The answers to these questions could be positive, negative or partial; if the answer was 'no' or 'partial', a narrative description was required. If the child was not in day care, a carer from home or a health nurse is expected to answer the questions.

The scoring of the forms enables the person answering the questions to construct a profile by feeding the answers to the questions into a model that is part of the screening tool. If there are areas of concern in the responses, the person answering the questions should offer solutions that may be tried out in the institution in cooperation with the child's home. The material should also be sent to the CECE and telephone advice could be given. Solutions or interventions to change a child's social situation should be taken whenever a partial or negative answer is given to the questions. Depending on the concerns, the person answering the questions might also be advised to contact a doctor or school psychologist.

How to evaluate differences between three- and five-year-old children – validating UBUS 3 and UBUS 5

One can formulate some general differences using handbooks of child development (e.g. Lightfood, Cole and Cole, 2012) to differentiate between three- and five-year-olds' competences. The differences in criteria one find in American psychological textbooks do not quite reflect what is expected of children in day-care institutions located in different societies (Rogoff, 2003), nor do they reflect the educational conditions they have. Even though we name it three- and five-year-olds' competence, these competences also reflect the educational situation. An example that was mentioned in the task force group is of a day-care mother in a county of North Greenland who did not allow her children to play outside because there could be sled dogs on the loose, and she was afraid they would attack her children. In this case, the three-year-old children might get a score of 'partial' or 'no' for questions relating to movement and knowledge of nature.

Across the Nordic countries, there are some shared views on what should be expected of a three-year-old and a five-year-old child. At three years, children are expected to be ready to go to preschool, be able to control their own movement and not use diapers at daytime, imitate other people and start to play. At five years, they are expected to be ready for school. Expectations of three- and five-year-old children are therefore built into institutional practice in day care and the routines children meet here. Consequently, we cannot evaluate a child's competences in isolation. Areas that are seen as important in the Nordic countries are an ability to trust others and control oneself, explore and play, and to initiate and cooperate in activities. An example of how the difference between three- and five-year-old children's social competence of interaction were put into questions can be seen in Table 5.1.

Educational values

To construct an assessment tool like UBUS 3 and UBUS 5, it is central that it captures important values in Greenland in relation to children's development. Therefore, the task force group had to represent different institutions related to child care in Greenland, and its members were assigned to represent a broad spectrum of institutional values in Greenland. The task force group had several meetings and created minutes from these meetings before coming to an agreement. After the first versions of UBUS 3 and UBUS 5 were agreed upon, the CECE created three test trials together with Hedegaard, sending the material to selected day-care institutions in the four counties in Greenland.[6] Parallel to the trials, CECE personnel visited the institutions to help support the use of the material and make observations, interviews, and later send questionnaires to the staff in the test institutions (an overview of the testing can be seen in Table 5.2). Between the test trials, the task force group met and discussed the results. Two of the trials focused on how both the well-trained and untrained employees

Table 5.1 The difference in area (2), social competence and interaction between three- and five-year-old children in how they make contacts and establish friendships

	UBUS 3 area 2	UBUS 5 area 2
Question 1	The child may play with others	The child contacts other children with ideas for play activity
Question 2	The child contacts other children to participate in play	The child accepts decisions and is led by shared rules, that is, accepting guidelines and rules in play and games
Question 3	The child accepts being close to adults	The child accepts bodily contact as well as contact at a distance, can express wishes for nearness or create boundaries for this

Table 5.2 Design for validating UBUS 3 and UBUS 5's screening of three- and five-year-old Children's Social Situation of Development, 2013–2016

	Involved day-care centres	Children being screened	Focus children observed	Interview of staff	Questionnaires
Trial 1	7	14	14	10	0
Trial 2	5	12	0	0	12
Trial 3	6	42	0	0	42

Three-year-old children screened and observed in all four counties. Interviews and questionnaires of staff

Trial 1	6	22	20	5	0
Trial 2	5	17	0	0	17
Trial 3	6	61	0	0	61

Five-year-old children screened and observed in all four counties. Interviews and questionnaires of staff could understand and fill in the forms. Through the trialling, interviews and questionnaires, the questions in the screening material were adapted to reflect Greenlandic staff's understanding of the issues in the different counties of North, Central, South and East Greenland.

CECE personnel carried out observations of focus children, by using interaction-based observations (Hedegaard, 2008). These focused on central aspects of children's development to ensure that UBUS 3 and UBUS 5 identified children that the day-care staff should be concerned about, as well as finding the criteria for concern. The observation method is based on the interaction between the child and the observer to understand the problems from the child's perspective. Through an active participation in the situation, the observer may gain insight into how the child participates in activities and relates to the demands placed on the child and what relationship there is between the surrounding people's intention and the child's intentions, and if this involves conflicts that also involve the child.

In addition to these three trials, two national conferences were held, one before and one after the last trial. Representatives of school psychologists and pedagogical consultancies as well as the staff in the test institutions were invited to the conferences. At the second conference, in addition to the same persons, members of the Department of Education were invited. Outlines of how UBUS 3 and UBUS 5 may be used in relation to school psychology practice were presented. Suggestions for adjustments from the participants were taken into consideration in developing the screening material and the instructions for its use.

The zone of concern: How to use the results from the UBUS 3 and UBUS 5

The outlines for using the screening tool built on creating profiles of the scores. Since staff can answer yes, partial or no in their assessment of children's activities, different profiles could be developed (see Figures 5.1 and 5.2). The scoring on the first area in the screening material (evaluation of children's health and well-being) needs to be positive; otherwise, the staff has to take immediate action and get medical help by contacting a doctor and or a school psychologist. They also need to involve the parents, so that shared care can be started. If the scoring at some of the other five areas is negative or there are more than two partial scores, the day-care institutions should contact the school psychologist, but they should also themselves suggest an intervention strategy that has to be realized immediately.

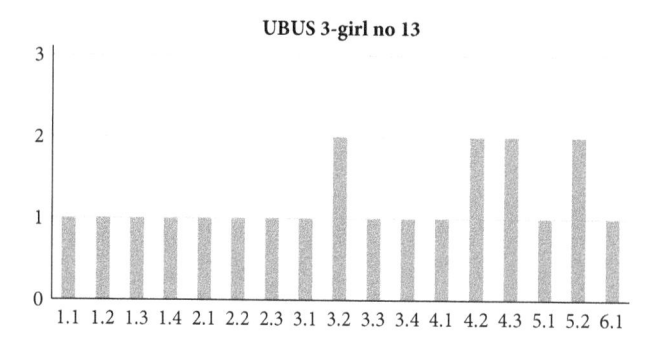

Radical-Local Screening of Preschool Children's Social Situations   105

UBUS 3-girl no 13

Figure 5.1 UBUS 3, profile of a three-year-old girl, first trial.

The vertical axis illustrates the answer (yes (1), partial (2) or no (3)).

The horizontal axis depicts the six areas – 1.1–1.4: social interaction and competences, 2.1–2.3: communication and language competences, 3.1–3.4: sensation and movement, 4.1–4.3: cooperation and initiation of activities, 5.1–5.2: knowledge of nature and culture, and 6.1: health and well-being.[7]

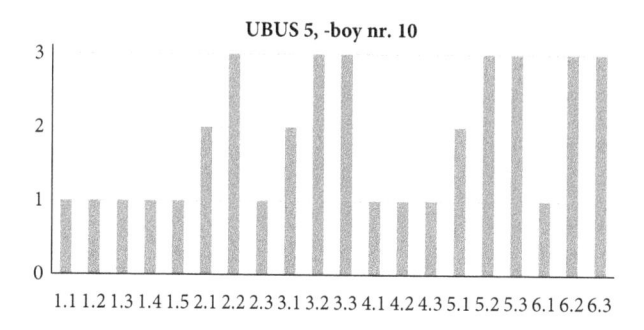

UBUS 5, -boy nr. 10

Figure 5.2 UBUS 5 profile of a five-year-old boy.

The vertical axis illustrates the answer (yes (1), partial (2) or no (3)).

The horizontal axis depicts the six areas – 1.1–1.5: health and well-being, 2.1–2.3: social interaction and competences, 3.1–3.3: communication and language competences, 4.1–4.3: sensation and movement, 5.1–5.3: cooperation and initiation of activities, and 6.1–6.3: knowledge of nature and culture.

Examples in Figures 5.1 and 5.2 illustrate differences that lead to different forms of intervention. The first profile shows that a three-year-old girl only partially masters age-relevant activities of *movement and sensation, cooperation and initiation of activities* and *cultural activities*. The instruction says that if this is the case also for other children in the institution, the kindergarten staff have to take this into consideration in their educational plan for all children. They may make the change for all children even if only one child has this problem, while ensuring that the specific child is particularly supported. After three months, they have to evaluate their progress by filling out a new form, so as to see if their interventions have supported the child in his or her activities.

The evaluation of a three-year-old girl

As demonstrated in the profile, the girl only partially mastered body activities, for example, taking clothes on and off, drawing, making puzzles, jumping, singing and dancing (3). She does not initiate activities (4) and does not yet participate in singing, music and dance (5).

Educational advice from CECE

The adults should pay attention to her when she takes clothes on and off to support her in doing this.

The adults, along with a small group of children, should initiate role-play activities as father, mother and children to demonstrate to the child the attributes of each of these roles. In the role of the doctors, you can merge songs and music. The adults should initiate song play to support the girl's imitation and play. The adults also may initiate doctor plays where the girl may explore her body or play where she may jump, roll and dance (or play dogs, monkeys and other animals).

The second profile (Figure 5.2) shows a five-year-old boy whose social situation of development is really problematic.

The pedagogue that filled out UBUS 5 wrote the following as a comment:

> He has difficulty accepting, for example, that he must not go outside the playground's fence despite explanations. He will not always wash hands before eating time. Nor does he want to participate when we are singing in the group or doing shared activities. After half a year in the kindergarten, the boy still cannot name the children and the adults. The boy never tells anything about what they do at home or in holidays. The adults find it hard to understand the boy when he talks.

The evaluation of the five-year-old boy

The boy seems healthy and in general happy (1). His way of communicating with the other children and adults is not the best, and he does not play with words or talk about his experiences (2). He knows that one has to accept rules in play and games, but he do not negotiate about these in play and he cannot distinguish between reality and fantasy when listening to stories and in play (3). He does not accept staff's decisions and will not be guided by decisions in a play group (5). He does not know the seasons of the year and cannot tell about animal or plants. He does not participate in cultural activities such as imitating singing or dancing (6).

Educational advice from CECE

While consulting school psychology in accordance with the municipality's rules, focusing especially on communicative and linguistic development, special pedagogical precautions must be taken immediately. In cooperation with the parents, a plan of action should be drawn up on how to teach the boy to participate in joint activities. The boy must learn to participate in a small group where the boy must learn to accept certain rules. Day-care staff and parents have to focus on the boy's positive activities and praise them, and in positive constructive ways talk about rules. The adults must be aware of the boy's learning about nature and culture to support him in this.

General evaluation of profiles

The evaluation of a child's screening profile creates a useful visual image that the day-care staff can share with the child's primary carers. It can therefore be used as a point of departure for creating common knowledge between home and day care (Edwards, 2010, 2017). As we explained in Chapter 1, common knowledge consists of what matters in a practice, enabling the problem being worked on to be expanded in discussions about what is important, and it also allows for a range of specialist knowledge, including that of parents, to be brought into play when working on a problem relating to the child's social situation of development. It can be used so that the different practitioners within the supporting systems of CECE, medical specialists and the school psychologists with their different strengths can act together in relation to what matters for them as professionals when supporting the child's well-being in his or her everyday social situation.

Conclusion

What we have aimed at in constructing UBUS 3 and UBUS 5 has been to create an instrument which can be used to evaluate children's well-being and activities in their everyday settings in the practices of day care and home. With this tool, we want to focus on the child's participation in different activities in interaction with early years workers and other children. For preschool children the conditions and how this participation takes place create the child's social situation of development. The focus in the assessment is on the interaction of a child with staff and other children, not their abilities as isolated and independent features.

In addition, UBUS 3 and UBUS 5 can be seen as an instrument with the potential to create common knowledge using relational expertise (Edwards, 2010, 2017) across the different institutions that comprise the child's life world. It can be used in ways that can support preschool children's social situations of development, in particular through liaison between home and preschool.

Our starting point has been that periods in children's development are closely connected with the traditions and values in the institutions they participate in. So when we have to assess children entering day care around three or becoming oriented to school at five, we need to consider how they fit with the practices in day care and school, but we also need to consider the cultural environments of the home. To support transitions from home to preschool and to school, it is important to have a tool that can be used to create common knowledge for parents, day-care staff and teachers to offer support that respects the traditions of both home and the different educational setting of day care and school. This requirement for common knowledge is also important for those working with vulnerable children, who need the support of medical and psychological specialists.

If children are not able to orient themselves to school when they are five or six, attention needs to be paid to the daily activities they participate in. They will need help in creating an orientation to school that also respects the family values that might be quite different. It is therefore important that those involved in supporting the child are also able to support each other. Our argument throughout this chapter has been that those adults who are central to the child's learning and development need to pay attention to helping the child create social situations of development which allow them to overcome the difficulties to be found in what we label a zone of concern.

The focus on the conditions in which the child develops as a learner is crucial. Our premise has been that children need to be able to access and evaluate powerful cultural concepts that operate across localities and situations as well as being sensitive to what is valued in the cultural traditions of their communities. Being able to do so, as we said earlier, give them choices in their future lives. There can be cultural differences within the same nation, as there is in Greenland, but day-care and school practice have to aim at giving children possibility for development so they can enter into the institutions that give equal opportunities for education independent of where they live in Greenland.

In Greenland, the government has been very focused on this aim by creating the CECE and its role in educating day-care staff in the standards of Effective Pedagogy stemming from CREDE and now initiating a screening material for evaluation preschool children social situation of development and readiness for school.

A parallel project to CREDE was initiated in 1989 in New York City by Hedegaard and Chaiklin (2005), as radical-local teaching and learning. Both this project and CREDE were oriented to cover diversity to create equal opportunities for children in the school system. But none of these projects have formulated an assessment system, which reflects their cultural-historical origins. This is what is realized with UBUS 3 and UBUS 5 with the idea that it should address the diversity that the different conditions give children in Greenland and at the same time initiate the building of common knowledge between different educational systems in relation to a child's zone of proximal development.

Notes

1 Inatsisartutlov nr. 16 af 3. December 2012 om pædagogisk udviklende tilbud til børn i førskolealderen, § 5, stk. 6.
2 The materials evaluated were:

   1. TRAS (Tidlig Registrering af Sprogudvikling), a Norwegian scale, by U. Espenak and J. Frost (2003).
   2. RABU, a Danish scale used by school psychologist in Greenland.
   3. Børne-linealen, a Danish-Greenlandic scale, created and used by health nurses in Greenland.
   4. Kuno Beller, Developmental Description, a Danish-German evaluation system.
   5. TRASMO, Early registration of motoric competences, a Norwegian scale, by U. Espenak and J. Frost.
   6. MPU (motoric–perceptual development) a Danish scale, 1977.
   7. SPU (school readiness test) by L. Pearson and J. Quinn (1986), used by school psychologist in Greenland.
   8. SDQ (Strength and Difficulty Questionnaires) by R. Goodman (2015), used by school psychologist in Greenland.
   9. EDI (Early Development Instrument) by M. Janus (2000).
   10. CBCL (child behaviour and emotional screening system) by T. Acherbach and I. Rescorla (2000).
   11. BASC-2 (behavioural and emotional screening system) by R. W. Kamphaus and R. Reynolds (2006).

12. ASQ (Age Stage Questioner) by J. Squires, D. Bricher and E. Twombly (2002).
13. BESS (Behavioural and Emotional Screening System) by T. Acherbach and I. Rescorla.

3 Pr. 1 August 2004: All day-care services according to the Service Act must prepare educational curricula that focus on

- the child's versatile personal development
- social competences
- language
- body and movement
- nature and natural phenomena
- cultural expressions and values

4 The seven standards of Effective Pedagogic stemming from CREDE are

1. joint productive activity
2. language and literacy
3. creating connection between home, community and institution
4. complex thinking through questions
5. learning dialogue
6. modelling, visualizing and demonstration
7. child guided activity

5 The assessment areas in UBUS 3 and UBUS 5 are

- the child's health and general feeling of well-being
- social interaction and competence
- communication and language competences
- sensation and movement
- cooperate and initiate activities
- culture and nature

6 In 2017, it became five counties.
7 Notice: The order of evaluation areas in the first trial was different from that in the final version and also the number of questions was less in areas 5 and 6.

References

Barker, R. G., and Wright, H. (1949). Psychological ecology and the problem of psychological development. *Child Development, 20,* 131–43.
Barker, R. G., and Wright, H. F. (1971). *The Midwestern and its children. The psychological ecology of an American Town.* North Haven, CT: Archon Books.
Bozhovich, L. I. (2009). The social situation of child development. *Journal of Russian and East European Psychology, 47,* 59–86.

Bronfenbrenner, U. (1979). *The ecology of human development*. Cambridge, MA: Harvard University Press.

Bøttcher, L. (2018). Using the child's perspective to support children with severe impairment in becoming active subjects. In M. Hedegaard, K. Aronsson, C. Højholt and O. S. Ulvik (Eds), *Children, childhood and everyday life. Children's perspectives* (pp. 149–66). Charlotte, NC: Information Age Publishing.

Bøttcher, L., and Dammeyer, J. (2016). *Development and learning of young children with disabilities: A Vygotskian perspective*. Dordrecht: Springer.

Christensen, E., Kristiansen, S. G., and Baviskar, S. (2008). *Børn i Grønland. En kortlægning af 0–14 årige børns og familiers trivsel*. København: Det Nationale forskningscenter for velfærd.

Davydov, V. V. (1990) Types of generalisation in instruction. Logical and psychological problems in the structuring of school curricula. *Soviet studies in mathematics education, Vol. 2*. Reston, VA: National Council of Teachers of Mathematics.

Edwards, A. (2010). *Being an expert professional practitioner: The relational turn in expertise*. Dordrecht: Springer.

Edwards, A. (2017). Revealing relational work. In A. Edwards (Ed.), *Working relationally in and across practices: A cultural-Historical approach to collaboration* (pp. 1–21). New York: Cambridge.

Elkonin, D. B. (1999). Towards the problem of stages in the mental development of children. *Journal of Russian and East European Psychology*, 37, 11–29.

Fleer, M. (2014). *Theorising play in the early years*. Cambridge: Cambridge University Press.

Hedegaard, M. (1988). *Skolebørns personlighedsudviklling set gennem orienteringsundervisning*. Aarhus: Aarhus University Press.

Hedegaard, M. (2002). *Learning and child development*. Aarhus: Aarhus University Press.

Hedegaard, M. (2008). A cultural-historical theory of children's development. In M. Hedegaard and M. Fleer (Eds), *Studying children. A cultural-historical approach* (pp. 10–29). New York: Open University Press.

Hedegaard, M. (2009). Child development from a cultural-historical approach: Children's activity in everyday local settings as foundation for their development. *Mind Culture and Activity*, 16, 64–81.

Hedegaard, M. (2012). Analyzing children's learning and development in everyday settings from a cultural-historical wholeness approach. *Mind Culture and Activity*, 19, 1–12.

Hedegaard, M. (2014). The significance of demands and motives across practices in children's learning and development: An analysis of learning in home and school. *Learning, Culture and Social Interaction*, 3, 188–94.

Hedegaard, M. (2016). Imagination and emotion in children's play: A cultural-historical approach. *International Research in Early Childhood Education*, 7, 57–72.

Hedegaard, M. (2018). Children's perspectives and institutional practices as keys in a wholeness approach to children's social situations of development. *Learning, Culture and Social Interaction*. DOI:10.1016/j.lcsi.2018.04.008.

Hedegaard, M., and Chaiklin, S. (2005). *Radical local teaching and learning*. Aarhus: Aarhus University Press.

Leontiev, A. N. (1978). *Activity, consciousness, and personality*. Englewood Cliffs, NJ: Prentice Hall.

Lightfood, C., Cole, M., and Cole, S. R. (2012). *The development of children*. New York: Worth Publishers and Palgrave Macmillan.

Mead, M. (1956). *Cultural transformation – Manus 1928-1953: New lives for old*. New York: William Morrow and Company.

Rogoff, B. (2003). *The cultural nature of human development*. New York: Oxford University Press.

Schousboe, I. (2013). The structure of fantasy play and its implication for good and evil games. In I. Schousboe and D. Winther-Lindqvist (Eds), *Play and playfulness* (pp. 13–28). Dordrecht: Springer.

Stern, W. (1985). *The interpersonal world of the infant*. New York: Basic Books.

Tharp, R. G., and Galimore, R. (1988). *Rousing mind to life*. Cambridge: Cambridge University Press.

Tharp, R. G., Estrada, P., Dalton, S. S., and Yamauchi, L. A. (2000). *Teaching transformed. Receiving excellence, fairness, inclusion and harmony*. Boulder CA: Westview Press.

Vygotsky, L. S. (1967). Play and its role in the mental development of the child. *Soviet Psychology*, 5(3), 6–18.

Vygotsky, L. S. (1993). *The collected work of L. S. Vygotsky: Vol. 2. The fundamentals of defectology*. New York: Plenum.

Vygotsky, L. S. (1997). *The collected works of L.S Vygotsky: Vol. 4. The history of the development of higher mental functions*. New York: Plenum.

Vygotsky, L. S. (1998). *Child psychology. The collected works of L. S. Vygotsky: Vol. 5* (pp. 151–66). New York: Plenum Press.

Wartofsky, M. (1983). The child's construction of the world and the world's construction of the child: From historical epistemology to historical psychology. In F. S. Kesse and A. W. Siegel (Eds), *The child and other cultural inventions. Houston Symposium 4* (pp. 188–215). New York: Praeger.

Weltzer, H. (1995). *Kuno Bellers udviklingsbeskrivelse af småbørn: Et pædagogisk hjælpemiddel*. Copenhagen: Dansk Psykologisk Forlag.

Winnicott, D. W. (1977). Leg, en teoretisk fremstilling, Chapter 3. In *Leg og virkelighed* (pp. 73–92). Copenhagen: Reitzels.

Part Two

Enabling Families as Supporters of Children's and Young People's Transitions

6

Easing Transitions into School for Children from Socially Excluded 'Hard to Reach' Families: From Risk and Resilience to Agency and Demand

Anne Edwards and Maria Evangelou

Introduction

The term 'hard to reach', when applied to families by the services that are set up to support them, is rightfully a contested term. At its most simplistic interpretation, the term refers to the most socially excluded families who rarely or never use community services, such as child and family clinics or drop-in centres. They are deemed to be hard to reach because they are almost invisible to members of the caring professions, who have no fail-safe way of making contact, engaging with them and building the trust necessary to support them. However, this label is frequently challenged by those who argue that the fault lies with the services and their approaches, rather than with the families (Boag-Munroe and Evangelou, 2012; Crozier and Davies, 2007). In line with the latter view, Landy and Menna suggest that

> working effectively with families who might be labelled 'hard-to-reach' involves a shift from perceiving the family as being hard-to-reach to thinking about what makes the service that is being offered hard to accept for a particular family and that working with such families involves a shift from providing information to listening and knowing how to respond to particular behaviours. (Landy and Menna, 2006, p. 180)

Whatever the reason, and we are in sympathy with the view that services need to rethink their approaches, this lack of contact with the most socially excluded families is particularly worrying for practitioners concerned with preparing children for transition into preschool or formal education. The argument is that a lack of contact with the services that might give support and access to other societal goods increases the likelihood of enhancing the families' disconnection from what society is able to offer them. Consequently, their children's transition to school is particularly challenging. For that reason, we have taken work with this particular group as our focus.

Disrupting the cycle of socio-economic deprivation, social exclusion and their educational implications was a priority for the Labour government in the UK between 1997 and 2010. It resulted in a plethora of locally based initiatives aimed at combating the social exclusion and poor educational performance of children from hard-to-reach families. In this chapter, we draw primarily on one English research study from this period: *Supporting Parents in Promoting Early Learning* (Evangelou, Sylva, Edwards and Smith, 2008). It was a 12-month mixed-methods national evaluation, led by Evangelou, of 12 different intervention projects run by 9 different agencies in 19 different sites that were all part of the 18-month government-funded Early Learning Parenting Project (ELPP). ELPP was set up to change cycles of socio-economic disadvantage and to prevent poor achievement at school for young children from these hard-to-reach families, by building the strengths of parents as early educators. The aim was to enrich the learning environment offered by the home by working directly with the most marginalized parents, putting in place family-based education as a protective factor in the lives of their children so that the children would be prepared for school entry. The evaluation examined the effect of ELPP on

- the work of the sites as organizations, the services delivered in those sites and the impact of ELPP on the development of service provision by local authorities;
- workforce development among practitioners who worked with parents and their children; and
- how parents engaged with their young children to support them as learners.

(The length of the evaluation was only 12 months, which prevented us from gathering data on children's subsequent school performance.)

This emphasis on education as a preventive factor drew on the prevailing framework of risk and resilience (Little, Ashford and Morpeth, 2004; Luthar, 2003). The framework underpinned initiatives which aimed at building resilience against the risk of social exclusion by inserting the environmental and interactional factors known to build the resilience that allows people to overcome adversity. The aims were laudable; but we shall be arguing that the resilience framing lacked an underpinning which saw the child as an active and agentic learner (Edwards, 2007; Edwards and Apostolov, 2007), with considerable implications for how school readiness is perceived in relation to parents' role in developing the agentic learner who is able to make the transition successfully.

Resilience has frequently been an area of debate in the literature on the prevention of social exclusion and other risks (Edwards, 2007; France and Utting, 2005; Little et al., 2004; Yates, Egeland and Soufre, 2003). Nonetheless, a risk and resilience framework for the interventions was at the time an entirely logical approach. During the first decade of this century, the concept shaped UK interventions which aimed at strengthening the attributes that parents and carers brought to children's developmental pathways; there was general agreement that the best predictors of individual resilience were relationships with caring prosocial adults and good intellectual functioning (Masten and Coatsworth, 1998). Social exclusion and the perpetuation of cycles of deprivation could, according to this view, be prevented by enhancing parental capacity to prevent vulnerability to adversity (Garmezy, 1991; Masten and Garmezy, 1985). Interventions aimed at prevention of social exclusion were therefore seen in terms of the development of competences that enabled children to adapt along appropriate developmental pathways, despite potentially adverse features in the environment.

Unfortunately, in our view, the importance of the relationship aspects of the protective factors rarely transferred into intervention programmes; rather, the emphasis was placed on competences within an educational framing. We are not alone in our unease; Yates et al. observe that 'relatively few [intervention] programs aim to improve the quality of the parent-child relationship' (2003, p. 255). Instead, the focus of these programmes is on competence building. We briefly explain the origins of our worries. Decades of research in developmental psychology have pointed to how infants develop a sense of who they are and who they might be in the context of intersubjective relationships with carers, who, over time, enable the child to move beyond the relationship and engage actively with the wider world (Bremner, 1994; Schaffer, 1996). These shifts, within a secure relationship with the caregiver, account for a developing sense of self and agency. A lack of these relationships can be remedied beyond infancy, if parents and carers are taught how to engage reciprocally with their children (Anning and Edwards, 2006); but Yates et al. (2003) emphasize the need for interventions to attend to parent-infant attachment relationships from the outset. These relationships are emotionally charged and therefore different from the more professionally distant relationships that children experience with staff at preschool or school, and they are a crucial element in the development of a sense of agentic self.

The focus of resilience building was, however, not exclusively on individuals; Masten and Coatsworth (1998) and Schoon (2006) are among many resilience researchers who offer accounts that include analyses of the contexts in which competences are developed and exercised. In doing so, they, however, take interactionist and largely normative views of individual development, which separate the individual and the context. Within their framing, formal education and qualifications are seen as one of the main routes to successful adaptation to and capacity to withstand adversity. As Schoon explained, 'Academic attainment is vitally important in our culture, and success or failure in school can have serious long-term individual and social consequences' (Schoon, 2006, p. 6). ELPP's concern with school readiness very much reflected this view.

The projects funded under the ELPP umbrella were run locally, drawing heavily but not exclusively on the services offered by voluntary and community sector (VCS) agencies. There was therefore the opportunity for considerable sensitivity to the strengths, needs, resources and opportunities that were offered in localities, but the workers had little or no backgrounds in child development; indeed, some had no prior experience of work with children. The projects themselves differed vastly. Some, such as Bookstart (Wade and Moore, 1998), were well-established interventions with some research backing, while others had grown directly from initiatives taken within a community, such as Thurrock Community Mothers. Most of the interventions offered training: the Peers Early Education Partnership (PEEP) provided a curriculum; others, such as Parents Early Years and Learning (PEAL), offered ideas to help guide the work of the staff. We do not go into the details of each approach in this chapter; we will instead draw on the study to identify some of the strategies for enhancing the learning environments offered by the home and consider them in relation to how they helped the children develop as agentic learners.

Unsurprisingly, given the focus on risk and resilience, rather than on ways of supporting the development of the agentic child, one key finding from the evaluation was that there was a change in how parents organized their children's environment – it was safer and the children had new experiences locally, such as library visits. However, 'there was no improvement in parenting behaviours that challenged children's thinking or extended their language' (Evangelou et al., 2008, p. 110). As we discuss the approaches taken under the ELPP umbrella, we will try to unpack the reasons for this lack of change in this aspect of parenting behaviours and recast the evaluation employing a cultural-historical approach to children's learning and development.

The social situation of development: motive orientation, common knowledge and learning

Central to a cultural-historical approach to learning and development is recognizing a motive to learn. In their book *Radical-Local Teaching and Learning for Education and Human Development*, drawing on their work in East Harlem, New York City (Hedegaard and Chaiklin, 2005), Hedegaard and Chaiklin enter debates about the weaknesses of culturally relative curricula, based on children's limited life experiences and their apparent lack of academic depth. They argue that cultural sensitivity and disciplinary standards in school curricula and pedagogy are not necessarily in opposition to each other. Instead, they explain that disciplinary knowledge can grow by helping primary-school-age children develop capacities that enable them to investigate and analyse their immediate life situations. Key to the programme they created to take forward those ideas was the development of children's motives for learning by focusing on topics that interested them. The development of a motive for learning, they argued, changes the child's relationship with his or her immediate world and is central to their development. There are, we suggest, strong links between a motive to learn and the unfolding of a learner's agency (see Edwards, Chan and Tan, forthcoming, for an extended discussion), and therefore that aspect of a child's development needs to be a feature of early intervention efforts.

Hedegaard and Chaiklin's analysis takes us back to how social exclusion and disconnection from what society values and offers have been interpreted within a risk and resilience framing. The very definition of hard to reach is a lack of connection with locally valued cultural resources such as libraries and child-welfare clinics, and therefore with much of what is valued within social and education systems. There is therefore the assumption that children's early alienation from school arises because they cannot make connections with what is culturally valued. The solution adopted by the Labour government was, following the prevailing emphasis on risk and resilience, to fund initiatives that aimed at enriching the home environment so that the differences between home and school were reduced. As we have seen, FLPP succeeded in improving the families' connections with local resources, but did little to prepare the children for the intellectual demands of school. We are suggesting that attention to the relational aspects of parent–child interactions and the development of the child as an agentic learner would have strengthened the interventions.

Reducing the differences in practices at home and school has long been a feature of the UK parental involvement initiatives aimed at getting parents of school-age children to support their children's engagement with school curricula: a process one of us described as the colonization of the home by the school (Edwards and Warin, 1999). The approaches to enriching the home environment for preschool children in ELPP were intended to be more subtle and, as we have indicated, aimed at inserting protective factors, such as the carer's engagement as a prosocial adult with the child, into the day-to-day interactions of the home. However, the wide diversity of the programmes involved, and the lack of change in parenting behaviours that might stretch children cognitively, indicates that perhaps not enough thought had been put into the initiative for considering how parents might support their children.

We are suggesting that ELPP's aim of enhancing the home environment as preparation for school can readily and usefully be recast in terms of the child's social situation of development (SSD) at home and at school. In doing so, we consider the development of the child as an agentic learner who relishes being stretched and challenged. Such a focus places the gaze firmly on the child as she or he moves in and between settings. This is because the SSD is not simply the social situation in which a person's development occurs; rather the SSD is always potential and created by the learner. Vygotsky described the SSD as 'a system of relations between a child of a given age and social reality' (Vygotsky, 1998, p. 199). For an SSD to be realized, a learner needs to be able to act agentically, take forward their own intentions, what matters to them, and connect their individual sense making with the more powerful publicly validated ideas that constitute the culture that is being mediated in the practices of the family or the school. If the two cultures demand very different things of them, the transition between them is challenging. But, we shall argue, the two sets of practices don't need to be the same: what is important is the opportunity for the child's agency to unfold in relation to play and learning in both sets of practices.

Hedegaard has quite recently added two ideas which can help us conceptualize and evaluate the ELPP interventions in relation to the SSD; these ideas are demands and motive orientations. In a 2012 chapter on children's motives, Hedegaard argued that, while trying to understand learning, we need to attend as much to the demands of activities within practices as we do to what the learner brings to the activity. These demands may be explicit – for example, 'Go clean your teeth before I read you a story' at bedtime – or embedded in routines such as putting today's used clothes in the laundry basket. In school, they are frequently the latter, sitting quietly on the carpet; or putting your books away when the bell goes, and are only made explicit when breached: 'Jane you forgot your book!'. By interpreting these tacit demands embedded in school routines, children learn to become pupils. Tacit or implicit demands may also be cognitively stretching, such as when children undertake careful matching activities when playing in the home corner; but much depends on their capacity to recognize the demands and respond to them.

For children to create an SSD at school, they need to be able to seek out, recognize and relish new demands, push themselves to make sense and connect their sense making with the public meanings valued in the practices of the school (Fleer, forthcoming). In the process of connecting their personal sense making with publicly validated meanings, they reposition themselves within the practices, see the familiar afresh, make new connections and use them to act in and on the practices. But they need to be able to recognize and make use of the opportunities to seek out the demands. They need to be accustomed to being stretched and challenged and to allowing their agency to unfold in productive actions.

This is where motive orientation becomes a key concept. Hedegaard described it as follows: 'Motive development can then be seen as a movement initiated by the learner's emotional experience related to the activity setting' (Hedegaard, 2012, p. 21). The attention to emotional experience in relation to an activity in this definition is crucial. It allows us to recognize that a child navigates and orients to the demands of the practices of home and school in ways that sustain their sense of who they are and what matters for them. If what matters for them at home and school are very different they not only need to navigate different practices but may also need to develop radically new motive orientations in order to approach to school demands and create the SSD that is supported by the resources of the school.

While we have been emphasizing the agency of the child and the SSD as a trajectory of learning that leads to development, adults are nonetheless important for the creation of an SSD. Adults present demands and make available the resources that enable young children's responses to them. This is done in so many subtle ways ranging from, for example, helping a child select the outside pieces of a jigsaw puzzle, to asking her to make table decorations and name cards for the family guests at dinner. It also involves exploring the natural environment together as a fun activity, and making up stories about his toys to encourage imaginative play. All such activities help develop a child's motivation to play, problem-solve through play and learn ways of tackling external reality. It is these kinds of activities that characterize the relational actions of prosocial adults who, as we indicated earlier, help engender resilience in children. Once the child enters school, this motive orientation to play shifts to a motive orientation to learn, if the child can recognize learning demands and has a history of relationships with adults in activities which allow them to develop as agentic problem-solvers and decision-makers.

Using the framing of the SSD foregrounds that it is the child who makes the transition to school and whose motive orientations need to adjust to the new demands. The major theme in this book is a discussion of how difficult transitions can be eased by building common knowledge between the practices in which initial motive orientations have been generated and those the learner is entering (see Chapter 1). As we explained in Chapter 1, common knowledge consists of the motives, the *what matters*, in the different collaborating practices and becomes a resource for mediating collaborative working on shared problems (Edwards, 2011, 2012, 2017). It is perhaps all too easy to see common knowledge as a bridge which ensures that what matters in the receiving practice (preschool or school) is pre-figured in the initial practice (family), or what matters in family is reflected in the receiving practice. But that would be too simplistic an interpretation in the cases we are discussing and would be likely to lead to the colonization of the home by the school.

Common knowledge involves valuing what matters, the motives that shape each practice; but it isn't necessarily built up in a synchronous way; the valuable contributions may come at different times over a child's developmental trajectory. Hedegaard recently demonstrated that building common knowledge can lead to a valuing of what different people offer to support the SSDs of developing children at different points in the child's life. She employed the concept of common knowledge to explain how day-care practitioners learnt to work confidently with the young children in their care and to stop focusing on day care as a preparation for preschool. Here is an extract from her chapter:

> The list of principles that matter in professional work in kindergarten, which follows, was formulated at our last meeting [with the practitioners]. I suggest that it can be seen as a form of common knowledge within the kindergartens that enabled the day-care professionals to reach beyond their own practice.

- Practice in kindergarten is important for children's development and is not only preparation for children to attend school.
- Therefore it is important to formulate what is special for kindergarten: how the practitioners work.
- It is also important to be more explicit about the competences we want children to bring with them from the kindergarten when they enter school.
- This means we need to formulate how we think about play and life-competences and what our roles are in supporting children's acquisition of life-competences.
- It is important to see the pedagogy of daycare in a historical and political frame.

(Hedegaard, 2017, pp. 260–1)

We could easily replace day-care practitioners with parents and kindergarten with family life in this list of principles. We would then see how parents and practitioners in school might contribute to supporting the agentic learner at different points in time by making appropriate demands on them as thinkers and problem-solvers.

From this perspective, we can see how Hedegaard and Chaiklin's radical-local curriculum was employing common knowledge by valuing what matters in the home and community *and* what matters in school, and was then using that knowledge to inform a curriculum that engaged and motivated the learners. Rai has made a similar point in relation to common knowledge in his study of a successful primary school in Rajasthan (Rai, 2017). In both of these examples of curricula, the teachers emphasized the thought processes of the children, demanding that they ask questions, experiment and reach conclusions that they could justify with evidence. It was these processes that linked home and community with school, and they were missing from most of the ELPP projects. Let us therefore turn to the ELPP interventions and consider them in relation to how they helped the children develop as potentially engaged learners able to create their own SSDs.

Examining ELPP through the lens of the social situation of development

One striking finding of the ELPP evaluation was that most of the parents in the target group showed emotional warmth and support for their child's learning

(Evangelou et al., 2008, p. 111), and this attribute increased over the duration of the initiative. Nonetheless, as we have already said, there was no evidence of improvement in the levels of cognitive and language stimulation in the child. It seemed that the parents didn't know how to engage in the processes of supporting an SSD; they were, however, interested in learning more. Here, one senior practitioner describes the impact of ELPP on a colleague and how it helped in her work with hard-to-reach parents.

> What she's most excited about is something about ... and she's a bit surprised by it, about how the focus on the child's learning has really worked in engaging families who are very hard to engage, and that she's a bit surprised by that. So she's someone who has worked with families in a lot of difficulties for years but she's tended to have more kind of family support role. And now she's going, let's talk about your child's learning and she's saying, they love it, they absolutely love it and so she's got a few families like who would never let a social worker in the door kind of thing, who hate professionals, all that kind of stuff. ... And she's saying 'it's incredible this ELPP thing because, you know, they never let anyone come in before, they didn't send their children to school, they hate the social worker, they just sit at home and do nothing. You know, but they let me in because I'm doing ELPP.' (Evangelou et al., 2008, p. 54)

It seemed that ELPP was going some way to address the challenge set out by Landy and Menna in 2006: 'Working effectively with families who might be labeled "hard-to-reach" involves a shift from perceiving the family as being hard-to-reach to thinking about what makes the service that is being offered hard to accept for a particular family.' The success in this case seemed to be because activities with the child had become a focus around which the parent and the practitioner could collaborate and the prosocial aspects of interaction between parent and child could be encouraged. Here is another practitioner making a similar point: 'I have noticed that workers in the ELPP project continue to get into families, not always but often, when other workers are not being allowed through the door. And I think that it is because they come with this different task almost and are seen in a different way' (Evangelou et al., 2008, p. 72).

But much would depend on what *doing ELPP* meant once the practitioner was in the home with the parent or had welcomed them at a settings-based session. There was considerable emphasis on resources, such as Duplo, and activities, things to do with your child, in both the home visit and settings-based interventions. Activities ranged from playing with gloop (a sticky substance for messy play) to shared reading. Nonetheless, based on observations and interviews, the evaluation concluded that parental change was at a global level of valuing education, rather than though their own specific behaviours 'such as labeled praise or the use of household routines for vocabulary learning'. The evaluation continues: 'This suggests that future work with parents ought to focus more concretely on parenting behaviours in addition to attitudes and aspirations' (Evangelou et al., 2008, p. 118).

The lack of attention to the details of parental behaviours and to the rationales for those behaviours was also evident in interviews with the practitioners. The VCS staff and the volunteers mostly lacked understandings of child development and children's learning and were delighted when they were introduced to concepts on short courses that gave them labels for the work they were trying to do. We reported their 'thirst for knowledge' (Evangelou et al., 2008, p. 118); but the understandings gained from these courses were necessarily superficial and did not focus on how to support children as agentic learners. We suggest that this weakness in the initiative was due to its basis in a risk and resilience framing. The projects, as a consequence, focused on the parents and on developing parents as educators and did not actually focus on the child as a learner. As a result, efforts were made to enrich the resources for play at home, thereby reducing differences between home and preschool or school, but there was no theory of pedagogic support for the agentic learner informing the projects. There was attention to an SSD, but only to its lay or colloquial meaning of an array of resources available (gloop, Duplo, books etc.). However, there was no attention to how children are enabled to create their own SSD and motive orientation towards learning.

This conclusion is disappointing, particularly so as the practitioners had made the shift to see the people they were working with as parents and carers, rather than as vulnerable clients. They also discovered that these hard-to-reach parents already had warm and caring relationships with their children and welcomed ELPP. The evaluation noted that 'services for parents need to aim at more than "awareness" to bring about a positive change in parenting behaviours' (Evangelou et al., 2008, p. 111). Much more could have been done from the starting point of parental warmth to encourage the relational interactions that begin with intersubjective explorations of the world and lead to the independent questioning and seeking of novelty that, as we have said, is central to learning.

Rethinking resilience through a cultural-historical lens

The first step in this rethinking is to focus on the child as learner, their trajectory as they orient to what is valued in the practices of home and school. It is hoped that the trajectory reflects their motive orientation as a learner: to be someone who approaches novelty, asks questions, seeks evidence and is able to reposition his or herself when new understandings are grasped. This notion of the child creating their SSD as their own network of relations around their own trajectory is not only a feature of childhood. Dreier, working with the trajectories of patients in psychotherapy as they move across everyday settings, has argued that clients, not therapists, are the primary agents of therapy (Dreier, 2000), and it is they who interpret and navigate new practices. Here, there are some commonalities with the aim of building a resilience that enables adaptation. But, whereas adaptation in the resilience literature is seen in terms of coping with adversity, adaptation in a cultural-historical understanding involves a dialectic relationship between person and practice. We might adapt to a new setting, but we may also contribute to it with our actions as agents shaping our own lives (Edwards, 2007; Edwards and Apostolov, 2007). Sameroff makes a similar argument in his transactional account of human development (Sameroff, 2009).

The next step is to consider what we know from research on child development about what children can gain from warm reciprocal relationships with parents. Yates and colleagues pick up on children's agency and summarize the role of parents as follows: 'We argue that the core of a developmental history of positive adaptation is a sensitive and emotionally responsive early caregiving relationship. These exchanges foster the development of children's positive expectations of the social world, and of their self-concepts as potent agents of change within that world' (Yates et al., 2003, p. 254)

Parents bring something distinctive to the unfolding of a child's agency and sense of self-efficacy. They do so through caring and responsive relationships, where they are attuned to what the child can and wants to do, and they can work alongside the child by relationally enabling the unfolding of their agency. This is not something that teachers can or arguably should do. Interventions which have focused on developing the sensitivity of marginalized parents to their infants' strengths and needs have been analysed within a cultural-historical framing of relational expertise and common knowledge in projects led by Hopwood in Sydney (Hopwood, Day and Edwards, 2016; Hopwood and Edwards, 2017).

They reveal the intimacy of the parent–child interactions and the time taken to develop parental sensitivity if it is lacking, for example, due to high anxiety. We therefore return to our argument that what home and school offer are necessarily different.

We next need to consider how the trajectory of an agentic learner is supported in the transitions between home and school. We have already argued that the support should not be a matter of the school colonizing the home. Rather, both families and schools should attend to how the dynamic of agency and demand is the engine for a child's SSD. They are likely to do this in different ways because, as we have argued, the adults' relationships with the child at home are fundamentally different from those at school. Hedegaard's conclusion in her 2017 chapter, that we should think of common knowledge in a linear manner spread over time, is helpful. We need to think of the movement both horizontally and vertically. From this perspective, we can highlight the different roles of parents and teachers when working relationally and encourage schools to attend to the insights that parents have about their children. At the same time, schools should be encouraging parents to help their children explore, question and seek evidence, thereby taking forward their SSD as agentic learners. The common knowledge here is the recognition of the different contributions parents and teachers make to children's development as learners and a mutual valuing of both.

What do our arguments mean for interventions with hard-to-reach or marginalized families to disrupt cycles of intergenerational social exclusion? First, interventions should seek and assess the parenting already in operation and not take a deficit model of parenting as the default starting point. Second, they should work with or, if necessary, build up the reciprocity that signals strong attachment between parent and child. Third, they should attend to the wider contexts in which the parents are trying to bring up their children and extend the interventions to disrupting the contextual challenges facing these families. This point is not unique to a cultural-historical view, but it is fundamental to it. The dialectic of person and practice that characterizes a cultural-historical view of learning requires analyses of the wider cultures in which the practices of families and schools are located and the need to intervene at societal as well as institutional levels if change is to be sustained. If we want children to be agentic learners, we need to create conditions in which the agency of their parents can also unfold, enabling them to move out of marginalization and to contribute to society.

References

Anning, A., and Edwards, A. (2006). *Promoting learning from birth to five: Developing professional practice in the pre-school*, 2nd edn. Buckingham: Open University Press.

Boag-Munroe, G., and Evangelou, M. (2012). From hard to reach to how to reach: A systematic review of the literature on hard-to-reach families. *Research Papers in Education, 27*(2), 209–39.

Bremner, G. (1994). *Infancy*, 2nd edn. Oxford: Blackwell.

Crozier, G., and Davies, J. (2007). Hard-to-reach parents or hard-to-reach schools? A discussion of home–school relations with particular reference to Bangladeshi and Pakistani parents. *British Educational Research Journal, 33*(3), 295–313.

Dreier, O. (2000). Psychotherapy in clients' trajectories across contexts. In C. Mattingly and L. Garro (Eds), *Narratives and the cultural construction of illness and healing* (pp. 237–58). Berkley: University of California Press.

Edwards, A. (2007). Working collaboratively to build resilience: A CHAT approach. *Social Policy and Society, 6*(2), 255–65.

Edwards, A. (2011). Building common knowledge at boundaries between professional practices. *International Journal of Educational Research, 50*, 33–9.

Edwards, A. (2012). The role of common knowledge in achieving collaboration across practices. *Learning, Culture and Social Interaction, 1*(1), 22–32.

Edwards, A. (Ed.) (2017). *Working relationally in and across practices: A cultural-historical approach to collaboration*. New York: Cambridge University Press.

Edwards, A., Chan, J., and Tan, D. (forthcoming). Motive orientation and the exercise of agency: Responding to recurrent demands in practices. In A. Edwards, M. Fleer and L. Bøttcher (Eds), *Cultural-historical approaches to studying learning and development: Societal, institutional and personal perspectives*. Dordrecht: Springer.

Edwards, A., and Apostolov, A. (2007). A cultural-historical interpretation of resilience: The implications for practice. *Outlines: Critical Social Studies, 9*(1), 70–84.

Edwards, A., and Warin, J. (1999). Parental involvement in raising pupils' achievement in primary schools: Why bother? *Oxford Review of Education, 25*(3), 325–41.

Evangelou, M., Sylva, K., Edwards, A., and Smith, T. (2008). *Supporting parents in promoting learning: The evaluation of the Early Learning Partnership Project*. London: Department for Children, Families and Schools.

Fleer, M. (forthcoming). Examining the psychological content of digital play through Hedegaard's model of child development. *Learning Culture and Social Interaction*.

France, A. and Utting, D. (2005). The paradigm of 'risk and protection-focused prevention' and its impact on services for children and families. *Children and Society, 19*, 77–90.

Garmezy, N. (1991). Resiliency and vulnerability to adverse developmental outcomes associated with poverty. *American Behavioural Scientist, 34*, 416–30.

Hedegaard, M. (2012). The dynamics aspects in children's learning and development. In M. Hedegaard, A. Edwards and M. Fleer (Eds), *Motives in children's development: Cultural-historical approaches* (pp. 9–27). Cambridge: Cambridge University Press.

Hedegaard. M. (2017). When daycare professionals' values for transition to school do not align with the educational demands from society and school. In A. Edwards (Ed.), *Working relationally in and across practices: A cultural-historical approach to collaboration* (pp. 247–64). New York: Cambridge University Press.

Hedegaard, M., and Chaiklin, S. (2005). *Radical-local teaching and learning*. Århus: Århus University Press.

Hopwood, N., Day, C., and Edwards, A. (2016). Partnership practice as collaborative knowledge work: Overcoming common dilemmas through an augmented view of professional expertise. *Journal of Children's Services, 11*(2), 111–23.

Hopwood, N., and Edwards, A. (2017). How common knowledge is constructed and why it matters in collaboration between professionals and clients. *International Journal of Educational Research, 83*, 107–19.

Landy, S., and Menna, R. (2006). *Early intervention with multi-risk families: An integrative Approach*. Baltimore, MD: Paul H. Brookes.

Little, M., Ashford, N., and Morpeth, L. (2004). Research review: Risk and protection in the context of services for children in need. *Children and Family Social Work, 9*, 105–17.

Luthar, S. (Ed.) (2003). *Resilience and vulnerability: Adaptation in the context of childhood adversities*. New York: Cambridge University Press.

Masten, A., and Coatsworth, J. D. (1998). The development of competence in favorable and unfavorable environments: Lessons from research on successful children. *American Psychologist, 53*, 205–20.

Masten, A., and Garmezy, N. (1985). Risk, vulnerability and protective factors in developmental psychopathology. In B. B. Lahey and A. E. Kazdin (Eds), *Advances in clinical child psychology, Vol. 8* (pp. 1–52). New York: Plenum.

Rai, P. (2017). Building and using common knowledge for developing school-community links. In A. Edwards (Ed.), *Working relationally in and across practices: A cultural-historical approach to collaboration* (pp. 96–112). New York: Cambridge University Press.

Sameroff, A. (2009). The transactional model. In A. Sameroff (Ed.), *The transactional model of development: How children and contexts shape each other* (pp. 3–21). Washington, DC: American Psychological Association.

Schaffer, R. (1996). *Social development*. Oxford: Blackwell.

Schoon, I. (2006). *Risk and resilience: Adaptations in changing times*. Cambridge: Cambridge University Press.

Vygotsky, L. S. (1998). *The collected works of L. S. Vygotsky: Vol. 5. Child psychology.* New York: Plenum.

Wade, B., and Moore, M. (1998). An early start with books: Literacy and mathematical evidence from a longitudinal study. *Educational Review, 50*(2), 135–45.

Yates, T., Egeland, B., and Sroufe, A. (2003). Rethinking resilience: A developmental process perspective. In S. Luthar (Ed.), *Resilience and vulnerability: Adaptation in the context of childhood adversities* (pp. 242–66). New York: Cambridge University Press.

7

Relational Approaches to Supporting Transitions into School: Families and Early Childhood Educators Working Together in Regional Chile

Christine Woodrow and Kerry Staples

Introduction

We conceive *transitions*, the central focus of this book, across two axes. First, our attention is directed towards the contribution of the educators' transformed practices to enhancing children's learning, social and educational well-being and thus supporting their transition into early childhood education and later to school. Typically, we know children in contexts of high vulnerability are more likely to experience less early school success than their more advantaged peers and that their transition to school is frequently problematic (Rosier and McDonald, 2011). The early childhood education and care (ECEC) setting forms a significant bridge between the two contexts of school and home. Children who have not participated in ECEC are frequently deemed less prepared for the rules and structure of the formal school learning environment (Dockett and Perry, 2013). Second, our interest is in the transition journey of the educators and their changing practices, as they negotiated new terrain, developed fresh understandings about the families and identified new possibilities for different kinds of relationships with them. This new and dynamic terrain was shaped by a range of factors that included exposure to new approaches and conceptual resources through which to think about, plan and reflect on their work, together with their encounters with families and community members triggered by the changed approach to their pedagogical work. These experiences challenged and interrupted previous assumptions and led to new understandings and pedagogies. The evidence from this study about the extent to which this disruption occurred is strong and brings to mind a phrase frequently invoked in interview data, 'cambiar la mirada' (literally – 'change the look'). This term was used by educators to describe how their view of educator-parent relations and of their practices had been transformed – how they had changed how they saw things, thus providing researchers with an indication of the significant impact of their participation in the action research component on familial relationships.

The importance of early learning in high-poverty communities

The persistent educational underachievement of children living in conditions of social and economic adversity is well documented (Portes, 2005) and was the central theme of the research described in this chapter. The consequences of educational underachievement are profound, including making it harder for children to break free from cycles of intergenerational poverty (Bradshaw and Bennett, 2014; Shonkoff, 2011). Indicators of trajectories of lack of educational success are frequently evident in children's early years of school (Arndt, Rothe, Urban and Werning, 2013; Webb, Knight and Busch, 2017). Research also shows that, typically, families in socially and economically disadvantaged circumstances often are, or feel, distanced from their children's formal learning, leading to a sense that they have little to contribute, thus reinforcing their marginalization. In educational discourse, families from disadvantaged communities are often pathologized as a problem and their children are positioned as 'at risk of failure' (Crozier and Davies, 2007; Dockett and Perry, 2013), despite research showing that families are frequently interested in their children's education (Crozier and Davies, 2007); are keen to, and often do, provide rich learning opportunities for their children, although not always recognizing they are doing so (Ogbu, 1995; Volk and Long, 2005; Woodrow, Somerville Naidoo, and Power, 2016); and have high aspirations for their children's learning (Delgado-Gaitan, 2005; Mohr, Zygmunt and Clark, 2012). The deficit positioning of families from disadvantaged communities is manifest in constructions of families as being 'indifferent' to their children's schooling and 'hard to reach' (Cortis, Katz and Patulny, 2009; see also Chapter 6, this volume). These research findings also aligned with baseline data collected for the project.

Research has also shown that when learning is contextualized, draws on and connects to experiences and lived realities, children living in poverty have improved educational trajectories (Sylva, 2014). By contrast, the dominant educational discourse emphasizes routines and decontextualized instructional approaches for children of disadvantaged families. But alternative interventions can work. Studies such as the Effective Provision of Pre-school Education (EPPE) research, a 20-year longitudinal, multi-sited study (Sammons et al., 2014; Taggart, Sylva, Melhuish, Sammons and Siraj, 2015), emphasized that high-quality early learning programmes can enhance and sustain children's achievement over time (Ishmine and Tayler, 2014). Essential elements of such high-quality environments have been shown to include responsive engagement involving educators and children (Cohrssen, Church and Taylor, 2014; Mayo and Siraj, 2015; Sylva, 2014), learning opportunities that are connected to and draw on children's realities, and families' involvement through which parents know about and support children's learning (Sylva, 2014).

Children who progress to school via ECEC settings are usually already familiar with some of the artefacts and structures of schooling, such as the role of teachers, structured routines, sharing with peers and group learning. Evidence shows that children who have participated in high-quality early education before school entry make good transitions to school and enter formal learning with an enhanced chance of success (Dockett and Perry, 2013; Howes et al. 2008; Sylva, Melhuish, Sammons, Siraj-Blatchford and Taggart, 2010). The literature regarding the importance of quality early learning experiences, particularly, significance for young children in disadvantaged contexts, strongly informed the development and implementation of the Futuro Infantil Hoy (Young Children's Future Today) (FIH) research project described in this chapter. The chapters in this collection exhibit motive orientations in connection with the demands of schooling (Hedegaard, 2014).

Research context

The FIH project was conducted in three northern Chile locations and was an element of a multifaceted government initiatives to address the issue of widespread inequality through expanded provision of quality ECEC centres. A unique collaboration involving an Australian university, agencies of the Chilean government, Chilean community organizations operating in early childhood centres and the Chile-based social responsibility foundation of a large multinational mining company enabled a project investigating ways to better support educational success of young children living in contexts of vulnerability.

An initial situation analysis generated a powerful data set highlighting the complexities embedded in the physical and socio-politico-economic context. A comprehensive understanding of the current practices and challenges associated with this context was critical to informing the research methodology and ensuring it was responsive to the local communities (Woodrow, Arthur and Newman, 2014). What emerged from the situation analysis was a picture of families with low educational levels, experiencing significant financial hardship, poor housing, complicated family arrangements and high levels of children, being cared for by extended family or neighbours. Drugs, alcohol, violence and parent incarceration were salient features of the community and a source of great concern to educators in relation to children's well-being. As one educator said, 'This is a vulnerable area … [there are] very serious considerations, their social reality, the children that we work with, particularly in terms of their protection' (educator, focus group setting G). While staff saw possibilities for changes in children's trajectories through their work with them, these perspectives reinforced the idea of the settings as places of welfare rather than education. Not all educators conveyed a deficit view of families; however, such views were frequently expressed when recounting the perceived low educational level of the families and the difficulties in engaging with these families.

The sociopolitical history of Chile provided an important backdrop to the educators' lives and their work experiences, with educators making frequent references to ongoing issues of minimal institutional support and rigidly hierarchical administrative systems that were change averse. While the government viewed the investment in early childhood education in high-poverty contexts as a way to enhance social outcomes, the ECEC settings, catering to children from three months to five years, were not well resourced. Additionally, staffing was frequently problematic and educators identified multiple risks of working in these neighbourhoods. One said: 'We are all at risk here, the children, and ourselves' (educator, focus group setting G). The perception that it was not a safe place to work contributed to staff attrition and the temporary relocation of staff to fill gaps, further adding to inconsistent parent-educator relationships.

Interactions with families were primarily unidirectional and relationships hierarchical. Traditionally, parents were only contacted to discuss 'wrong things their kids have done' (educator, focus group G). Parents were not otherwise welcome inside the classroom, with teachers seeing parents' presence as 'an invasion' or even expressing concern about being judged by parents. These perceptions were reinforced by safety protocols that involved educators receiving children at the gates, which remained padlocked for the remainder of the day. When parents were permitted to contribute, their participation was conditional, subject to the direction of the staff, and usually involved routine preparation of materials. There was a common perception that families needed to be educated. Educators planned workshops based on parental surveys and their perceptions of parents' needs. As this educator explained, 'What we do is we create [meetings], bring people especially in those areas to talk to the parents and, you know, teach them and talk to them about what they want to know' (educator, focus group setting G). The ECEC setting was viewed by families with some suspicion partially due to a more traditional view that families had a primary responsibility to care for the child rather than the state. There was also a pervasive community suspicion resulting from Chile's sociopolitical history, which influenced interactions with government agencies. Families reiterated the minimal role they were expected to play in the ECEC setting and in schools, as well as the scant interaction with staff beyond problem situations, greetings, farewells and 'special' events.

Teaching and learning in the sites were guided by a national curriculum, interpreted and administered somewhat rigidly. Despite the long traditions of aspiration for quality early childhood provision (Peralta, 2011), evaluation studies indicated that, across the Chilean system, ECEC programme quality in contemporary terms remained a challenge (Villalón, Suzuki, Herrera and Mathiesen, 2002). Classroom observations revealed warm, caring settings where learning was teacher-centric. Children were often involved in whole group activities or spending significant amounts of time as passive recipients of frequently decontextualized knowledge such as rote learning of the alphabet. Educators mostly supervised children's play in under-resourced classrooms, decorated with adult drawings and displays. A heavy emphasis on health routines and cultural norms of politeness was evident, with lessons and activities typically delivered with a great deal of energy, warmth and affection.

Research design and methodology

The Australian project team recognized the imperative to embed a multilayered research design in the FIH project. This was to ensure ongoing responsiveness to the local context and to establish an evidence base about processes, outcomes, challenges and impact of the work. The research design included:

- site-based and documentary situation analysis to inform the initial design decisions and conceptual framings;

- annual focus groups with educators and interviews with centre directors in each;
- collection of teaching artefacts at each setting annually;
- semi-structured interviews with key stakeholders annually (regional managers, funding body managers and project mentors);
- classroom observations using a context-specific protocol biannually;
- action research embedded in the project design; and
- annual regional workshops/focus groups with family members.

Data was collected over the eight years of the project during which time 20 early childhood settings participated. Phase 1 of the research involved situation analysis and design; phase 2 involved researching the pilot project involving five early childhood centres; phase 3 researched the consolidated project involving a further 15 early childhood settings.

Reflecting the findings from the situation analysis and an international literature review, a critical sociocultural approach was designed to provide the overall framings of the FIH project. Iterative cycles of practitioner action research involving early years educators in innovations in their pedagogical approaches were supported through the establishment of critical communities known as *Leadership Round Tables*. Regular sessions of professional learning featured the introduction of new concepts and theories to support their pedagogical innovations, reflection and evidence analysis. Three study tours to Australia were funded by the funding body, allowing a number of participants to observe alternative early childhood pedagogical practices. The researchers positioned themselves as collaborators in partnership with the educators, working hard to resist constructions of themselves as foreign experts, who some Chilean educators had come across in other projects. Educators explored understandings of what it meant to be knowledge creators and were provided with professional learning opportunities to develop skills relevant to researching local practice. Locally based *mentoras* (mentors) were employed to support the educators and their innovation, reflection and evaluation processes. The pedagogical change model, based on principles of activism, agency, connection, mutuality, distributed leadership (Harris, 2014) and sustainability evolved over time.

The findings and examples presented in this chapter have been drawn from a synthesis of data gathered from educators, directors, family members during focus groups and interviews during phase 2 of the research. Each focus group or interview during this period was arbitrarily assigned an alphabetical classification.

Theoretical framing

A range of theoretical resources were assembled to inform the processes supporting the educators' efforts in reconceptualizing how they worked, drawing particularly on findings from the EPPE study (Mayo and Siraj, 2015; Sammons et al., 2014) and a Vygotskian focus on learners constructing new understandings through their active engagement within social practices. In brief, FIH aimed at repositioning children from being passive consumers of knowledge to being active agents in their own learning in ECEC settings. Finally, there was a reconceptualization of educators as collaborators and leaders of children's learning, which allowed them to see families and communities as potential partners in the children's learning.

Key conceptual resources were selected in response to the pedagogical challenges that surfaced during the situation analysis and in successive cycles of action research in the Leadership Round Tables. These resources included the concepts of scaffolding, co-construction and sustained shared thinking, the latter arising from an analysis as part of the EPPE study (Sylva et al., 2010). Most importantly, an invented concept, *Literacidad*, developed as part of the project, drew attention to the concept of literacy as a social practice, reinforcing the social and cultural ways of doing things through the use of text rather than a set of skills and processes that must be learnt and internalized (Comber and Cormack, 1997). This prefaced a shift away from the rote learning processes framed and influenced by the term *alfabetización* (reading and writing).

Lastly, the concept of 'funds of knowledge' (Moll, Amanti, Neff and Gonzalez, 1992; Gonzalez, Moll and Armanti, 2005) was introduced. Funds of knowledge are defined by Moll and his colleagues 'to refer to the historically accumulated and culturally developed bodies of knowledge and skills essential for household or individual functioning and well-being' (1992, p. 133). This concept, with its origins in work done in disadvantaged Hispanic communities documenting the everyday practices of families and identifying and presenting these as richly contextualized resources for children's learning, provided a key mobilizing resource in helping educators conceptualize how they might engage with families.

The concepts of common knowledge, relational agency and relational expertise developed by Edwards (2010, 2017 and Chapter 1, this volume) have also contributed a significant resource for the analysis of the educators' work with the children, families, community as well as with each other. In particular, the concepts have enabled us, as researchers, to better understand what was at stake in these attempts at reconceptualizing educators' practices and engagement with families and what key resources, skills, knowledge and understandings might be demanded of the educators.

Edwards (2010, 2011, 2012) describes common knowledge as understanding other's deeper motives, values and purposes when engaging in joint efforts. Knowing *what matters* to each other mediates interactions and is seen as fundamental to collaborative professional practice and collaborations between professionals and families. The desired outcome for FIH, through such collaboration, was the children's long-term educational success, with children's literacy learning being viewed as a way of supporting the children's transition to school.

Our position was that the productive engagement of children in the educational setting is enhanced when values, motives and intentions are shared between key stakeholders in children's lives. Rai (2016), for example, argues that developing common knowledge when working with families and communities fosters families' agentic involvement in supporting children's education. Reciprocal understanding of what matters to both the school and the family helps in aligning the support each gives to the child as a learner. For example, our research showed us that for educators to engage parents as interested protagonists in their children's learning, they needed to develop more meaningful relationships with them and to better understand their realities. In brief, they needed to exercise relational expertise in both building and using common knowledge with parents.

This project therefore saw educators develop their relational expertise both with each other and with parents. Edwards (2011, 2012) identifies relational expertise as an additional expertise that involves finding out what is important to the collaborating partner; understanding their stance, strengths and their motives; and working towards aligning responses to the problem being worked on.

In this way, educators were challenged to move away from their traditional ways of working in which their own motives/intentions were the primary reason for their actions. Instead, educators were encouraged to form partnerships with each other and with families that were mediated by common knowledge to enable the different expertise offered in each practice to be brought into play. This development of relational expertise was most relevant to educators in the research sites and to the *mentoras* working with them. The capacity of the *mentoras* was built through the leadership roundtables. Together the *mentoras* explored the complexity of their work with educators, developing their own common knowledge about mentoring, and contributed to each other's development of professional expertise in that new role.

Putting concepts to work

By working with the idea of relational expertise, we could see that forming and sustaining relationships with families requires educators to recognize what matters in the expertise of the families and make what matters for them as educators explicit. Over time, educators developed this relational expertise and, through this, gained new understandings of what was important to families. Activities were instigated to promote sharing of this new knowledge and perceptions among educators and families. Through these learning encounters, participants were encouraged to question the traditional and normative views of literacy acquisition, early learning and the parent-teacher relationship. These activities lead to conceptual shifts in what was important to each group as a collective and as individuals. Most importantly, educators moved from a deficit view of families, and families realized how they could uniquely contribute to and gain from the ECEC. In effect, transformations in the relationships in the family setting occurred as common knowledge about 'what matters' to families and educators became better understood as being essential to the parent-educator partnership.

The concept of 'funds of knowledge' was pertinent to the process of developing relational expertise and forging understandings of common knowledge as it provided the educators with a language and tangible ideas about how to enter into different relations with families and ensure that family and community knowledge was recognized and respected. In interview and focus group data, educators consistently identified funds of knowledge as the primary mobilizer for their changed understandings and knowledge about how to work differently with families: 'We use methodologies that are a great motivation not only for the team, but for the parents, this has enriched our work ... it [funds of knowledge] has helped us improve the quality of teaching ... and more than anything, the relationship with parents' (director, interview setting Y). Similarly, Rai (2016) reminds us that Moll and his colleagues argue that when educational settings seek to understand children's funds of knowledge, they also make the institution's funds of knowledge more accessible, thus creating greater opportunity for mutuality in the relationships.

From this new perspective, educators developed a range of locally relevant strategies to engage with families and elicit their motivations, interests and capabilities together with the resources of the local communities. These resources included the Literacy Café, discussed later, which became an iconic feature across the 20 sites as well as other smaller scale projects. The funds of knowledge approach was also taken up in planning the children's learning. Educators shifted towards a more investigative approach with children and drew on local events such as earthquakes, government elections and sporting events as topics for children's research.

This change in curriculum focus also changed the relationships between educators and children, with one early years supervisor observing that the funds of knowledge approach 'enabled educators to place the child at centre of the pedagogical proposal' (curriculum advisor, Interview Central Office). Parents noticed the difference too, with many observing the increased independence of their children, irrespective of their age. As one father observed, 'This centre helps them to work. Compared with the education I had, today we can see children are more independent than we were. The values are well set here. I have confidence in the centre. We are a community – we work very much together' (father, family focus group setting P).

These changes in perspective and ways of working were significant to establishing the groundwork for the development of more sophisticated relationality in the form of relational agency in joint action on problems and challenges. This joint action is mediated by the common knowledge that has been built up (Edwards, 2010, 2015; Rai, 2016).

Edwards (2010) explains how the recognition of how and why others interpret and react to problems and alignment of one's own interpretations and response to theirs produces enriched understandings of the problem being worked on. What the research showed was a change in how both educators and families began to share and value each other's contribution, which led to dramatic shifts in the institutional practices of the ECEC. Educators no longer worked in isolation; they offered support to families and asked for support from families. Requests for support were different though – more authentic, not tokenistic – and linked to the families' expertise. Families valued their new sense of agency, and their level and depth of participation deepened as they began to appreciate the importance of their contribution – they were eager to participate in new ways so as to change their child's educational trajectory.

Pedagogies in transition

So far in this chapter, we have outlined the FIH project and explored some insights about the related research that the use of Edwards's 'gardening tools' of common knowledge, relational expertise and relational agency has made possible.

In this section, we present three exemplars of pedagogical innovations that illustrate the changing ethos and development of common knowledge, relational expertise and relational agency. To begin, educators were encouraged to think about the usefulness of Australian examples of pedagogical practice in a Chilean context and to reimagine what would be appropriate in their ECEC settings. Accessing families' funds of knowledge was an important first step in transforming how educators worked (Newman, Arthur, Staples and Woodrow, 2016) and is reflected in the descriptions below. What follows are illustrative of some of the many innovations that educators undertook to strengthen parent-teacher relationships and build common knowledge and a sense of community around the ECEC. Many of these ways of working were significant disruptions to traditional practices and triggered spinoffs that permeated many aspects of the ECEC operations, including changes to greeting procedures, locking the gate protocols and were evidence of professionals and their pedagogies in transition.

Through each of the activities involving families, there were opportunities for educators to understand what mattered to the families and for families to understand the intentions of the educators.

Exemplar 1: Literacy Café

The Literacy Café was initially developed at one of the original research sites as a way of engaging families in conversations with the educators, although it quickly developed as a forum for more substantial exchanges of information. Its success in gaining parents' and other family members' attention and their willingness to participate quickly became legendary and all participating centres were soon adopting the practice. Essentially, it involved small groups of parents being invited to attend a group meeting with an educator at an appointed time in their child's ECEC. Typically, educators took some care in preparing the invitations in the style of an event. Conversation cards covering a range of topics were created by educators and modest refreshments were provided. In understanding the significance of this innovation, it's important to recognize the sociocultural context in which clearly established class boundaries meant that families from poor communities rarely engaged with educators except in times of trouble. The Literacy Café interrupted these social norms and established a dialogic space which carried the emergent relations fostered through earlier activities forward. The parent data abounds with parents' enthusiasm for this opportunity 'to have a coffee with a teacher'. As this mother said, 'We like the literacy cafes because we can interchange experiences. We learn from each other' (family focus group setting P). It was viewed as an opportunity to know more about their children's learning, ask questions and share knowledge about their children and aspects of family life, in other words, as an opportunity to build common knowledge. Educators reported that parents were asking for them to occur more frequently and this was also confirmed in the parent data. The conversation cards were scaffolds for educators to hear from parents about what mattered to them, but they also enabled the development of relationships among parents and between parents and educators. It was evident that, as the practice developed, exchange of information became two way and subsequent iterations of conversation cards and topics reflected parents' choices.

The Literacy Café enabled:

- generation of common knowledge through more dialogic sharing of knowledge and perspectives (more than giving information);
- fostering of relational expertise by clarifying intentions and motives; and
- development of relational agency, as educators worked with what they learnt from parents to adapt the processes and learning environment to what was known, and specific and parents felt armed with more knowledge about how to support their child as a learner.

Exemplar 2: Technology enabled travelling media (camera, journal)

The introduction of technology to the early childhood centres was made possible through the generous resourcing of the project. Digital cameras, data projectors and printers were made available to each centre; yet, their introduction highlighted the negative views held by schools and teachers about children and children's home life. Digital cameras were intended to provide a means of documenting learning activities as well as recording events and 'funds of knowledge' of children, families and the local community. These were quickly placed under lock and key. In one school, the principal insisted on locking them in his own office, a considerable distance from the ECEC. Most educators were reluctant to allow children to use the cameras and were openly resistant to the idea of sending them home with children for family use. Over time, these attitudes changed as knowledge and experiences were exchanged between educators in the forum of the Leadership Round Table. Educators quickly recognized the value of children's engagement and the learning opportunities inherent in their use, especially when used in conjunction with the data projectors. The technology and the cameras in particular were significant artefacts/instruments for instigating change both in terms of children's engagement in learning and in building common knowledge and developing relationships with families. This educator recognized the importance of the devices in providing new ways/opportunities for communicating and literacy learning: 'I think the more substantial thing is the use of technology, and the way that we can organize all these worlds for the kids to be able to manipulate, use the camera, take pictures, to build stories, to take, I mean, to construct things that have relationships with literacy' (educator, interview setting F).

Another educator observed that the cameras were seen as 'tremendously attractive' to the families and 'now they are asking about their children's work, showing interest and involvement … as a consequence of seeing the photos, its made them interested and easier for them to understand our work' (educator, focus group setting Y).

The success of one centre instigating a travelling box in which the camera was carefully secured, together with a set of suggestions as to how the family might use the camera to document family activities to be later shared with children and educators at the centre, engendered great enthusiasm in both parents and educators. Parents reported this as being a highly valued activity. It generated meaningful understandings of what mattered to the families and educators and was significant in building common knowledge as a resource they could use in their work with families and in easing children's orientation to the opportunities and demands of the ECEC.

The resulting photo journals produced by the families therefore enriched relationships. The photo journals became a way of sharing family and community knowledge and changing the dynamic between educators and families and inserting local 'funds of knowledge' in the curriculum. Although initially families were thought not to understand the use of technology, educators found they were capable. As this educator said, 'We showed them the technology we thought that they didn't know about what this activity was for, useful for and we realized that they know far more than we did' (educator, focus group setting F).

Another educator observed that this approach enabled the parents to 'become participants'. The views of parents also changed:

> We have improved a lot, our relationship with the family. We started with these stories, exchange, and the family feels very proud and they are very engaged with this idea of stories, ... through this story telling process, we have discovered a lot of knowledge that families have, that people have. We have a kind of learner learning improvement through the project. (Director, interview setting F)

A parent describing her family's involvement through the use of the travelling photo journal said: 'Last time the children were learning about professional work. The parents came and explained their work. My husband is a truck driver so we did something about trucks for the children to take home' (mother, family focus group setting P). What is significant here is to understand the change in families' participation from that of being locked out of settings, to being resource providers of materials for teachers' use in the classroom, to becoming active contributors to the curriculum, valued and appreciated for the knowledge they share with the children.

The use of technology enabled:

- generation of funds of knowledge through sharing images and stories generated by parents in the home environment, including family members, activities and community events;
- fostering common knowledge by clarifying intentions and motives in exchanges between the early childhood centre and the family home;
- development of educators' relational expertise as they sought to learn about families' funds of knowledge in the home learning environment and construct learning experiences based on family contributions; and
- recognition of distributed expertise and exercising relational agency by negotiating and repositioning of families as curriculum collaborators in a process of democratic acknowledgement and re-distribution of expertise.

Exemplar 3: Gathering and sharing information

Educators across the research sites devised a range of initial strategies to signal to families their interest in engaging with them differently. These entry-level activities gathered information in creative and visible ways. The *Family Literacy Tree* comprised a large paper or cardboard tree with blank leaves and provided a static space for families to identify knowledge and skills that they could contribute to the ECEC. It was a feature that emerged early in the life of the project and represented a tentative step in educators engaging families, but was an innovation based on understandings of parents as resource.

Variations of the *Tree of Dreams*, which was similar in format to the Literacy Tree, provided safe ways for parents to reveal their aspirations for their children. Parents were encouraged to describe their career aspirations for their children, their immediate hopes/goals for the current ECEC experience or the values they hoped would characterize their children's lives. This early activity helped educators develop common knowledge and challenge their perceptions of what matters to families. As families' motives were made explicit through this activity, educators began to view families more positively. Educators used the technology tools to produce colourfully illustrated panels depicting learning activities so as to exchange information with families so that they were better informed about their children's learning and able to understand the purpose of different learning experiences better. These panels communicated to parents a respect for their rights and interest in knowing.

Discussion: Educators, children, families and pedagogies in transition

The exemplars described above relate to pedagogies designed to support a different kind of engagement with families with the understanding that enhancing family connectedness to children's learning has a beneficial effect on children's transition to school and subsequent school success. They are indicative of many pedagogical innovations that occurred in this project. Others were more directly focused on children's learning, including the use of technology in the classroom, the establishment of dramatic play spaces equipped with literacy materials to foster literacy-related play, incorporation of community events and issues in the curriculum, and the use of the outdoors as a learning space. Many of these strengthened children's learning by connecting learning to their life worlds, making the transition from home to school easier for them.

The pedagogical innovations reveal some of the ways educators transformed their work with each other, the children, families and communities. Long-held beliefs that guided their traditional pedagogical approaches were challenged, and transformational shifts in values and beliefs saw the educators develop new practices and understandings. In the interviews, educators made frequent reference to how they worked before and how their perspectives and pedagogies changed, demonstrating how they were in transition as professionals.

There were changes in the way educators viewed their role over the course of the project. One outcome of developing common knowledge and relational expertise as a practitioner is becoming more aware of one's own specialist expertise and what matters in one's own professional practice. These processes were evident among the educators. As their sense of professional identity grew, so did their confidence to go out into the community and advocate the importance of ECEC. As one director indicated, 'I think there is also part of the misunderstanding, mis-value of the way others see our work because we are working closed door, you know, behind the gate, and now we are trying to communicate better with the rest of the school, try to go out and let them know what we are doing' (director, focus group setting E).

The style of ECEC leadership also shifted from being an autocratic one to one in which relational skills were practised, as this director explained:

> In the past I was told that the director was at a level higher than the teachers, and therefore had to tell them what to do. During the capacity building sessions, the mentor of this programme pointed out that leadership was a shared endeavour, and that I had to learn to delegate tasks to other people. It was not a question of making my work easier, but of enabling people to do. (Director, interview setting P)

The importance of the family context, home-school communication and parent engagement in children's learning are factors frequently highlighted as being important to children's transitions to school (Melhuish et al., 2008; Crosnoe and Cooper, 2010; Rimm-Kaufman and Pianta, 2005). As educators sought, gathered and incorporated families' funds of knowledge and local community events into children's learning experiences, they also increased children's chances of educational success (Crosno and Cooper, 2010; Dockett and Perry, 2013). In one interview at the end of the project, this director describes the transformations in planning for children's learning when local contextual events are incorporated in this interview.

> When they [educators] finally understood that this was like a network ... that I could teach ... if I have to teach numeracy, to give you an example, I can start off anywhere ... if a child wants to talk about a ball, then we can talk about the golden ball award. Likewise, the topic of being the president of a country was brought up. A child asked, 'How is an election for president carried out?'. The scope of the project widened and we ended up doing a mock election in

class. The whole voting process was organized step by step, including the setting up of the election table, issuing identity cards, having a voting urn and a secret chamber. Not only the children, but all the adults involved in the Kindergarten took part in this project. At that moment, the educators finally realized the usefulness of such concrete projects. I hope we will continue to do such projects every month, instead of being old-fashioned like before. (Director, interview setting W)

However, socializing the world of institutional learning is not the only function of the ECEC setting. Social awareness, social coherence and inclusion were also engendered by the educators' changed engagement with families, the pursuit of common knowledge and the seeking and documentation of community and family funds of knowledge as observed by this educator: 'The classmates get to know who the children are, who their family is, their dog, their house. …This gives them motivation to learn literacy because it is about their classmates. It is not the same as learning from a magazine that is unrelated to them' (educators, focus group setting W).

As educators began to see the importance of involving families in meaningful ways and valuing their contributions to the children's learning, they expanded their relationship with families over time. These new ways of working enabled the transition of families from being outside observers to being inside participants. As meaningful relationships with families and the community were built, early childhood centres became a valued institution in the families' lives as they recognized its contribution to achieving their aspirations for their children.

> Now we have a different relationship with the family in the sense before we used to say 'can't bring this, can't do this, can't do that, can't fix that, can't do painting like that', things like that. Now actually we interact and relate to the family in a more about, well, she is talking about the funds of knowledge, and how they are incorporating the knowledge that the family have to work with them. Before they used to impose children should or could learn, and now they are taking the children interest and family background knowledge to the learning. (Educators, focus group setting F)

Through these new family-focused activities, educators developed a more nuanced understanding of what matters for families; they were able to identify the parents' aspirations for their children, as well as recognize and harness families' funds of knowledge. Educators also noted that the parents were more open and comfortable, developing an 'understanding about what we do here with their kids, what they are learning. … The [FIH] programme has helped the communication, what are the things happening during the day, and what are the things they do with them' (educators, focus group setting F). One educator encapsulated this idea, saying:

> Now the family is far more involved in this learning process. I think that has made a considerable change in the sense of the kids feel supported. Now it's not just us doing the work, but the family as well. So they have two different opportunities of where to source their knowledge. (Educator, focus group setting F)

These transformed pedagogies and practices supported children's transitions to formal education. Importantly, children transitioned through these transformed pedagogies from passive receivers of the programme to active protagonists in their own learning with motive orientations to what mattered in school. However, despite improvement in the transition from home to ECEC, *mentoras* identified that more could be done to support the transition of children from the ECEC settings to school, and this would be a new focus as they encourage directors to reflect on how they might work with school teachers. One *mentora* noted that 'educators are now seeing that their work is similar to that of the teachers in schools' (reunion focus group). Educators' changing perspectives of their professional role and their developing relational expertise will contribute to relational agency engaging with school teachers to address the challenges of supporting children from high-poverty areas successfully transitioning to school. However, we sound a note of caution and look to Hedegaard (2017) for a nuanced account of the different kinds of expertise offered by the ECEC and schools. It is to be hoped that the new confidence of the ECEC educators means that they don't see themselves as just teachers, but as also having a distinct role and specialist insights about children as learners and the communities in which they live, from which the teachers might learn.

Conclusion

The project saw the transformation of the relationship between educators and families to support children's transitions into the ECEC setting, enabling them to more easily orient themselves to what mattered in the ECEC. The intention was that easing that transition would help prepare the children for their later transition to more formal schooling.

A number of other transitions also occurred during this project. Educators' articulated the conceptual framework they employed through a common language. The development of relational expertise saw educators discuss the motives of their work with each other and with families so as to address the ways in which children's learning and transition to the ECEC could be enhanced. Ultimately, through this project, common knowledge emerged as participants brought their different perspectives to the ECEC curriculum, routines and processes. Above all, the educators were repositioned in ECEC practices and were open to responsive innovations. As this participant said, 'It is a change in the way we view things … a change of perspective … a change in the way we do our work' (director, interview setting V).

References

Arndt, A.-K., Rothe, A., Urban, M., and Werning, R. (2013). Supporting and stimulating the learning of socioeconomically disadvantaged children – perspectives of parents and educators in the transition from preschool to primary school. *European Early Childhood Education Research Journal*, 21(1), 23–38. doi:10.1080/1350293X.2012.760336.

Bradshaw, J., and Bennett, F. (2014). *Investing in children: Breaking the cycle of disadvantage – A study of national policies*. Country Report-UK. European Commission.

Comber, B., and Cormack, P. (1997). Looking beyond 'skills' and 'processes': Literacy as social and cultural practices in classrooms. *Literacy*, 33(3), 22–9.

Cortis, N., Katz, I., and Patulny, R. (2009). *Engaging hard to reach families and their children. Occasional paper Number 6 Stronger Families and Communities Strategy 2004-2009*. Canberra, ACT: Australian Government. Department Families, Housing, Communities and Indigenous Affairs.

Cohrssen, C., Church, A., and Tayler, C. (2014). Purposeful pauses: Teacher talk during early childhood mathematics activities. *International Journal of Early Years Education*, 22(2), 169–83. doi:10.1080/09669760.2014.900476.

Crozier, G., and Davies, J. (2007). Hard to reach parents or hard to reach schools? A discussion of home-school relations, with particular reference to Bangladeshi and Pakistani parents. *British Educational Research Journal*, 33(3), 295–313. doi:10.1080/01411920701243578.

Crosnoe, R., and Cooper, C. E. (2010). Economically disadvantaged children's transitions into Elementary School: Linking family processes, school contexts and educational policy. *American Educational Research Journal*, 47(2), 258–91. doi:10.3102/0002831209351564.

Delgado-Gaitan, C. (2005). Reflections from the field: Family narratives in multiple literacies. *Anthropology and Education Quarterly, 36*(3), 265–72. doi:10.1525/aeq.2005.36.3.265.

Dockett, S., and Perry, B. (2013). Trends and tensions: Australian and international research about starting school. *International Journal of Early Years Education, 21*(2–3), 163–77. doi:10.1080/09669760.2013.832943.

Edwards, A. (2010). *Being an expert professional practitioner: The relational turn in expertise.* Dordrecht, New York, NY: Springer.

Edwards, A. (2011). Building common knowledge at the boundaries between professional practices: Relational agency and relational expertise in systems of distributed expertise. *International Journal of Educational Research, 50*(1), 33–9. doi:10.1016/j.ijer.2011.04.007.

Edwards, A. (2012). The role of common knowledge in achieving collaboration across practices. *Learning, Culture and Social Interaction, 1*(1), 22–32. doi:10.1016/j.lcsi.2012.03.003.

Edwards, A. (2015). Recognising and realising teachers' professional agency. *Teachers and Teaching, 21*(6), 779–84. doi:10.1080/13540602.2015.1044333.

Edwards, A. (Ed.). (2017). *Working relationally in and across practices: A cultural-historical approach to collaboration.* New York, NY: Cambridge University Press.

González, N., Moll, L. C., and Amanti, C. (2005). *Funds of knowledge theorizing practice in households, communities, and classrooms.* Mahwah, NJ: L. Erlbaum Associates.

Harris, A. (2014). *Distributed leadership matters: Perspectives, practicalities, and potential.* London: SAGE.

Hedegaard, M. (2014). The significance of demands and motives across practices in children's learning and development: An analysis of learning in home and school. *Learning, Culture and Social Interaction, 3*(3), 188–94. doi:10.1016/j.lcsi.2014.02.008.

Hedegaard, M. (2017). When day care professionals' values for transition to school do not align with the educational demands from society and school. In A. Edwards (Ed.), *Working relationally in and across practices: A cultural-historical approach to collaboration* (pp. 247–64). New York, NY: Cambridge University Press. Retrieved from https://ebookcentral.proquest.com.

Howes, C., Burchinal, M., Pianta, R., Bryant, D., Early, D., Clifford, R., and Barbarin, O. (2008). Ready to learn? Children's pre-academic achievement in pre-kindergarten programmes. *Early Childhood Research Quarterly, 23*(1), 27–50. doi:10.1016/j.ecresq.2007.05.002.

Ishimine, K., and Tayler, C. (2014). Assessing quality in early childhood education and care. *European Journal of Education, 49*(2), 272–90. doi:10.1111/ejed.12043.

Mayo, A., and Siraj, I. (2015). Parenting practices and children's academic success in low-SES families. *Oxford Review of Education, 41*(1), 47–63. doi:10.1080/03054985.2014.995160.

Melhuish E. C., Phan Mai, B., Sylva, K., Sammons, P., Siraj-Blatchford, I., and Taggart, B. (2008). Effects of the home learning environment and preschool center experience upon literacy and numeracy development in early primary school. *Journal of Social Issues, 64*(1), 95–114. doi:10.1111/j.1540-4560.2008.00550.x.

Mohr, J., Zygmunt, E., and Clark, P. (2012). Becoming good human beings: Low-income mothers' dreams for children and their insight into children's needs. *Early Childhood Research and Practice, 14*(2). Retrieved from http://ecrp.uiuc.edu/v14n2/mohr.html.

Moll, L. C., Amanti, C., Neff, D., and Gonzalez, N. (1992). Funds of knowledge for teaching: Using a qualitative approach to connect homes and classrooms. *Theory Into Practice, 31*(2), 132–41. doi:10.1080/00405849209543534.

Newman, L., Arthur, L., Staples, K., and Woodrow, C. (2016). Accessing family knowledge: Conceptualising opportunities for recognition of family engagement in young children's literacy learning. *Australasian Journal of Early Childhood, 41*(1), 73–81.

Ogbu, J. (1995). Cultural problems in minority education: Their interpretations and consequences – part one: Theoretical background. *Urban Review, 27*(3), 189–205.

Peralta, M. V. (2011). Early childhood education and public care policies in Chile: A historical perspective to analyze the present. *International Journal of Child Care and Education Policy, 5*(1), 17–27. doi:10.1007/2288-6729-5-1-17.

Portes, P. R. (2005). *Dismantling educational inequality: A cultural-historical approach to closing the achievement gap.* Retrieved from http://www.peterlangusa.com.

Rai, C. P. (2016). Building and using common knowledge for developing school-community links. In A. Edwards (Ed.), *Working relationally in and across practices: A cultural-historical approach to collaboration* (pp. 96–113). New York, NY: Cambridge University Press. Retrieved from http://ebookcentral.proquest.com.

Rimm-Kaufmann, S. E., and Pianta, R. C. (2005). Family-school communication in pre-school and kindergarten in the context of a relationship enhancing intervention. *Early Education and Development, 16*(3), 287–316. doi:10.1207/s15566935eed1603_1.

Rosier, K., and McDonald, M. (2011). *Promoting positive education and care transitions for children.* Melbourne: Australian Institute of Family Studies.

Sammons, P., Sylva, K., Melhuish, E. C., Siraj, I., Taggart, B., Smees, R., Toth, K., and Welcomme, W. (2014). *The Effective Provision of Pre-School Education [EPPE] project: A longitudinal study funded by the DfES: (1997 – 2003), Technical Report.* London: Institute of Education.

Shonkoff, J. (2011). Building a foundation for prosperity on the science of early childhood development. In *Pathways: Poverty, inequality and social policy.* Stanford Centre for the Study of Poverty and Inequality. Retrieved from www.inequality.com.

Sylva, K. (2014). The role of families and preschools in educational disadvantage. *Oxford Review of Education, 40*(6), 680–95. doi:10.1080/03054985.2014.979581.

Sylva, K., Melhuish, E., Sammons, P., Siraj-Blatchford, I., and Taggart, B. (2010). *Early childhood matters: Evidence from the Effective Pre-school and Primary Education (EPPE) project.* London: Routledge.

Taggart, B., Sylva, K., Melhuish, E., Sammons, P., and Siraj, I. (2015). *Effective pre-school, primary and secondary education project (EPPSE 3-16+): How pre-school influences children and young people's attainment and developmental outcomes over time Research Brief*. London: Department for Education.

Villalón, M., Suzuki, E., Herrera, M., and Mathiesen, M. (2002). Quality of Chilean early childhood education from an international perspective. *International Journal of Early Years Education, 10*(1), 49–59. doi:10.1080/09669760220114845.

Volk, D., and Long, S. (2005). Challenging myths of the deficit perspective: Honoring children's literacy resources. *Young Children, 60*(6), 12–19.

Webb, G., Knight, B. A., and Busch, G. (2017). Children's transitions to school: 'So what about the parents'? or 'so, what about the parents'? *International Journal of Early Years Education, 25*(2), 204–17. doi:10.1080/09669760.2017.1301808.

Woodrow, C., Arthur, L., and Newman, L. (2014). Futuro Infantil Hoy and community capacity building: An international early childhood literacy project. In L. Arthur, J. Ashton and B. Beecher (Eds), *Diverse literacies in early childhood: A social justice approach* (pp. 86–105). Melbourne: Australian Council for Educational Research.

Woodrow, C., Somerville, M., Naidoo, L., and Power, K. (2016). *Researching parent engagement: A qualitative field study*. Retrieved from https://researchdirect.western sydney.edu.au/islandora/object/uws:34565

8

The Transition of Roma Children into School: Working Relationally Across Cultural Boundaries in Spain

José Luis Lalueza, Virginia Martínez-Lozano and
Beatriz Macías-Gomez-Estern

Introduction

From a cultural-historical perspective, human development is the product of participation in cultural practices that have historically been constructed within the framework of institutions such as the family and the school. Across these practices, there is always some type of discontinuity which must be addressed and overcome (Hedegaard, 2005; Rogoff, 1993, 2003). However, when the cultural framework of the family is far removed from that of the school, as is the case among certain ethnic minorities or immigrant populations, the discontinuities between the two scenarios may be very significant, and hence acceptance of the rationale for school tasks and achievement of a successful transition may be both arduous and protracted (Greenfield and Cocking, 1994; Poveda, 2001).

Therefore, schools, seeking the inclusion of members of minority groups such as Roma communities, must start from an awareness of the concerns and priorities of this cultural group in order to design interventions that will facilitate their transition between scenarios and to promote dialogue in this respect. A better understanding of this community's socializing practices and of other forms of behaviour would help teachers and education managers understand the difficulties sometimes encountered in ensuring school attendance.

At the same time, schools as institutions have their own values, norms and objectives that should be conveyed and shared among all involved. One aspect of this is the need to foster children's understanding of and response to the demands of the school environment. In this task, families can play an essential role, as supporters of their children's transition to a formal education setting. Of course, families must be informed of the school's concerns and ambitions for the children. Thus, establishing common knowledge of what matters in the two practices of school life and home life (Edwards, 2010, 2012, 2017) regarding the issues facing children is of crucial importance.

This chapter presents two experiences, one in Barcelona and the other in Seville, of the Roma community in their children's transitions to formal education. To place these experiences in context, we first present the main features of Roma culture, knowledge of which is fundamental to understanding how the educational practices described below are constructed. Knowledge of the evident discontinuities and contradictions between educational institutions and the values held by Roma families is an essential prerequisite for creating a system in which schools and families can work together effectively, and this question underlies all the main challenges facing an education establishment that claims to be inclusive. These challenges concern the acquisition of new motives by families and children entering the educational system, while retaining their established values and beliefs. A successful response to these challenges requires the mastery of new tools and cultural artefacts, together with the creation of shared practices and narratives in which participants from minority cultures feel represented and respected. We describe two episodes in this respect – one taking place in an out-of-school activity, the other within a primary school. In both cases, the neighbourhood contains many challenges, with high rates of absenteeism, academic failure and dropout. We illustrate how education professionals address these challenges and how they work closely with children and families in order to facilitate their transition to the surrounding 'normative' culture represented by schooling.

Discontinuities between family and school in activity contexts

The discontinuities between the educational practices of Roma communities and those commonly encountered in schools can usefully be examined by taking the activity as a unit of analysis (Leontiev, 1978). An activity is defined primarily by the relationships between the subject, the object and the artefacts that mediate this relationship. According to Engeström (2001, 2007), we must also take into account the institutional anchoring of the activity, which includes the rules and norms by which it is regulated, the community of reference and the division of labour. An analysis of each of these six activity parameters reveals clear differences between schools' educational practices and those of families in the Roma community.

For the school, *the subject* is the *individual*, as concerns all rights and duties. In the Roma community, on the other hand, the subject is always considered within the context of family membership. The family plays a central role, and the community is essentially an interconnected set of families. Children must be aware of their position in this framework and understand that their lives are woven into the network of family relationships. For the school, all students are equal, without distinction on the basis of family origin, community of origin or sex. Individual progress, then, is the sole responsibility of individuals, depending on their own effort and ability. In the Roma community, however, each member's progress is organized around the role played in the family, as a child, as a young person seeking a partner, as a spouse, as a parent or as a grandparent; as part of this progress, the goal of children's socialization is primarily that of marriage (Padrós, 2016). Hence, the primary task to be accomplished in the construction of personal identity is not that of fostering individual autonomy, but of ensuring the perpetuation of the family cycle.

In formal learning institutions, subjects are presented with *goals* focused on the individual acquiring knowledge, skills and appropriate language and behaviour. The broader educational goal is the internalization and the autonomous application of these goals to new situations. But in the Roma world, educational practices are oriented towards preparing young people to contribute to maintaining the established social order. The aim, therefore, is to equip 'good' Roma boys and girls with appropriate knowledge, skills and attitudes. In this society, knowledge is not transmitted via an institution staffed by specialists; instead, contexts based upon guided participation are organized to enable children to become adept in the world of adult activities, first as mere spectators, then as assistants and apprentices, until they are finally recognized to have sufficient skill and responsibility to carry out the necessary tasks themselves.

The pedagogical *instruments* employed by the school are exclusively dedicated to transmitting learning and are viewed as useful insofar as they enable each student to achieve this goal. But in Roma communities, the tools of traditional guided learning are the same as those used for productive activity, and they are useful only to the extent that they bring well-being or prestige to the group. These instruments are not created to transmit knowledge about how to engage in agriculture, livestock or craftwork, but focus mainly on trade (the purchase and resale of livestock or antiques, trade based on recycling or in street markets, etc.) and on artistic expression, especially music. The essential aspect of the Roma people's survival is not their knowledge of a natural world to be transformed, but that of a social world with which to interact.

The school *community* is composed of individuals organized exclusively according to their role in that context, that is, as students, teachers or service personnel. This role disappears as soon as they leave the building and the school door closes behind them. On the contrary, the Roma community comprises a network of families, and each person's role is maintained in all his/her social actions. Any individual conduct outside the home is a matter that involves the family (whether positively or negatively) with the rest of the community.

School *rules* are a means of shaping individual responsibility through rewards, punishments, evaluations, merits and demerits, and are fundamentally oriented towards the individual. Everyone is responsible for his/her own actions and is evaluated according to the knowledge shown to have been acquired. The fruits of endeavour, in the form of certificates and titles, are individual and guarantee a personal future. In contrast, the Roma law that governs relations within the ethnic community places the emphasis on collective values. Responsibility is not confined to individuals; each social act includes the family, and the transgression of a law is a matter that involves the family as a whole. Just as the entire family is 'stained' by the guilt of one of its own, it is affronted by an attack on any of its members.

At school, the *division of labour* is organized according to roles that are determined by the complex legitimizing mechanisms of society, one of which is teachers' possession of certificates that entitle them to perform their function. There is also a distribution of functions between parents and teachers, within limits that are sometimes equivocal, but unarguably present. In Roma society, with regard to teaching/learning practices, the question of who teaches is not determined by a role created to carry out this function; instead, the teachers are simply those who perform the tasks pertaining to teaching and who have a prior relationship (family or community) with the learner. Knowledge is intimately linked to experience, and hence to sex and age. It is the mother who shows her daughter the ins and outs of working in the market, the father who instructs his son in making a deal. In the discourse of Roma people about their own culture (Cerreruela et al., 2001; Lalueza and Crespo, 2009), it is the elders who possess the fundamental knowledge required for social life, and Roma society defers explicitly and implicitly to accumulated wisdom, to knowledge that is profoundly dependent on experience that only the senior members of the community can possess. There is accumulated knowledge in a slowly changing environment, and it is transmitted in the form of stories from which lessons must be drawn. Recognition of knowledge based on the experience of those who become grandparents is at the heart of the community's power and legitimacy. Thus, elders have direct authority over their descendants and are granted the capacity to mediate in community conflicts.

We see, thus, a pattern of individual versus collective subject, individual versus group goals, formal versus traditional instruments, institutional versus blood-tie community, individual versus shared responsibility and role division by professionalization versus division by sex and age. There are two sets of practices that reflect different goals, use different instruments, establish different references and, above all, define different subjects. All of these differences, in themselves, impose multiple difficulties on those who must respond to the demands of both universes, but the task becomes even more arduous when the power relations between the respective communities are profoundly asymmetric. In the following pages, we examine how the school tries to facilitate transitions between these different cultural scenarios and to soften the discontinuities between them.

Challenges in Roma children's transition to school

From a cultural-historical perspective, development is the result of participation in sociocultural practices. This participation facilitates appropriation of the artefacts required to form an active part of the community. According to Barbara Rogoff, 'To understand cognitive development, it is necessary to take into account the particular problems that children try to solve and their significance within the culture' (1990, p. 156). Accordingly, educational processes must address the challenges that emerge in a context of increasing participation within the community.

In designing a culturally inclusive school, certain questions arise regarding discontinuities between the Roma community's educational practices and those of the school. First, we must consider whether school practice is a meaningful sociocultural scenario for Roma students, that is, its practices might not make sense to them. Second, according to the above considerations, it is problematic to affirm that the school's goals are identifiable to those of the Roma or shared by them. Third, in a context of meaningfulness and contrasting educational goals, it is necessary to inquire into how school practices are incorporated into the identity of Roma students. In relation to these questions, ethnographic research (see, for example, Crespo, Pallí and Lalueza, 2002; Lalueza and Crespo, 2009; Lamas and Lalueza, 2012; Padrós, Sánchez-Busqués, Lalueza and Crespo, 2015) have identified three areas in which schools have difficulty in achieving the inclusion of Roma students: (a) the appropriation of motives that give meaning to participation in school practices and which facilitate their incorporation within the students' identity; (b) the acquisition of cultural tools that enable participation in the school's institutional practices; and (c) the construction of narratives for sharing meanings and establishing common goals.

The appropriation of motives to participate in school. According to Hedegaard (2005), 'The development of children can be understood as the appropriation of competence and motives to manage daily practices within different institutions, and also to build a sense of who they are and who they want to be in the future' (p. 188). The challenge facing the school is that of constituting a meaningful activity and of setting goals shared by the participants, such that they will incorporate this practice into their identity. Progress in education, understood as the acquisition of skills through school practices, cannot exist without consideration for students' motives or for the orientation of their goal-directed activity and the meaning given to it. Citing Leontiev, Hedegaard explains the relationship in these terms: 'Through shared activities motivated by social practices at home and school, the child learns to combine needs with objects, and then acquires new motives' (2005, p. 193). The presence of shared motives, and engagement in goal-directed activity, is what gives meaning to the subject and is essential to the active participation that is necessary for development.

Motives are a fundamental aspect of identity construction. Identity is transformed through participation in different practices and as the individual becomes a member of new institutions. Only through active participation (goal oriented, with meaning) can schooling be incorporated into the identity of its members. Conversely, when the school practice is peripheral, resistance phenomena appear, together with ethnic differentiation processes by which identity is constructed outside or in opposition to the school, as indicated by Ogbu (1994), referring to the secondary cultural traits of African Americans, and as occurs in the Spanish context with groups of Roma students (Fernández-Enguita, 2004; Fernández-Enguita, Mena and Riviere, 2010). An educational alternative should make the objectives of its daily practices intelligible and promote their incorporation as motives for the participants.

The appropriation of cultural tools. The basic skills (reading, mathematics and science, but also rituals, scripts and routines) acquired in school are the artefacts we need to mediate relationships with our social environment. Their acquisition allows us to participate in social practices and, therefore, to form part of the reference community. In consequence, failure to acquire them hinders social inclusion. Such mediating artefacts embody cultural heritage in that they are an 'aspect of the material world that has changed during the history of their incorporation into goal-directed human action' (Cole, 1996, p. 113). Artefacts transform the environment in which we live, but also transform us by defining the activities we perform. When students participate in a goal-oriented activity, they appropriate the cultural heritage embodied in the artefacts.

The historical emergence of reading and writing was a revolutionary form of mediation to which Vygotsky and Luria gave great importance in their explanation of the mental functioning of the modern subject. Michael Cole (Laboratory of Comparative Human Cognition, 1983), in referring to the latter, observed that it is not just the acquisition of writing that produces the mental changes attributed to literacy, but also the characteristics of the activity in which the acquisition occurs and the practices that are incorporated within that activity. Learning to read is important, but equally important is how one learns, in what context and for what purposes. Regarding schools, the key issue here is the appropriation of artefacts by students – not only primary artefacts (writing, language appropriated to describe the objects of knowledge, etc.) but the secondary ones as well (scripts, forms of action appropriated for each activity, addressing others, etc.). The appropriation of school activity requires knowledge of its goals and standards, and of the terms that guide the conduct of its members (Edwards and Mercer, 2013). In the case of Roma students, failure in the acquisition of primary artefacts cannot be separated from the non-appropriation of secondary artefacts in the form of routines, rituals and uses of language – the set of daily practices whose appropriation is needed to make sense of the school experience. An educational alternative would be an institutional framework that promotes the appropriation of practices of cultural artefacts.

Establishing shared narratives. Every culture has a set of narratives that objectify reality (Moghadam, 2003), a common way of understanding the world, a shared definition of reality that includes values, hierarchy, priorities, belongings, ways of interpreting the past, desirable goals and so on. Overlying this objectified world, intersubjective agreements are established that enable communication and joint activity. Belonging to a cultural community involves the sharing of terms, that is, the ways of categorizing reality that need not be explained because they are taken as a given. Schweder and Levine (1984) refer to them as the preconceived ideas that are not discussed and are unspoken, which each cultural community establishes as the basis for understanding.

Understanding the goals of an activity is only possible when a 'story' is shared with the other members of the community (Bruner, 1996). Participation in an institution (family, school, work, etc.) involves sharing the stories that indicate and justify the goals of the institution's activities. The ecological transitions that occur on entering a new scenario can be effected without much difficulty when the intersubjective agreement about reality is maintained. The entry into school of a child from a dominant cultural group is facilitated by the narratives of the institution, which share the same referents as those of the family; this forms part of a basic agreement on their joint aims and understandings. However, when members of an ethnic minority group with little power in the dominant society attend school, they encounter a world where the rules, language, relationships and objectives of the activity are different from or may even contradict those of their family and cultural group. Although schools generate narratives of all kinds, the ones that are especially relevant are those oriented towards the future; practices are justified not by their immediate usefulness, but by their contribution to a child's progress.

This idea of progress does not correspond with the views of certain cultures, such as the Roma population, and the discontinuity hampers the joint construction of community and family discourses with those of the school. Consequently, the peripheral participation of children from these ethnic groups tends to be supported by narratives of the present and immediate future (Sebastián, Gallardo and Calderón, 2016). Furthermore, the narrative of the school often excludes other narratives that are foreign to them, viewing them as interference (Poveda, 2001). When narratives are not shared, alternative stories emerge, usually constructed in opposition to the dominant narrative, such as the refusal to use the language the school considers to be correct or reluctance to adopt the behaviour patterns of the 'good' student. According to Ogbu (1994), it is the identity characteristics built in opposition to the dominant culture that stimulate the development of secondary cultural differences (Lalueza, 2012).

Thus, a key issue for intercultural education is how the school, an institution that helps define reality according to the dominant culture, can create spaces of intersubjectivity with members of minority groups that support objectifications of the world which differ from or are even in opposition to their own. The failure to establish a shared narrative that is meaningful to all members explains the disaffection on the part of those who do not understand, share or appropriate those of the school. The aim of the educational proposals that we present below is to contribute to the design of activity systems that favour the incorporation and creation of new motives, practices and narratives in contexts of transition between a minority culture and that of the school.

Educational experiences to support the transition to school of Roma children

Experience has shown that the challenges described above can be addressed and overcome when schoolchildren are involved in contexts of significant educational activity, thus generating motives for participation, facilitating the appropriation of formal artefacts, and sharing narratives. If a school can achieve this, it will bring about an important change in its institutional dynamics. This understanding underlies the approach adopted in the educational models of La Casa de Shere Rom in Barcelona and La Clase Mágica in Seville.

Both of these experiences are inspired by a network of out-of-school learning opportunities for children developed by Michael Cole and the Laboratory of Comparative Human Cognition at the University of California, termed Fifth Dimension (Cole, 1996; Cole and Distributive Literacy Consortium, 2006; Nilsson and Nocon, 2005), and later by La Clase Mágica (Vásquez, 2003; Macías-Gomez-Estern and Vásquez, 2015). These projects foreground two key ideas: the continuity with the community environment and the collaborative nature of the educational practice. The first is related to the notion that educational activity must be associated with the community in which it takes place in order to make the learning meaningful and connected to the community's objectives and concerns. The students and their families must be respected and acknowledged as interlocutors with the capacity to formulate and pursue objectives and, therefore, to transform the activity. The second assumes that the construction of knowledge is a social process based on participation and collaboration among actors (including teachers, researchers, practitioners, university students and schoolchildren) each of whom has different areas of knowledge and experience.

The Shere Rom project: After-school experiences as a bridge to school

La Casa de Shere Rom was founded in Barcelona in 1998, following negotiations with the leaders of a Roma community in the metropolitan area of the city (Crespo et al., 2002). This initiative gave rise to a joint extracurricular project in the premises of a local Roma association. La Casa de Shere Rom is a laboratory for the design of new educational practices and empowerment strategies for the Roma community and has demonstrated its capacity to improve the skills of the children who attend it (Crespo, Lalueza, Portell and Sánchez-Busqués, 2005). The project has been applied at 16 different sites, including elementary schools, secondary schools, civic centres, libraries and Roma associations (Luque and Lalueza, 2013). At all of these sites, the project was coordinated by a specialist, combining the roles of researcher and practitioner, provided by the university, and staffed by a group of university students engaged in service-learning practices. The Shere Rom project aims to build an intercultural school where the voices of participants in this educational meeting are explicitly recognized. To this end, in the intervention, special attention is paid to establishing a climate of mutual trust, one that is inextricably bound to recognizing the motives of others and their legitimacy. This involves creating channels for dialogue by means of which shared knowledge can be constructed, informing each interlocutor of 'what matters' to the other. We analyse some elements that make this possible and examine precisely how motives, cultural tools, practices and narratives are shared and created, through what Edwards terms *sites of intersecting practices* (2010). In these spaces, participants can be explicit about their real concerns, in a climate of mutual respect, and may build common knowledge without the restrictions of the institutional barriers that often impede communication and understanding.

The Shere Rom project, as a non-formal educational activity, was designed taking into account the reasons underlying the potential participation of the parties addressed. In fact, the Roma families took very little part initially, either in the parents' associations or at the meetings and interviews to which they were invited. Our inquiry into the reasons for this (Sánchez-Busqués, Padrós and Lalueza, 2015) revealed that the families distrusted the school, in part because they felt that the institutional discourse (i.e. the teachers' words and their implications) censured how the Roma families brought up their children. This delegitimization was resented, as was the functioning of an institution whose decision mechanisms were alien to them and over which they had no power of decision. Contrary to a widespread belief among teachers, the parents of Roma children want their children to learn, but they are mistrustful of an institution that seems to reproach the traditional Roma ways of transmitting their culture.

In response, the Shere Rom project as a non-formal and non-compulsory activity seeks to avoid creating institutional barriers, such as restrictions on the times and spaces in which adults could participate. By using the premises of the Gypsy Association, which is perceived as a community meeting place, families do not feel intimidated by an institutional space seen as foreign. The meetings held are informal but, at the same time, the families are legitimized as valid interlocutors, endowed in many respects with decision-making capacities. Spaces are created in which there are relationships of mutual trust, where the reasons for educators and families acting together are known and taken into account in their organization. Families participate in these spaces because they consider their motives to be legitimized: the educational activity provides the children with valuable tools, without delegitimizing them or making them feel like outsiders. When the project was later moved to schools, that is, into the space of a hegemonic institution, we learnt from this experience and as first step initiated non-formal meetings between teachers and families in hybrid spaces such as the entrance courtyard. As we will see in the Seville example, the legitimization of families is deepened through their incorporation into educational tasks within the formal institution.

In the same way, the reasons that make children willing to take part in educational activities must be taken into account. We have compiled a set of narratives created by the children about the activity, and these accounts reveal that one of the reasons for them being happy to attend is because they view it as a great game, one that continues week after week and is maintained thanks to a degree of fantasy, whereby a mysterious character (the wizard Shere Rom) writes letters to them. At first the children may be reluctant to engage in reading and writing tasks, but in time they realize that they will receive a personal reply, addressed to them by name. In reality, they know that behind the identity of the magician there is one of the educators or someone related to them, but they help uphold the fiction, by sharing the belief that there is really someone or something called Shere Rom and that he knows them intimately because he writes them personalized letters. Another motivation for the children to participate is the possibility of establishing new relationships, with the university students, who are interesting because of their age and the role they play in the activities. These reasons and motivations provide educators with resources to create spaces of interaction in which to teach the children, using this interaction as an incentive for the children to take ownership of the aims underlying the educational activity.

The assumption of standards and rules is another crucial aspect of the transition from family practices to those of the educational institution, involving the acquisition of new tools and cultural artefacts, and bringing into play motives and practice. Educators must be aware of the community's values and of their grounding in domestic practices in order to facilitate the child's transition from the home environment to school. Thus, knowledge of the importance of collective responsibility in Roma culture will help educators achieve compliance with the rules for the new activity. For example, if one member of the Roma community harms another, this is not a problem that affects only these two individuals; it involves their families, too. Likewise, the description of two persons as *compadres* (brothers, companions) implies the existence of a loyalty agreement between members of different families.

Awareness of this aspect of Roma culture enabled us to resolve cases of serious breach of the centre's rules, such as physical assault. The offender was allowed to return to the activity only if two *compadres* vouched for him, committing themselves to his good behaviour, in the understanding that if he did not behave well, all three would be expelled. This approach may clash with the hegemonic mentality based on individual responsibility, but it is perfectly intelligible in the space of cultural transition designed at Shere Rom. A norm has been generated to which the children adhere, and it has been created taking into account the practices and motivations of their culture. But in addition, a relationship of trust has been achieved, based on the fact that the children's families believe that the educators comprehend and respect their motives, values and practices; and this means that the entire community taking part in the educational activity, in turn, is aware of the values and goals of the school environment and respects them.

An illustrative example of how this mutual knowledge is woven into a shared narrative that captures the common knowledge of what mattered in each practice comes from an initiative taken to combat high rates of school dropout. The narrative was built at meetings held between the educator leading one of the project sites, the families of the children at this centre and the social educators in the neighbourhood. The highest levels of premature school leaving are found among girls in Roma communities, at the beginning of secondary school education, at around 12 years of age. The teachers and school managers usually interpret this as a 'lack of motivation to learn', or 'difficulty in abiding by school rules and discipline', conceptualizing these girls as 'demotivated'. However, the specialist knowledge and participation of the educator who coordinated the project with the community made it possible to reconceptualize this problem.

In fact, the problem was not an 'absence of motives', or demotivation, but rather a conflict between motives oriented towards different contexts of activity. These girls were approaching the age of marriage, a fundamental goal in the life cycle of this community, and one to which everything else, including schooling, was subordinated. In addition, in a cultural context that places such a high value on virginity, a powerful factor is that of families' mistrust of high schools as uncontrolled meeting spaces between adolescents. On the other hand, there was also concern among the mothers of these girls, worried about their daughters' loss of job and social opportunities through leaving school at such an early age. This worry, moreover, was grounded in their own experience. These mothers, thus, had a twofold ambition. They wanted their daughters to respect the dynamics of their community, arising from family relationships based upon marriage, and at the same time to receive an education going beyond their own limited experience.

The problem is that previously they had been unable to talk with anyone at the school or in the social services who could understand, let alone legitimize their position. In this context, the key to achieving change lay in joint action, based on the educators' knowledge of what was important for the mothers, together with the mothers' understanding that their beliefs, values and ambitions were respected by the professionals. For the education planners, this was the starting point in the construction of shared goals towards which joint action could be aimed with the ultimate purpose of reducing rates of school dropout (Padrós, 2016). In addition, through the mediation of the project leader, sites of interacting practices were created whereby the families and the social services workers could begin to trust each other. Each group had its own interests, but was aware of the others' ideas and goals, thus enabling a relationship of trust to be established and for all concerned to begin working towards their common objectives. New practices (in this case, concerted action to combat premature school leaving by Roma children) were constructed from a multiplicity of voices expressing their diverse reasons for participating and co-creating a new narrative.

The practices described above are aimed at facilitating children's transition to the institutional environment, a process in which the roles played by educators and their relational expertise (Edwards, 2010, 2012, 2017) are fundamental in order to create spaces of trust and communication. This outcome, however, has been achieved in an after-school environment of 'low-level institutionalization', disconnected from school and proximal to the families of the community in question. In the next section of the chapter, we consider a contrasting experience in Seville, revealing how such processes can be addressed within an institutional context.

La Clase Mágica in Seville: A within-school learning community

The second experience we present as an example of the institutional inclusion of Roma children is of a severely marginalized area of Seville, in southern Spain (Macías-Gomez-Estern, Martínez-Lozano and Mateos, 2014; Macías-Gomez-Estern, Martínez-Lozano and Vásquez, 2014). Here too, as in the case of the Shere Rom project, social agents and local educational institutions entered into a process of negotiation, in 2010. This gave rise to the creation of a service-learning project (Blázquez and Martínez-Lozano, 2012; Macías-Gomez-Estern and Vásquez, 2014) in which university students collaborated with various schools in the area. At present, this collaboration mainly takes place in a primary school, where 90 per cent of the children are from the Roma population. This institution had previously experienced high rates of violence in the classrooms, absenteeism and school failure, and therefore decided to transform its methodology. This new approach is described below.

In 2006, with the agreement of teachers, governors and families, the school decided to convert itself into a learning community (Elboj, Valls and Fort, 2000), in which the participants would share spaces and decision-making, where the school would be open to all and used by all. Under this new system of participatory management, parents, children, teachers, volunteer helpers and everybody else involved in the educational process can take decisions and put forward suggestions for the school and its activities, such as the 'dreams', chosen annually as goals that the educational community wishes to achieve. Everyone has their own dreams, and a democratic choice is made of which ones will be that particular year's goals. A soda fountain, a playground painted in bright colours, a school where there is respect for all, and clean, well-dressed children are just some of the dreams that have been sought. Such spaces for interaction enable parents and educators to know each other's hopes and fears and show that they have more in common than may at first have appeared.

Hence, the construction of shared motivations in the school environment can be achieved by incorporating the values and practices of the Roma community into the daily life of the school. It does not take place in a decontextualized or abstract way, by treating the 'Roma culture' as a fixed, static object, but arises from the voices and actions of the children and their families. The teachers and other staff are in close contact with all the children and their parents, in a warm, personal relationship that is far removed from what is usually found in the traditional educational context. Thus, a bridge for interaction is created, supporting the transition towards adoption of more formal relational styles. An example of this different approach is the fact that, every morning, the staff at the school dedicate the first hour of the day to greeting and welcoming the children and their parents when they arrive. During this time, questions can be answered, needs addressed and problems resolved; moreover, the school obtains an up-to-the-minute view of each family's situation.

This setting replaces the common practice elsewhere in which the interaction between teachers and families is restricted to scheduled encounters, usually during a specific afternoon after the classes have finished. The school, aware of the families' way of life, has adapted the latter scenario to one that is better suited to the population being served, seeing them at more convenient times, and has achieved a much more effective level of intercommunication. These spaces also help bring people together and let them know each other's daily concerns, facilitating information exchange and the construction of shared knowledge, thus easing the children's transition to the school environment.

The following example illustrates how the school works: an eight-year-old boy, accompanied by his mother, was refusing to enter school and crying. Together, the teacher and the child's mother persuaded him to enter his classroom. Later, the mother told the school's head teacher a possible reason for the child's behaviour: he had stayed up very late the night before because he was present at a *pedida* (a festive ceremony that is very important in Roma culture, in which the family of a husband-to-be visits the family of the bride-to-be to request their consent for the marriage). On hearing this, the teacher was sympathetic and understanding, expressing acceptance of this cultural practice, although the timing of the occasion was hardly compatible with the child's need to attend school in the morning, and encouraged the mother to accompany her son to the classroom. A more punitive, rigid attitude by the teacher would probably have resulted in the boy's absenteeism, consented to by the family. However, by expressing understanding and respect for a typical cultural practice of the Roma community, an immediate positive result was obtained: the family collaborated in ensuring the child attended school, as usual.

But the scene witnessed did not end there, in what might otherwise have been an unreflexive adoption by the school of cultural practices that, in certain aspects, might not facilitate the children's adherence to the norms (and their justifications) in the school environment. What in fact took place was a real process of negotiation and dialogue between contrasting motivations. In subsequent meetings with the families, the teacher encouraged discussion about the possible disruption caused by children's attendance at festive events in the middle of the school week and the harm caused by the consequent loss of rest and sleep. This attitude to the question shows how the school institution respects and legitimizes the understandings and practices of the Roma community, but also uses them to foster acceptance of its own goals and values.

The children's transition is also facilitated in this learning community via the appropriation of school-related cultural tools. Through active participation, the knowledge base that is constructed in the school is not presented as something decontextualized and alien to the community, but is attained by means of projects that are agreed upon and negotiated by the class groups and the teaching staff, within the framework where 'normal' school work is carried out. In this way, the class content reaches the children as an appropriate outcome to their particular needs, responding to problems or dilemmas affecting them directly and providing knowledge that is functional, instrumental and useful. An accumulated fund of knowledge (Gonzalez, Moll and Amanti, 2006) is used in day-to-day school life, presenting in the classroom examples and experiences related to children's lives and using them as a gateway to introducing standard academic content. For example, the children's experience of street markets and the arithmetic of the commercial exchanges that take place there motivate their addressing the mathematical concepts included in the school curriculum. At the same time, this orientation lends legitimacy to the Roma community's ways of life, implicitly recognizing its norms and values.

The creation of new practices and spaces is another of the elements that facilitate the Roma students' appropriation of academic content. The arrangement of the classroom into interactive groups is well suited to the heterogeneity usually found in class groups. Thus, subgroups of three or four children, guided by an adult, are organized so that problem-solving is carried out in a cooperative way, applying the participants' collective knowledge. The knowledge derived from the academic context is not imposed authoritatively, but is accessed through dialogue among the different members of each micro-group and the coordinating adult.

These practices are also expressed by means of the regular discourse constructed by the teachers, seeking to promote a permanent sense of fellowship, through shared narratives that reinforce the idea of belonging to the same educational community. These participatory practices foster a shared sense of identity, as does the teacher's incorporation of communicative and symbolic elements of the Roma community into the class activities. Thus, the International Day of the Roma People is celebrated at the school, as a tribute to the cultural heritage of the vast majority of these children and their families, acknowledging the value and importance of their practices. In addition, when addressing the children, the teachers voluntarily and naturally make use of words and expressions from the Caló[1] language, part of the families' culture, thus producing a form of language in the school that incorporates elements related to the Roma community's forms of speech and narration. A third tangible element in the construction of a shared narrative, one that creates a sense of belonging to the school, is the use of physical spaces for the expression of messages produced by children that inspire intercultural cohesion, such as arts and crafts or the products of their own educational projects, which often refer to their community's norms, values and beliefs. Thus, the educational space is occupied in a way that is both symbolic and real, producing a sense of identification with the school that extends beyond the frontiers of the Roma community.

Conclusions: Learning from experience – how schools can achieve the inclusion of Roma children

When Roma perceive the school as a 'space of domination' (Ruiz-Román, Calderón-Almendros and Torres-Moya, 2011), it generates attitudes of rejection and promotes dynamics of alienation. To overcome this, an inclusive education must convert the institution into a 'meeting place', in which goals and values of diverse origins are legitimated, together with those corresponding to the school. The legitimation of minority cultures means opening up the school to the voices of the communities of origin, to include them as a starting point in the construction of knowledge.

In this chapter, we have described two experiences aimed at helping Roma children in their transition to school life: one is an after-hours project and the other takes place within the school. Although these approaches have different characteristics, there are common elements in how they address the task of enabling children to make the transition to school education. In both cases, the project managers seek to construct a common understanding of what matters in each practice among very diverse participants, through three identifiable strategies.

First, by accepting the legitimacy of existing motivations and fostering new ones, the projects adjust their approach to suit the local culture, matching activities to the characteristics of the group, the interests of the teacher and the dynamics of the school. Moreover, they take into account the social context, the characteristics of the neighbourhood and the cultural framework of the community to which the families and students belong, thus explicitly acknowledging the existence of convergent cultures. Motives are not imposed; rather, a space is created in which different concerns and interests can be expressed and acknowledged.

The second strategy is that of mediational practices that enable the appropriation of tools and artefacts. Relationships between the participants are based on collaboration and on the recognition of competence and decision-making capability in the 'cultural other'. This collaborative learning philosophy promotes the construction of a microculture in which adults and children cooperate in the acquisition of new tools and in the creation of a shared project/artefact. In this collaboration, the adult figure acts as a partner, not as an evaluator, helping create strong emotional ties that promote the learning process and facilitate the acquisition of tools. Thirdly, the incorporation of a shared narrative helps integrate different tools into a goal-directed, meaningful activity, which is presented to children as a common challenge, one that is shared with a sense of complicity among the whole community, and oriented towards an outcome that is seen as the result of collective work.

As the various artefacts of the activity are appropriated by all the participants, a microculture takes shape from which shared narratives and new goals emerge. As a mediational practice, this microculture creates an interagency space (composed of the university, the school and social organizations), an intergenerational space (the adult educators, the student collaborators and the children) and an intercultural space (diverse institutional, generational and community cultures) in which different voices are expressed and where power relationships related to age, gender and cultural background are diluted, thus generating a work dynamic where norms and roles are explicitly negotiated. When this takes place, it means that the participants have appropriated the model and have made it theirs. Furthermore, they have become empowered to address the subsequent development of the programme.

All these strategies require collaboration between different managers/ planners/educators, families and university students. Everyone arrives at the activity with their own motives and goals, and all converge in an activity space 'at the border'. This space has great potential for developing common knowledge, but only when participants create a new 'common microculture'. And this is possible when relational expertise is applied (Edwards, 2010), by which educators generate forms of knowledge about the symbolic framework of the community, producing the following outcomes: (a) a shared evaluation of occurrences, so that appropriate solutions may be applied, respectful of the motives of all involved; (b) an understanding of community practices and of their use as funds of knowledge (Llopart and Esteban-Guitart, 2018) for the implementation of new practices, these too being coherent with the participants' motives; and (c) the maintenance of this coherence through a shared narrative that contributes to giving meaning and continuity to the activity.

Note

1 A variant of Romany, used in Spain, which consists of a mixture of Romany and Castilian Spanish.

References

Blázquez, A., and Martínez-Lozano, V. (2012). La Residencia Universitaria Flora Tristán: un ejemplo de formación humana y de compromiso con la sociedad. *Revista de Educación, 358*, 618–30.

Bruner, J. S. (1996). *The culture of education*. Cambridge, MA: Harvard University Press.

Cerreruela, E., Crespo, I., Jiménez, R., Lalueza, J. L., Pallí, C., and Santiago, R. (2001). *Hechos Gitanales*. Cerdanyola del Vallès: Publicacions UAB.

Cole, M. (1996). *Cultural psychology*. Hillsdale, NJ: LEA.

Cole, M., and Distributive Literacy Consortium. (2006). *The fifth dimension: An after-school program built on diversity*. New York: Russell Sage.

Crespo, I., Pallí, C., and Lalueza, J. L. (2002). Moving communities: A process of negotiation with a gypsy minority for empowerment. *Community, Work and Family*, 5(1), 49–66.

Crespo, I., Lalueza, J. L., Portell, M., and Sánchez-Busqués, S. (2005). Communities for intercultural education: Interweaving practices. In M. Nilsson and H. Nocon (Eds), *School of tomorrow. Teaching and technology in local and global communities* (pp. 27–62). Oxford: Peter Lang.

Edwards, A. (2010). *Being an expert professional practitioner: The relational turn in expertise* (Vol. 3). London: Springer Science and Business Media.

Edwards, A. (2012). The role of common knowledge in achieving collaboration across practices. *Learning, Culture and Social Interaction*, 1(1), 22–32.

Edwards, A. (Ed.). (2017). *Working relationally in and across practices: A cultural-historical approach to collaboration.* Cambridge: Cambridge University Press.

Edwards, D., and Mercer, N. (2013). *Common knowledge: The development of understanding in the classroom.* London: Routledge.

Elboj, C., Valls, R., and Fort, M. (2000). Comunidades de aprendizaje. Una práctica educativa para la sociedad de la información. *Cultura y educación*, 12(1–2), 129–41.

Engeström, Y. (2001). Expansive learning at work: Toward an activity theoretical reconceptualization. *Journal of Education and Work*, 14(1), 133–56.

Engeström, Y. (2007). Enriching the theory of expansive learning: Lessons from journeys toward coconfiguration. *Mind, Culture, and Activity*, 14(1–2), 23–39.

Fernández-Enguita, M. (2004). Educación, economía y sociedad en España. In J. L. García-Delgado, P. Solbes and M. Fernández-Enguita (Eds), *La educación que queremos: Educación, formación y empleo* (pp. 29–79). Madrid: Fundación Santillana.

Fernández-Enguita, M., Mena, L., and Riviere, J. (2010). *Fracaso y abandono escolar en España.* Barcelona: Fundació La Caixa.

Gonzalez, N., Moll, L. C., and Amanti, C. (Eds). (2006). *Funds of knowledge: Theorizing practices in households, communities, and classrooms.* London: Routledge.

Greenfield, P. M. and Cocking, R. R. (Eds). (1994). *Cross-cultural roots of minority child development.* Hillsdale, NJ: LEA.

Hedegaard, M. (2005). Strategies for dealing with conflicts in value positions between home and school: Influences on ethnic minority students' development of motives and identity. *Culture and Psychology*, 11(2), 187–205.

Laboratory of Comparative Human Cognition. (1983). Culture and cognitive development. In W. Kessen (Ed.), *Handbook of child psychology; Vol. 1. History, Theory, and Methods* (4th edn). New York: Wiley.

Lalueza, J. L. (2012). Modelos psicológicos para la explicación de la diversidad cultural. *Cultura y Educación*, 24(2), 149–62.

Lalueza, J. L., and Crespo, I. (2009). Voices in the Gypsy developmental Project. *Mind, Culture, and Activity*, 16(3), 263–80.

Lamas, M., and Lalueza, J. L. (2012). Apropiación de un modelo colaborativo en escuelas multiculturales con alumnado en situación de exclusión social. *Cultura y educación*, 24(2), 177–91.

Leontiev, A. N. (1978). *Activity, consciousness, and personality.* Englewood Cliffs, NJ: Prentice-Hall.

Llopart, M., and Esteban-Guitart, M. (2018). Funds of knowledge in 21st century societies: Inclusive educational practices for under-represented students. A literature review. *Journal of Curriculum Studies, 50*(2), 145–61.

Luque, M. J., and Lalueza, J. L. (2013). *Aprendizaje colaborativo en comunidades de práctica en entornos de exclusión social. Un análisis de las interacciones.* Madrid: Ministerio de Educación.

Macías-Gomez-Estern, B., Martínez-Lozano, V., and Mateos, C. (2014). 'Clase Mágica-Sevilla'. Una experiencia de aprendizaje-servicio y de transformación identitaria. *Psicología, Conocimiento y Sociedad, 4*(2), 109–37.

Macías-Gomez-Estern, B., Martínez-Lozano, V., and Vásquez, O. A. (2014). 'Real learning' in service learning: Lessons from La Clase Mágica in the US and Spain. *International Journal for Research on Extended Education, 2*(2), 63–78.

Macías-Gomez-Estern, B., and Vásquez, O. (2014). La Clase Mágica goes international: Adapting to new sociocultural contexts. In B. Flores, O. Vasquez and E. Clark (Eds), *Generating transworld pedagogy: Reimagining La Clase Mágica* (pp. 193–208). Lanham, MD: Lexington Books.

Macías-Gomez-Estern, B., and Vásquez, O. (2015). Identity construction in narratives of migration. In T. Hansen and K. Jensen (Eds), *Self in culture in mind. Conceptional and applied perspectives* (pp. 177–200). Aalborg: Aalborg University Press.

Moghadam, V. M. (2003). *Modernizing women: Gender and social change in the Middle East.* Boulder, CO: Lynne Rienner Publishers.

Nilsson, M. and Nocon, H. (Eds). (2005). *School of tomorrow: Teaching and technology in local and global communities.* Oxford: Peter Lang.

Ogbu, J. U. (1994). From cultural differences to differences in cultural frame of reference. In P. M. Greenfield and R. R. Cocking (Eds), *Cross-cultural roots of minority child development* (pp. 365–91). Hillsdale, NJ: LEA.

Padrós, M. (2016). 9 anys sent paya, 9 anys agitanant-me. Un estudio del ciclo vital en una comunidad gitana. Doctoral thesis. Barcelona: Universidad Autónoma de Barcelona.

Padrós, M., Sánchez-Busqués, S., Lalueza, J. L., and Crespo, I. (2015). The Shere Rom project: Looking for alternatives to the educational exclusion of Roma. *International Journal for Research on Extended Education, 2*(2), 46–62.

Poveda, D. (2001). La educación de las minorías étnicas desde el marco de las continuidades-discontinuidades familia-escuela. *Gazeta de Antropología, 17,* 17–31.

Rogoff, B. (1990). *Apprenticeship in thinking. Cognitive development in social context.* New York: Oxford University Press.

Rogoff, B. (1993). Children's guided participation and participatory appropriation in sociocultural activity. In R. H. Wozniak and K. W. Fischer (Eds), *Development in context: Acting and thinking in specific environments* (pp. 121–53). New York: Lawrence Erlbaum.

Rogoff, B. (2003). *The cultural nature of human development.* New York: Oxford University Press.

Ruiz-Román, C., Calderón-Almendros, I., and Torres-Moya, F. J. (2011). Construir la identidad en los márgenes de la globalización: educación, participación y aprendizaje. *Cultura y Educación, 23*(4), 589–99.

Sánchez-Busqués, S., Padrós, M., and Lalueza, J. L. (2015). La escuela vista por las familias. Proyecto migratorio frente a construcción minoritaria. *Papeles de Trabajo sobre Cultura, Educación y Desarrollo Humano, 11*(2), 65–9.

Schweder, R. A., and Levine, R. A. (1984). *Culture theory: Essays in mind.* New York: Cambridge University Press.

Sebastián, C., Gallardo, G., and Calderón, M. (2016). Sentido identitario de la formación.Una propuesta para articular el desarrollo de la identidad y el aprendizaje en contextos educativos. *Papeles de Trabajo sobre Cultura, Educación y Desarrollo Humano, 12*(3), 2–9.

Vásquez, O. (2003). *La Clase Mágica: Imagining Optimal Possibilities in a Bilingual Community of Learners.* New York: Laurence Erlbaum.

Small Children's Movements across Residential Care and Day Care: How Professionals Build Common Knowledge and Practice That Matter for Children

Ida Schwartz

Introduction

How day-care teachers and child-welfare workers work together, relate to one another and to parents are often crucial to the successful support of children's social participation in and across contexts. Drawing on a critical theoretical perspective (Dreier, 2008; Schraube and Osterkamp, 2013), I present analyses of the conditions of cooperation across children's contexts and the kind of knowledge the different parties consider vital to exchange. A special focus is directed on how the interaction between the different parties establishes conditions that provide parents the opportunities to support their children's participation in kindergarten. The aim is to contribute to theoretical discussions on how to understand the construct of common knowledge in inter-professional work (Edwards, 2010, 2011) in relation to children's transitions between residential and day care. Different professional perspectives and disagreements are at stake in inter-professional cooperation due to professionals' different practices, positions and tasks (Højholt, 2006). Drawing on a critical psychological concept of *conflictual cooperation* (Axel, 2011), the chapter outlines how a theoretical way of understanding these conflicts goes through the recognition that childcare work is, in itself, contradictory and filled with dilemmas (Højholt and Kousholt, 2018).

Theoretical and conceptual frameworks and empirical study

This chapter is based on the premise that human beings learn and develop through their participation in social practices (Hedegaard, Chaiklin and Jensen, 1999; Dreier, 2008; Holland and Lave, 2001; Lave, 2008; Schraube and Osterkamp, 2013). The concept of *social participation* highlights how subjects try to arrange and influence their conditions in their everyday lives together with others (Dreier, 2016; Schraube and Højholt, 2016). Thus, in a social practice perspective, children develop through their participation in and across various societal contexts and communities in everyday life (Dreier, 2009; Hedegaard, Aronsson, Højholt and Ulvik, 2018; Hedegaard and Fleer, 2013; Højholt, 2008; Juhl, 2015). For children in general, participation in play and educational activities together with other children during childhood is considered the most important ways of learning how to get access to and take part in social practices in society (Hedegaard and Fleer, 2013; Højholt and Kousholt, 2017). Likewise, in critical psychological and in cultural-historical theory, *cooperation* is seen as central in the understanding of human beings' *collective construction* of their societal conditions.

Regarding welfare-based childcare, Edwards argues from a cultural-historical activity approach that we need to develop new forms of inter-professional cooperation across contexts in order to meet increasingly complex social problems in social child welfare (Edwards, 2005, 2010, 2011). She argues that professionals should align their work with that of professionals in other contexts, and she refers to this perspective as 'the relational turn' in professional expertise (2010). Professionals need to be responsive to complex social problems *together* and work relationally across contexts (Edwards, 2009, p. 207). From this perspective, shared goals should not be seen as permanently defined and fixed, but as negotiable in professionals' work with difficult dilemmas in practice (Edwards and Daniels, 2012). She argues that, as a consequence, 'the distributed nature of expertise in multi-professional children's services turns attention to how knowledge is mobilised across practices' (Edwards and Daniels, 2012). The knowledge that Edwards focuses on, however, is not knowledge of how to be a pedagogue or a social worker, but knowledge of what matters, and with that she understands the professional motives in each professional practice. What she calls common knowledge consists of shared knowledge of these professional perspectives and can, of course, include the perspectives of the clients. She suggests turning attention to how this knowledge of what matters in each practice is mobilized across practices (ibid.). Building common knowledge becomes necessary when working on a complex problem such as a child's trajectory towards social exclusion. In this perspective, the construct of common knowledge means that professionals come to recognize what is important for each other when tackling the complexity of the task and aligning their contributions (Edwards, 2010).

Edwards's recognition of the different professional perspectives anchored in different professional practices has much in common with a critical psychological perspective. Axel (2011) also argues that human beings act together and work with the same objects across contexts under contradictory social conditions. In a historically developed division of labour, however, how social practices are interconnected becomes increasingly invisible. Different subjects have different views of the same issues in and across practices, not just because they have different attitudes or professional knowledge, but because they are positioned differently and handle different aspects of the same common cause (Højholt, 2006). This means that conflicts should always be seen as embedded in cooperation, which Axel (2011) has conceptualized as 'conflictual cooperation'.

In this chapter, I explore how to understand the development of common knowledge as a part of conflictual cooperation embedded in contradictory societal conditions and thus interwoven with general dilemmas of childcare. Drawing on Højholt (2016, p. 147), we need to explore dilemmas and conflicts as situated in social practices in order to deepen our understanding of what kind of knowledge professionals need to exchange across contexts. The common cause in inter-professional cooperation in child welfare is to work towards providing children and their parents equal opportunities to take part in institutional arrangements. I argue that professionals need to work differently with different aspects of childcare in order to contribute to the common cause. The point is to show how the meaning of inter-professional cooperation must be understood from the perspectives of children and parents and the ways interventions matter in their everyday lives.

The study

This chapter is a conceptual reworking of empirical material collected and presented as part of a PhD project conducted at a residential home from 2003 to

2005 and published in Schwartz (2007, 2018). The research was conducted in a practice research tradition (Højholt and Kousholt, 2012), which means exploring participants' different perspectives, actions and involvement as situated and connected through their engagements in common matters in social practices. In this approach, particular observations or insights are reflected *together with* the participants drawing on their knowledge from different perspectives in order to understand more about how practical issues and challenges in childcare are connected with structural conditions.

The chapter presents analyses of two cases that provide different examples of how cooperation between parents, professionals in day-care and residential-care facilities can influence small children's social participation. I use the term 'day care' to emphasize that it is the preschool institution that is in focus. The chapter is based on interviews with two day-care teachers, two child-welfare workers working in residential care and two parents. All interviews focused on the children's everyday lives across their homes, residential care and day care. In addition, I made observations and followed the children in and across residential home and the day-care centres. The purpose of the research project was to explore professional approaches and practices from a decentred perspective, that is, from the perspective of children in their everyday lives across social contexts (Dreier, 2008).

A childhood in trouble

In a Danish context, children between three and six years of age spend a large part of their everyday lives in day-care centres which are highly professionally organized environments (Ringsmose and Kragh-Müller, 2016). Researchers such as Andenæs (2011) and Kousholt (2011) in the field of childhood and child development have shown how parents and day-care teachers build relationships and exchange knowledge about children's well-being, development and challenges in their everyday lives. In connection with children living under stressful living conditions, day care is also considered to be of particular importance, because it allows children to participate in an ordinary childhood context.

Children in out-of-home care face very different problems owing to their lives under disadvantaged social conditions. How something becomes a problem in a child's life is connected to their family life, their everyday life across childhood contexts and the ways these problems are professionally understood and handled. In the last 10 years, in Denmark, there have been major changes in relation to the placements of children within the broad system of residential care. The responsibility for residential care has been increasingly transferred from the state to municipalities, while more children are being placed in family care rather than in residential institutions (Lausten, 2015). Thus, a historical development in the out-of-home care of children and adolescents is the move away from the treatment of individuals in isolated centres to the attempt to normalize the children's living conditions and enhance their inclusion in the local environment. The aim is to prevent social exclusion by making it possible for all children to take part in the general life of kindergartens and schools, a move which is in line with international policies, as formulated in the Salamanca declaration (UNESCO, 1994). This educational emphasis is followed by a general development in day care from an individualizing and deficit-oriented perspective on specific children to a focus on the provision of social possibilities for their participation (Warming, 2011). However, as Armstrong, Armstrong and Spandagou (2011) point out, there seems to be quite a distance between these overall visions of inclusion and the actual practices of diversity in childhood institutions.

Children placed in out-of-home care, whether in residential or family-care settings, within a Danish context, will often maintain their everyday lives in their kindergarten during their placements. Zooming in on these children's everyday life, a picture is displayed of many caregivers being involved in their daily care. There are at least three parties: the parents (often living separately), professionals at the residential institution (here named child-welfare workers) and the day-care teachers. The cases to be presented show that different approaches to and perspectives on child development and children in difficulties are at stake in day-care and residential-care institutions in Denmark.

The children's places

In the study, the residential institution 'Solhøj' was located in a suburban area and most of the families it served were living quite nearby. This made it possible for most of the small children to remain in their ordinary kindergarten when placed in out-of-home care. The residential home invited the parents to take part in caring for their children as often as they could manage, which was a rather unusual practice in Denmark. If possible, the children often stayed at home during the weekends. This meant that parents picked up their children from the kindergarten on Friday and brought them back again on Monday morning. When a placement takes place in an environment familiar to the children, the kindergarten is often a well-known context in their lives and hence a stable base as the children can continue their usual everyday life. The day-care teachers may be the professionals who have known both the children and their parents the longest. This does not necessarily signify that the relationships of children and their parents with the children's kindergarten are exclusively positive.

The two children focused on in the analyses are both in residential care, but have very different conditions in their day-care institutions. Emil, a five-year-old boy, attends a regular kindergarten located in a residential area designated as socially disadvantaged. A support teacher is assigned to Emil for 10 hours every week. The second child, Winnie, is also five years old, and she attends a special needs education group, located in a separate room of an ordinary kindergarten. In Winnie's case, the day-care teachers are specially trained to work with children in vulnerable situations.

In an interview, Emil's day-care teacher reports that Emil is physically violent towards the other children. The kindergarten has received many complaints from parents whose children have been hurt by him, and this is a cause for concern for the teachers. It is Emil, as a person, who is pointed out as problematic, and teachers believe that the problems are owing to something Emil has 'in himself' as a person, which the day-care teachers cannot cope with. There have been two support assistants who have worked differently with Emil. The first support teacher takes him out of the children's group and engages him in massage and sensory exercises in a special room. The second support teacher assists Emil in the children's group, but the day-care teachers do not actually know what the support teacher's efforts are. Emil is the support teacher's assignment when she is in the kindergarten. However, the support teacher's efforts are not coordinated in relation to the overall educational approach of the kindergarten. The day-care teachers mostly experience the support as time that is freed up for them so that they can concentrate on the other children.

In the course of my observations, it is apparent that Emil faces difficult opportunities of participation. The play with the other children soon becomes violent and conflict-ridden, and often Emil seems to be left to his own devices, running around on his own without joining with children's groups. At lunchtime, however, he seems happy and proud to provide cups for his group. While picking up cups, the children discuss who should sit next to Emil:

Girl: Oh no, Emil is going to sit here (in this group).
Boy takes his hands to the head and makes a deep sigh.
The children push Emil's lunchbox around on the table. Nobody wants to sit next to him.
A girl places the lunch box in the centre of the table.

The problems in Emil's everyday life are not seen in relation to his difficulties with respect to his being a part of the children's communities, and the day-care teachers do not consider it their job to work professionally to prevent his social exclusion. On observing Emil's everyday life, we gather that the educators act spontaneously with limited strategies, which primarily constitute scolding, reprimanding and restricting his liberty of action, efforts, which in turn seems to aggravate Emil's chaotic actions.

In Winnie's day care, her specially trained teacher reports that 7 out of the 13 children in her group are from particularly socially disadvantaged families. At the day care, they work systematically with a structured set of routines aimed at supporting the children's participation. The social educator describes Winnie as being 'rootless in her head'. However, in this special group, teachers have the opportunity to structure everyday life down to the smallest elements, and the adults enact their special educational work with clear rules and consistent intervention against unacceptable behaviour.

The two day-care centres and the residential-care home represent very different childhood contexts, which provide Emil and Winnie with significantly different developmental conditions. First, the two kindergartens are not equally equipped for coping with the political objectives of inclusion, and there are huge differences in educational competences of the staff and the resources available. Second, the three institutions do not share the same perspectives on childcare. Individualizing and behavioural therapy approaches dominate in different ways in the two day-care centres while the residential care represents a child-centred and dialogue-based educational approach. This draws a picture of a complex cooperation between caregivers located in different places, performing different tasks related to childcare and with highly different views on child development.

Problems in Emil's kindergarten, seen from the perspective of his mother

When children are placed in residential care, this is frequently preceded by problematic collaborative relations between parents and the day care.

Emil's mother tells that Emil has a history of being involved in many conflicts with other children. This elicits angry reactions from the other parents. Emil's mother reports that when picking him up at the kindergarten, she only gets negative reports about Emil, and she feels that her son is being made a scapegoat:

> I'm afraid that they only see the negative things. He's always a troublemaker, and he's the one who's stupid or doing stupid things. It really is a wrong approach to have. They should be more open about things, saying: he's beginning to become a scapegoat, what shall we do?

Emil's mother thinks that the day-care teachers are of the opinion that Emil does not belong in the kindergarten and that he should move so as to get the 'right' kind of help.

When the day-care teachers express their frustrations about having to cope with their daily workload, Emil's mother gets the impression that her child is a burden. Emil's mother feels that her child is portrayed as not fitting in anywhere so that it would be easier to get him diagnosed and the municipality would know in which 'box' to put him. The professionals' complaining in itself creates barriers to the cooperation between a parent and the educators.

Specific support organized for a particular child, such as time with the support assistant, is not always experienced as a help. Emil's mother expresses her concern about her child being taken away from the children's group. She thinks it is the interaction with the other children that is the problem, and it does not help him to take him out of the group. Support that is intended to provide help becomes a special condition for children as well as parents, which, paradoxically, may lead to new problems. The problem of not feeling good enough as a parent adds to all the other concerns and strains parents and children experience in their lives. It is hard to be confronted with difficult problems that are rooted in contexts where the parents themselves have limited influence.

Cooperation between residential care, kindergarten and parents

In relation to Emil, the cooperation between kindergarten and residential care is problematic too. The child-welfare workers think that the kindergarten teachers are not sufficiently qualified and that they have a negative perception of Emil. When the child-welfare workers report that Emil is developing well at Solhøj, this almost seems to intensify the experience of frustration in his kindergarten. The efforts undertaken to help Emil in the two institutions remain uncoordinated and do not contribute to an overall improvement of his situation.

The kindergarten is generally critical of the residential institution because different staff come to pick up the children. The children's permanent place in life is the kindergarten, while the changes in their lives take place elsewhere. Because different child-welfare workers bring the children to the kindergarten, the day-care teachers do not get to meet and talk to parents daily. Emil's day-care teacher says:

> We do not have the daily dialogue. I have also thought that we may not be sufficiently outreaching. There are many different people coming from Solhøj, and always someone new. Whenever a new person arrives, I will say who are you so? So, maybe, I think, I unconsciously withdraw. That's what you do.

When the place of placement is an institution rather than a family, the changing of staff is a normal condition. Regular contact between the kindergarten staff and those of the residential institution does not take place, and this calls for special conditions for the ways in which cooperation with the kindergartens may be organized. The day-care teachers I interviewed think that, prior to the residential-care placement, they represented a firm basis in the child's life, but afterwards they often feel left out with respect to cooperation. When they ask the child-welfare workers at Solhøj about the family's current life situation, they are told that the child-welfare workers are under an obligation to maintain confidentiality. A child-welfare worker says:

> How much should they know (in day-care)? And should they know everything? I think it's up to the parents to tell them what they want to be revealed. Of course, in order to take care of the children in a particularly tense situation, the parents may provide information – or the parents together with me.

How the parties may exchange knowledge without talking behind the back of parents is a problem. It is also debatable how much kindergartens need to know about problems in the parents' lives. What belongs to the private sphere, and how much do the parents themselves wish to reveal? In an interview, Winnie's mother, for instance, reported that a day-care teacher suddenly mentioned Winnie's mothers' alcohol treatment. The mother was not aware that the day-care teacher knew about this problem. How the parties can work closely together while respecting parents' rights to privacy is a serious dilemma.

Emil's mother finds that the educators 'release the problems with their cooperation with the residential institution on her':

> Emil's mother: Then they (day-care teachers) may for instance say that they find it confusing with all these different adults bringing Emil: 'Emil does not have any spare clothes', and so on. When I pick up Emil three days later, I'll get the same message. Solhøj does not do so and so.
> I: Okay. So, they complained about Solhøj to you?
> Emil's mother: Yes, they did, and also about the many different adults at Solhøj.
> And about how dissatisfied they were about Emil having to stay at the institution. It was very, very hard for them to understand the situation. It was very difficult to establish collaboration all the way round.
> I: So, what did you do?
> Mother: Well, I talked back and forth: I discussed the problems about Solhøj with the kindergarten, I talked with Solhøj, and then the child-welfare workers went to talk with the kindergarten.

It is very problematic for the parents when cooperation between professionals has reached a deadlock. Much responsibility can be taken away from parents, but when trouble arises, it still seems to be the mother who must coordinate and do so from a position with very little influence.

The question is what kind of knowledge day-care teachers need and which kind of personal information about the family's life situation is necessary. There is a tendency to look for answers to children's actions in the child, in the family or in the past rather than in the actual context in which they as professionals take part. It seems necessary that the day-care teachers are informed of significant changes in a child's life, but that does not alter the fact that the main responsibility of the day-care teacher is to make the child's everyday life work for them, despite problems. This again leads to questions about conditions and resources.

A joint exploration of action opportunities

Cooperation between Winnie's special educational group and the residential institution is better than the relations around Emil. The child-welfare workers believe that the kindergarten has a good feeling about Winnie, and, in addition, they note that she is happy at her kindergarten, which is in itself conducive to the cooperation. However, good cooperation does not mean that the parties act quite similarly. Winnie's teacher in the special kindergarten reports, for example, how she works with the residential institution on getting Winnie to stop using a diaper. She believes that it is important to make a coordinated effort so that Winnie is not met with different attitudes in the three different life settings: at home, in day care and in residential care. However, it is difficult because it involves not only cooperation between the two caregivers placed in each institution but also the professionals in the two staff groups as well as Winnie's parents, who are divorced. They all have widely different opinions on how to help a child stop using a diaper.

The child-welfare workers believe that the diaper provides comfort to Winnie in an unstable period of her life, and therefore she herself has to help decide when to give it up. In the kindergarten, they take a different stance, namely that it is time that she slowly starts to do without the diaper because she's soon going to attend school. Winnie's mother is of a third opinion, namely, that Winnie is far too old to use a diaper, and Winnie's mother thinks it should be taken away immediately. These different attitudes affect what can be done in practice in each place. The day-care teacher believes that it does not make sense to do anything different because this will confuse the child, whereas the child-welfare workers express the opposite attitude:

> Winnie's day-care teacher thought we should intervene and decide that it should be *now*; otherwise Winnie would not get the general idea. Where I think that if she uses diaper at night, and sometimes it's off during the day, this would mean that Winnie would be more involved, and I believe this would work well.

The child-welfare workers believe that the most important thing is that Winnie helps determine when it is time. Here, their educational view of the importance of involving the child is evident. The child-welfare workers believe that adults should coordinate their actions towards the same aim, but the ways to reach the aim may differ for the different places. Winnie can, for example, be without a diaper at the day-care centre and still use it at night at the residential institution. The child-welfare workers believe that the parties can cooperate without actually coordinating exactly similar actions.

However, in the day-care centre, they are in favour of structure and strict guidelines for the children, and they find it difficult to accept the problem being addressed differently from different perspectives. Here, their philosophy of behavioural therapy appears in their seeking a uniform response. While these discussions go on, it is ultimately the mother who, on a summer trip with Winnie, decides to put away the diaper. She reports, not without considerable pride, that it happened without any fuss. This corresponds to ordinary practice of upbringing where parents spend time with a child on holiday, supporting them in making a crucial change in habits.

This example demonstrates how a complicated problem may be solved in spite of disagreements and through many parties' different contributions. Attempts to coordinate take place, leaving room for addressing the child's situation differently in different places. At the same time, the different parties' open search for solutions also allows the mother to contribute. These issues are very similar to conventional parent and day-care teacher cooperation on key care topics, such as eating, sleeping and cleanliness, in areas where several parties collaborate on the same issue without necessarily acting in concert (Andenæs, 2011; Højholt, Juhl and Kousholt, 2018; Røn Larsen and Stanek, 2015).

In an interview, the child-welfare workers also reported that Winnie's kindergarten was hosting an event in which children themselves could decide whom they wanted to invite. Winnie wanted to invite her mother and brother; this caused difficulties because Winnie's mother had given up on all cooperation with her children's kindergartens many years ago. She felt she was criticized by the professionals and by other parents as well, because sometimes she drank too much. Therefore, the most likely outcome was that she would not appear at all. However, the child-welfare workers at the residential care had established a good relationship with Winnie's mother and therefore the parties agreed that, together with Winnie and her brother, a child-welfare worker would pick up Winnie's mother so that all four would attend the children's event together.

Winnie's day-care teacher says that she has experienced how important it is for the children that 'their adults' know each other across contexts and that the educators know about the children's lives in both places. The day-care teacher says:

> I have clearly noticed that Winnie knows we are talking together. She knows that I know Pernille [residential institution] and that I'm going to talk to her. It is a good experience for the children, one way or another, and it contributes to the establishment of connections in their lives.

Both the day-care and residential institutions express that it is conducive to cooperation to talk regularly about all the small practical things and events in everyday life and continuously attune their impressions of the child's well-being at both places. It is similar to the exchange of everyday life events and challenges which, generally, characterizes cooperation between parents and educators in day-care centres (Andenæs, 2011). The point is that, in flexible cooperation, the contribution of many parties can help establish meaning and coherence in children's lives while, at the same time, encouraging parents to participate in their children's care to the widest extent possible. If it is not achieved as the common goal to establish consensus, it can pave the way for flexible reflection and action.

Conflicts and possibilities in cooperation across contexts

Emil develops new ways of participating in the residential care, but due to the lack of cooperation between the two institutions, his participation in the day-care institution is nevertheless conflict-ridden, and the child is mostly isolated in relation to the children's communities. Between the two institutions stands a powerless and despairing mother. In the case of Winnie, educators in the kindergarten and the residential institution work closely together to support her daily life, in such a way that it creates room for different approaches and practices and allow a vulnerable mother to be able to play a part in caring for her daughter. In a welfare society, the task of following children's lives at home and across different locations outside the home is traditionally carried out by parents (Kousholt, 2011). In these two cases, however, this important work of childcare must take place through cooperation between the two institutions, who should also work in cooperation with parents in order to exchange knowledge about what matters for the child.

Owing to their family situations, the children live very stressful lives, and at the same time face major difficulties with respect to gaining access to the children's communities which constitute important living conditions in their everyday lives. As Højholt (2016) puts it, in order to understand inequality, we must investigate social conflicts situated and in the ways they become problems *for* children. The analyses discussed above indicate that an improvement in the cooperation between parents, day-care teachers and child-welfare workers in relation to the everyday lives of children across locations could support the children's participation opportunities. The children are in the midst of these relationships, and they may become squeezed and affected by adults' mutual conflicts and irritation. The case with Winnie also shows that collaboration between adults can facilitate a more closely knitted network of support for a child that creates the space for different perspectives and actions without being deadlocked in conflicts.

When cooperation between the parties reaches a deadlock, it can limit the scope of action of parents and children, as in the case of Emil. Day-care teachers constantly approaching the authorities about problems with the child may leave the parents with the impression that their child is unwanted and marginalized in the day-care institution, and with the feeling of having failed as parents. Thus, conflicts between authorities and other professionals contribute to increased stress levels in family life. This helps us understand how children's marginalization can be seen to be linked to an experience of limited action possibilities among those who might otherwise support the child. Children's situations make parents experience stress and affect their confidence in handling their tasks as parents.

Day-care teachers easily feel insecure and excluded from cooperation while the child-welfare workers focus on cooperation with the parents and less on developing a cooperative relationship with the day care. The child-welfare workers do not consider themselves an important element in the support of the children's participation opportunities in the kindergarten. They believe this to be the task of the day care. In this case, professionals look at each other's efforts as distinct islands, and they act in isolation, without understanding that, collectively, the various efforts contribute important elements to the overall care of a child.

Controversies about which knowledge should be exchanged seem, on their own, to create barriers between the cooperating parties. The day-care teachers want more insight into the problems of the family and into the perspectives of the child's future, which they regard as prerequisites for their professional efforts. As this chapter points out, it may not be the exchange of insight into problems in the family's situation and background they lack, as much as the fact that the parties need to consider themselves as participants in a cooperative relationship that provides insight into the child's situation outside their own functional area and creates room for exchange about different action possibilities in relation to dilemmas within the work of childcare. They seem to need this knowledge about what other parties do in order to understand how to strengthen their own contribution.

The dilemma as to whether the diaper should be removed from Winnie immediately, or whether she, herself, should be able to participate in the process illustrates very well how professionals can posit very different perspectives on the same problem, act very differently in relation to this and yet, through flexible open and exploratory cooperation, arrive at a good conclusion. Additionally, the professional's exchange and negotiation allowed room for a mother to act.

In both cases, the shared knowledge in inter-professional cooperation can be understood as multifaceted, conflictual and contradictory.

Dilemmas in childcare: Exploring the work of childcare as multifaceted

Defining children's needs is a highly controversial and conflictual matter in psychological theory, child service politics and in professional practices (Burman, 1994; Schwartz, 2017, 2018; Woodhead, 2015). Difficulties, contradictions and dilemmas can be understood at the core of child care in general (Højholt et al., 2018; Kousholt, 2012) and, thereby, no less so in the case of children in child welfare. In the case of placement, dilemmas between caring and demands are constantly in play (Bijleveld, Dedding and Bunders-Aelen, 2013; Schwartz, 2018). Dichotomized approaches to children's needs show up in practical discussions about how to support them. In Winnie's day care, for example, their treatment-oriented approach is often opposed to the child-centred and dialogue-based educational method practised at Solhøj. The staff in both places must work hard to find ways in which to overcome their very different views of what kind of support the children need. Here is an example:

> The day-care teachers have for some time been missing an important key. They suspect that Winnie has taken it, but she denies any knowledge of it. The day-care teacher approaches the child-welfare workers at the residential institution about it, and they question Winnie without results. Suddenly, one morning at Solhøj, Winnie comes down from her room with the key. The child-welfare worker chooses to show pleasure in the appearance of the key and emphasizes that it is very nice that she herself has found the key and handed it over. They decide together that Winnie will deliver the key back the same day. Winnie gives the key to the day-care teacher who tells her that they were sure that she had taken it and, also, that they believe she takes other things. The day-care teacher shows clearly that she is worried about Winnie not admitting to have stolen the key. Later, the child-welfare worker explains to me that he is highly frustrated about the reaction of the day-care teacher. In his opinion, such a key cannot be such a big problem to justify so much fuss. He also believes that the day-care teacher is accusing Winnie for a lot of things for which she has no way of knowing whether Winnie is actually guilty. Moreover, the child-welfare worker disapproves of the day-care teachers' angry and upset behaviour as Winnie is facing up to handing over the key.

At the residential-care home, the child-welfare workers offer the view that Winnie is a 'passionate collector'. She usually has pockets full of stuff that the child-welfare workers regularly help to sort. For example, they find rusty nails and fittings in her pockets mixed with clips and tape from the office of the residential institution. Much of it has no value and other things have to be returned to their rightful owners. At the residential care, they consider it an important task not to accuse Winnie of theft, but to teach her to distinguish between yours and mine, and between valuable objects and things that are the property of everybody. By showing Winnie confidence, the child-welfare workers gain access to help her to sort the things and to distinguish between what she is allowed to take and what she cannot take. The child-welfare workers believe that allegations of theft may cause Winnie to withdraw, which will leave her on her own in such an important learning process. The case points to the question of understanding how a child can learn how to distinguish between her own things and those of others by taking part in different educational practices.

There are two complementary ways of reading this event. From Edwards's view of common knowledge, the workers in both settings would have benefitted from understanding the professional reasons in play in the other setting. The child-welfare worker's emphasis on a developmental process that involves the child's active contribution and the day-care professional's emphasis on behavioural conditioning would, in Edwards's terms, comprise the common knowledge that both sets of professionals could have deployed to support Winnie's developmental trajectory. Doing so would have involved each set of professionals in coordinating their responses.

The other way of reading it is to emphasize the contradictory aspects of the event. This response can augment the common knowledge concept. The example shows how professionals have very different views on upbringing and how they also react very differently. My point is to demonstrate how the work of child care itself must be understood as contradictory. The argument here is that acceptance of differences in perspectives contributes to opening up the diversity in the work of child care, so that all parties in the process can nuance their own perspectives in relation to a shared, varied and flexible adaptation to the child's process.

In addition, personal problems can be understood as linked with general dilemmas of taking part in social practices with different conflicting social demands and expectation (Schwartz, 2018; Højholt, 2011). When the day-care teachers assume it as their task to spell out their standards, the child-welfare workers can afford to immerse themselves in others aspects of the child's process as focusing on her personal interest in collecting things. The child meets different reactions from different parties in her social environment, and this allows her to recognize that adults will not always respond in the same way. A problem may have many perspectives and contain aspects that one must consider and relate to.

If the professionals across the different locations and practices the child inhabits explore how social demands, possibilities and expectations differ in different places, seen from the children's perspectives, this may create a space in which the parties can explore how they can contribute differently in their common handling of dilemmas and problems. It is the parties' insight into the child's situation in and across contexts that allows the different professionals to relate relevantly to the various contributions of others. The child is about to learn how to handle different expectations in different places. This leads to an understanding of common knowledge as consisting of different and, at times, contradictory perspectives on the same matter. Differences in professional practices could then be seen as resources that potentially create the space for children's development of agency. Understanding child care as multifaceted and filled with dilemmas opens up for the possibility that children, young people and parents themselves may explore and learn how to organize their participation and contribute in relation to challenges in their lives.

References

Andenæs, A. (2011). Chains of care: Organising the everyday life of young children attending day care. *Nordic Psychology, 63*(2), 49–67.

Armstrong, D., Armstrong, A. C., and Spandagou, I. (2011). Inclusion: By choice or by chance? *International Journal of Inclusive Education, 15*(1), 29–39.

Axel, E. (2011). Conflictual cooperation. *Nordic Psychology, 63*(4), 56–78.

Bijleveld, G. G., Dedding, C. W., and Bunders-Aelen, J. F. (2013). Children's and young people's participation within child welfare and child protection services:
A state-of-the-art review. *Child and Family Social Work, 20*, 129–38.

Burman, E. (1994). *Deconstructing developmental psychology*. London: Routledge.

Dreier, O. (2008). *Psychotherapy in everyday life*. Cambridge: Cambridge University Press.

Dreier, O. (2009). The development of a personal conduct of life in childhood. In T. Teo, P. Stenner, E. Park, A. Rutherford, C. Baerveldt and International Society for Theoretical Psychology. Conference (12: 2007: Toronto, Ont.) (Eds), *Varieties of theoretical psychology: International philosophical and practical concerns* (pp. 175–83). Concord, ON: Captus University Publications.

Dreier, O. (2016). Conduct of everyday life. Implications for critical psychology. In E. Schraube and C. Højholt (Eds), *Psychology and the conduct of everyday life* (pp. 15–33). New York: Routledge.

Edwards, A. (2005). Relational agency: Learning to be a resourceful practitioner. *International Journal of Educational Research*, 43(3), 168–82.

Edwards, A. (2009). From the systemic to the relational: Relational agency and activity theory. In A. D. Sannino and K. H. Guttierez (Eds), *Learning and expanding with activity theory* (pp. 197–211). Cambridge: Cambridge: University Press.

Edwards, A. (2010). *Being an expert professional practitioner: The relational turn in expertise*. London and New York: Springer.

Edwards, A. (2011). Building common knowledge at the boundaries between professional practices: Relational agency and relational expertise in systems of distributed expertise. *International Journal of Educational Research*, 50(1), 33–9.

Edwards, A., and Daniels, H. (2012). The knowledge that matters in professional practices. *Journal of Education and Work*, 25(1), 39–58.

Hedegaard, M., Chaiklin, S., and Jensen, U. J. (1999). Activity theory and social practice: An introduction. In S. Chaiklin, M. Hedegaard and U. J. Jensen (Eds), *Activity theory and social practice* (pp. 12–30). Aarhus, Denmark: Aarhus University.

Hedegaard, M., Aronsson, K., Højholt, C., and Ulvik, O. S. (Eds). (2018). *Children, childhood, and everyday life: Children's perspectives* (2nd edn). Charlotte, NC: Information Age Publishing.

Hedegaard, M., and Fleer, M. (2013). *Play, learning, and children's development: Everyday life in families and transition to school*. Cambbridge: Cambridge University Press.

Højholt, C. (2006). Knowledge and professionalism from the perspectives of children. *Critical Psychology: International Journal of Critical Psychology*, 19, 81–106.

Højholt, C. (2008). Participation in communities – living and learning across different contexts. *Australian Research in Early Childhood Education*, 15(1), 1–12.

Højholt, C. (2011). Cooperation between professionals in educational psychology – children's specific problems are connected to general dilemmas in relation to taking part. In H. Daniels and M. Hedegaard (Eds), *Vygotsky and special needs education: Rethinking support for children and schools* (pp. 67–86). London: Continuum Press.

Højholt, C., and Kousholt, D. (2012). Practice research. In T. Teo (Ed.), *Encyclopedia of critical psychology* (pp. 1485–8). Singapore: Springer Science Business Media BV.

Højholt, C. (2016). Situated inequality and the conflictuality of children's conduct of life. In E. Schraube and C. Højholt (Eds), *Psychology and the conduct of everyday life* (pp. 145–75). Oxon: Routledge.

Højholt, C., and Kousholt, D. (2017). Children participating and developing agency in and across various social practices. In M. Fleer and B. v. Oers (Eds), *International handbook on early childhood education* (pp. 1581–98). Dordrecht: Springer.

Højholt, C., and Kousholt, D. (Eds). (2018). *Konflikter om børns skoleliv* [Conflicts about children's everyday lives in school]. Copenhagen: Dansk Psykologisk Forlag.

Højholt, C., Juhl, P., and Kousholt, D. (2018). The collectivity of family conduct of life and parental self-understanding. In S. Garvis and E. E. Ødegaard (Eds), *Nordic dialogues on children and families* (pp. 13–27). London and New York: Routledge.

Holland, D., and Lave, J. (2001). *History in person: Enduring struggles, contentious practice, intimate identities.* Santa Fe, NM: School of American Research Press.

Juhl, P. (2015). Toddlers collaboratively explore possibilities for actions across contexts: Developing the concept conduct of everyday life in relation to young children. In G. B. Sullivan, J. Cresswell, A. Larraín, A. Haye and M. Morgan (Eds), *Dialogue and debate in the making of theoretical psychology* (pp. 202–10). Concord, ON: Captus Press Inc.

Kousholt, D. (2011). *Børnefællesskaber og familieliv* [Children's communities and family lives]. Copenhagen: Dansk Psykologisk Forlag.

Kousholt, D. (2012). Family problems. Exploring dilemmas and complexities of organizing everyday family life. In M. Hedegaard, K. Aronsson, C. Højholt and O. S. Ulvik (Eds), *Children, childhood, and everyday life: Children's perspective* (pp. 125–39). Charlotte, NC: Information Age Publishing, incorporated.

Lausten, M. (2015). Needs and characteristics of high-resource using children and youth. In J. K. Whittaker, J. Fernandez del Valle and L. Holmes (Eds), *Therapeutic residential care for children and youth: Developing evidence-based international practice* (pp. 73–84). London: Jessica Kingsley Publishers.

Lave, J. (2008). Situated learning and changing practice. In A. Amin and J. Roberts (Eds), *Community, economic creativity, and organization* (pp. 283–96). Oxford: Oxford University Press.

Ringsmose, C., and Kragh-Müller, G. (Eds). (2016). *Nordic social pedagogical approach to early years.* Switzerland: Springer.

Røn Larsen, M., and Stanek, A. H. (2015). Young children and their conduct of everyday life. *Nordic Psychology, 67*(3), 195–209.

Schraube, E., and Højholt, C. (2016). *Psychology and the conduct of everyday life* (1st edn). London and New York: Routledge.

Schraube, E., and Osterkamp, U. (2013). *Psychology from the standpoint of the subject: Selected writings of Klaus Holzkamp.* Basingstoke: Palgrave Macmillan.

Schwartz, I. (2007). Børneliv på døgninstitution. Socialpædagogik på tværs af børns livssammenhænge [Children's lives in residential care. Social Pedagogy across children's contexts of life]. PhD thesis, University of Southern Denmark.

Schwartz, I. (2017). Putting the child at the center of inter-professional cooperation in out-of-home care. *Child and Family Social Work, 22,* 992–9.

Schwartz, I. (2018). Residential care and children's development of agency in everyday life. In M. Hedegaard, K. Aronsson, C. Højholt and O. S. Ulvik (Eds), *Children, childhood, and everyday life: Children's perspective* (2nd edn, pp. 167–84). Charlotte, NC: Information Age Publishing.

UNESCO. (1994). *The Salamanca statement and framework for action on special needs education*. Salamanca: UNESCO.

Warming, H. (2011). Children's participation and citizenship in a global age: Empowerment, tokenism or discriminatory disciplining? *Social Work and Society*, 9(1), 119-34.

Woodhead, M. (2015). Psychology and the cultural construction of children's needs. In A. James and A. Prout (Eds), *Constructing and reconstructing childhood: Contemporary issues in the sociological study of childhood* (pp. 72-91). London: Routledge.

10

Helping Children in Cross-Cultural Post-Disaster settings: Creating Relational Pathways to Resilience

Pernille Hansen

Conceptualizing children's psychological reaction to disasters and the help provided

Children are particularly vulnerable to the negative effects of natural disasters that lead to mass structural destruction. How they react depends on factors such as their personality, past experiences and learnt coping behaviour. Other influencing factors include whether they are separated from caregivers, how others around them react and the level of disruption of their day-to-day lives (Belfer, 2006; Margolin, Ramos and Guran, 2010). Common approaches to helping children in and after disasters have focused on identifying and treating post-traumatic stress reactions (Weiss, Saraceno, Saxena and van Ommeren, 2003). Post-traumatic stress disorder (PTSD) has been referred to as 'the most frequent and debilitating psychological disorder that occurs after traumatic events and disasters' (Galea, Nandi and Vlahov, 2005, p. 78). However, controversy exists around how valuable diagnoses and treatment of PTSD and other psychological disorders are in post-disaster settings, especially across different cultures and in low-income environments with limited mental health services that cannot offer recommended interventions such as cognitive-behavioural therapy, trauma-focused psychotherapy or eye movement desensitization and reprocessing (Belfer, 2006; Bisson et al., 2007). Most of the screening tools commonly used to identify children at risk of PTSD in post-disaster settings, such as the children's revised impact of events scale (CRIES-13) and the UCLA post-traumatic stress disorder reaction index (PTSD RI), are developed for use in European and

North American contexts and not culturally adapted, reducing their validity and reliability (Summerfield, 2001; Weiss et al., 2003).

Diagnosing children with psychological disorders where there are no services and/or high risks of stigma and discrimination, or providing care that is not culturally adapted, can result in long-lasting negative unintended consequences that are not easily reversed (Belfer, 2006). A significant task of a disaster health care response has therefore become the prevention of interventions that may potentially cause harm, initiated by either local or international agencies (Komesaroff and Sundram, 2006). Finally, while many children may report elevated symptoms of mental distress shortly after disaster exposure, a relatively small minority of children report elevated chronic, persistent mental health symptoms over time. The majority of children do extraordinarily well in post-disaster settings (La Greca et al., 2013). Thus, instead of focusing on treating the minority who display complicated reactions, there is instead now a shift towards exploring and promoting what makes people stronger and better able to cope. It is a mindset shift from focusing on 'damage to the child' to 'opportunities for the child' to grow and develop.

Individual, family and community resilience

Resilience is when a person, or group of people, manage(s) to cope and function well, despite facing adversity. Resilience in and after disasters refers to the ability of an individual, group, community or nation to survive, adapt to and recover from the loss and disruption caused by a disaster (Boon et al., 2012). Strengthening children's resilience in these situations involves a focus on individual, family and community resilience. Individual resilience is explained as a 'shared quality of the individual and the individual's social ecology, with the social ecology likely to be more important than individual factors for recovery and sustainable well-being for populations under stress' (Ungar, 2012, p. 17). Family resilience is when the family functions well as a unit and all family members and the unit have the potential and opportunities to adapt (Walsh, 2012). Community resilience is described as a high prevalence of wellness in the community, demonstrated through high and non-disparate levels of mental and behavioural health, role-functioning and quality of life in constituent populations (Norris, Stevens, Pfefferbaum, Wyche and Pfefferbaum, 2008).

There are two overarching foci of current resilience research. The first is identifying protective mediating factors that can help mitigate or prevent negative impacts of potential risks. The second focuses on how children actively negotiate access to the health-sustaining resources they need – the pathways to resilience (Skovdal and Daniel, 2012; Ungar, 2005). Making resources available is not enough in itself, they have to be accessible, relevant and effective (Ungar, 2005). My concern is how we, as psychology practitioners, can help to enable these pathways. I join other authors in viewing pathways to resilience as similar to opportunities for development, and regard the experience of resilience as an experience of positive development in adverse circumstances (Liebenberg and Ungar, 2009; Masten and Obradovic, 2008; Ungar, 2011).

Disaster: The earthquake in Haiti

The earthquake in Haiti on 12 January 2010 occurred at around 16.43. The epicentre was near Leogane, about 25 kilometres west of Port-au-Prince. Thousands of homes slid down the terraced slopes in the hills of Port-au-Prince, each crushing the house below it. Many survivors were injured and trapped in collapsed buildings for days before they were rescued. The disaster directly affected around 3.9 million people, with 222,570 reported deaths. Between 750,000 and 1.2 million of those affected were children (UNICEF, 2011). As it was late afternoon, many of the children were in school and separated from their parents. Before the earthquake, Haiti was the poorest nation in the Western Hemisphere. It had a detrimental history of foreign exploitation and an internal division by class with very overt social inequalities (Raviola, Eustache, Oswald and Belkin, 2012).

Shelters in Santo Domingo

Neighbouring Dominican Republic was the first country to respond, with provisions and medical care and by opening their borders and providing access to medical treatment and local hospitals. However, the government of the Dominican Republic quickly faced an unprecedented health emergency. Soon hospitals and clinics were overwhelmed by the surge of patients needing urgent surgical and medical care. Non-governmental organizations and bodies – such as churches, community organizations, wealthy individuals and businesses – provided assistance with 'shelters', that provided care and provisions to post-operative patients who were well enough to leave the hospitals but were not yet well enough to return to Haiti. Their establishment was spontaneous and not part of the official coordinated response. By the third week after the earthquake, there were at least 16 shelters known to the official services. The patients in them were not in critical conditions, but still needed continued medical care and accessed this as outpatients. The nature of the shelters varied. Some were pre-existing institutions that cared for specific vulnerable groups, others were monasteries and convents, and some were private homes. One shelter, for example, usually housed children living with physical disabilities and was very spacious. Many of the patients who were bedridden or in wheelchairs were sent here. The core staff in the pre-existing institutions remained the same, with added help from volunteers or paid staff assigned to the shelters.

Mental health and psychosocial support

The National Programme for Mental Health (NPMH), of the Ministry of Health of the government of the Dominican Republic, joined in the response to the earthquake from 13 January to help coordinate mental health and psychosocial support in the border areas of Jimani and Fond Parisien, and in the shelters in Santo Domingo. A crisis intervention team was established with locally practising psychiatrists and psychologists and Haitian and Dominican student volunteers from tertiary institutions. After a short training, the team starting working: mostly alone, but a few in small teams. Most of the Spanish-speaking psychologists worked through translators to speak with the Creole-speaking Haitians. They provided emotional support; gave information and practical help; and referred those who needed psychiatric treatment. The intervention team also supported Dominican helpers who were affected by the suffering they witnessed and from working for long hours.

After the first few weeks, several challenges were identified. First, the number of available mental health providers was limited, putting an immense load on those involved. Second, most of the volunteering private psychologists usually worked as individual therapists and were not experienced in disaster responses or community-based psychosocial support. Third, in some shelters there was resistance to help from outside and follow-up action was not carried out. Fourth, the language barrier and an extreme shortage of translators limited in-depth communication. Many psychologists were frustrated over the lack of time and resources to support everyone in need, and were concerned about the growing number of children and adults showing severe symptoms of depression and anxiety. Some Dominican helpers were also beginning to show signs of severe stress and occupational burnout.

The NPMH recognized the need for a different approach to providing mental health and psychosocial support, and sought guidance from the psychology department of the Universidad Iberoamericana (UNIBE) on setting up a more community-based psychosocial response. I was invited to join the team working on this task as a PhD researcher and a mental health and psychosocial support technical advisor and practitioner. I worked with a team of staff and students from the psychology department to (i) conduct initial intervention research to recommend interventions to the NPMH, (ii) support direct interventions in two shelters and (iii) conduct case study research. The research was conducted over a period of a year and three months, with two 5-day visits to Santo Domingo in February and March 2010, and a 10-day visit to Haiti in April 2011. The aim of the research was to help strengthen the methods used to support children and families to experience resilience in and after disasters. The research questions were as follows: (i) How did the Haitian children and their families and the Dominican helpers experience the situation and how did it affect their well-being? (ii) What resources and support did they have and what did they need? What interventions were relevant and possible? and (iii) How can we help promote children's resilience in and after disasters? In the rest of this chapter, I describe how I interpreted some of the case study research data to address the third research question by using concepts from ecological and cultural-historical theories of development.

Using development theories to create a framework to explore resilience

The bioecological perspective

Bronfenbrenner's bioecological model (Bronfenbrenner, 2005; Bronfenbrenner and Morris, 2006) of human development provides a useful framework to analyse resilience at individual, family and community levels in post-disaster settings as resilience has repeatedly been found to rest on relationships between social and community infrastructure factors (Boon et al., 2012; Masten and Obradovic, 2008; Ungar, 2012). His model is based on the hypothesis that well-being is influenced by the social context and the function and quality of relationships one has with others, such as family, neighbours and institutional systems.

He reveals that development is influenced by the interactions and events that occur in different layers of the child's social and environmental milieu and by context and time. Bronfenbrenner focuses not only on the direct interactions the child has with others but also on the conditions for development, that are determined by the ecological systems the child is a part of. This calls for consideration of the child's within-person characteristics, such as adaptive coping, self-efficacy and optimism, and external factors, such as family support, neighbourhood networks, healthy systems and government support systems (Boon et al., 2012). Resilience takes place within this multidimensional system of interaction between biological functioning, risk factors, environmental issues and protective factors (Goldstein and Brooks, 2005).

In Figure 10.1 Bronfenbrenner's model, applied to the research context, shows the Haitian child embedded in integrated ecological systems with interactions at different levels that all play a part in the child's experience of well-being and resilience. The child's personal characteristics: dispositions, bioecological resources of ability, experience, knowledge and skills, and demand characteristics that invite or discourage reactions from the social environment

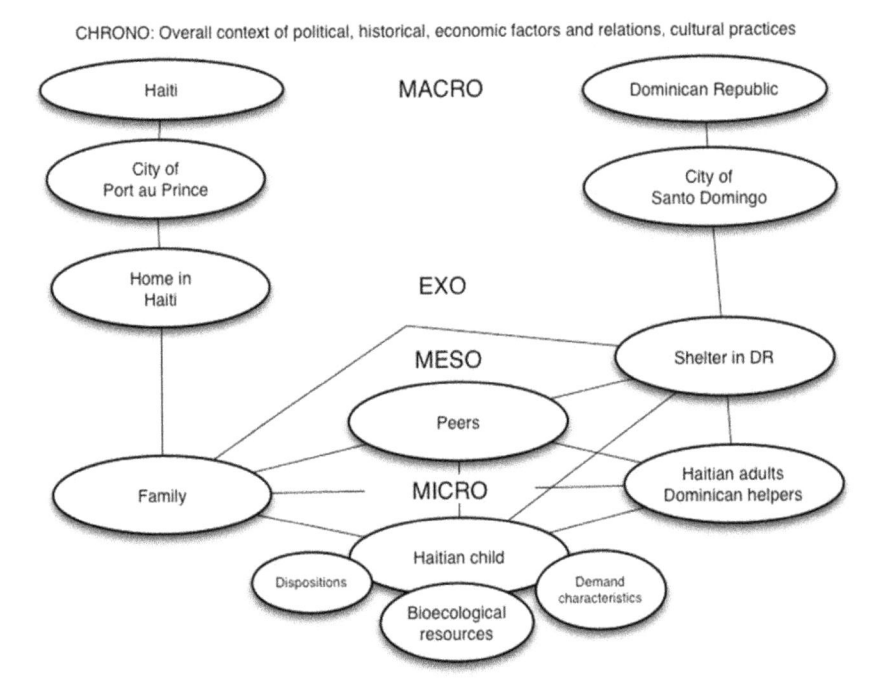

Figure 10.1 The application of Bronfenbrenner's (2005) bioecological system to the research context.

are considered as within factors; the external factors are the micro-, meso-, exo-, macro- and the chrono-systems. The micro-system is where the Haitian child takes part in proximal processes with others: family, peers, and other Haitian and Dominican adults. The meso-system refers to interactions between the children and adults in the shelter that take place independently of the focal child: the interactions of others around the child. The exo-system refers to the institutions (shelters) in the city of Santo Domingo, embedded in the macro-systems of the government and the country. The chrono-system refers to the time the events took place in, interlinked with the analysis at the macro level of the historical, political, economic relationship between the two countries. Ungar (2012) employs Bronfenbrenner's model to provide an 'interactional, environmental and cultural perspective on resilience' (p. 14), where he suggests that it is the *goodness of fit* between elements of the meso-system (interactions between family, school and community systems) that predict positive growth/development in adverse situations.

This perspective allows for analysis of contextual factors and indigenous coping strategies instead of imposing a standard set of outcome measures as determinants of resilience. Ungar (2012, p. 15) describes this 'complex, multidimensional way of understanding resilience as, or more, dependent on the capacity of the individual's physical and social ecology to potentiate positive development under stress than the capacity of individuals to exercise personal agency'. While this shift in focus from the individual as the primary unit of analysis to a contextually relevant understanding of resilience is useful, it does not provide us with the theoretical tools needed to understand the complexities of the interaction between the child and environment and what it is that leads to successful navigation and negotiation of resources needed for resilience. I turned to particular aspects of the cultural-historical approach to development to explore this, specifically the role of crisis, zone of proximal development, activity settings and institutional practices.

The cultural-historical approach

The cultural-historical approach examines the relationships between the human mind and activity. Vygotsky (1998) presented a holistic model of development that included the dialectic relations between psychological, biological and cultural dimensions of a person's life. He introduced the concept of mediated action as the semiotic process that enables the development of human consciousness through interaction with artefacts, tools and social others in an environment, which leads to individuals finding new meanings in their world (Yamagata-Lynch, 2010). Vygotsky was explaining the relationship between an individual's mental processes and their interaction with cultural, historical and institutional settings, pointing out that humans' relations with the world are always mediated by symbols and tools (Wertsch, del Río and Alvarez, 1995). Edwards and Apostovlov (2007, p. 72) explain that through the cultural-historical lens, 'people are not passive recipients of a culture, they are shaped by their culture, but through the processes of externalisation they also act on and in turn shape it'. Through their interactions they create meanings, and they also create and modify activities that lead to changes in the artefacts, tools and people in their environment (Scribner, 1997). Thus, while Bronfenbrenner explained how different social ecologies impact the child, Vygotsky's theory highlights the crucial role the child has on shaping the world they live in.

Vygotsky (1998) was among the first theorists to bring attention to the role of crisis in development. He explained that children go through stable age periods where development appears to be smooth and unremarkable, but in between stable age periods, children experience crises that present them with new demands and call for the development of new competences and different motives in behaviour. I applied this concept to the disaster context and suggested that everyone involved faced crises that presented them with novel demands that called for new competences and skills. The Haitian adults and children faced physical, emotional and social losses in addition to the stress of being in a foreign country and being wholly dependent on their hosts for survival. Many children had lost one or more caregiver, heightening already-existing vulnerabilities and the risk of harm or exploitation. Dominican helpers faced crises from secondary trauma and exhaustion. Vygotsky (1998) explained that crises are 'social situations of development' which are realized through the child's interaction with others. He stressed the dialectic relations between the child and his or her surroundings. While the surroundings impact the child's experiences, motives and actions, the child's action simultaneously impacts the surroundings. In short, the child is seen to be part of creating the conditions for his or her development. To explain children's learning through social interaction, Vygotsky introduced the concept of the zone of proximal development, describing it as: 'What the child can do today in cooperation and with guidance, tomorrow he will be able to do independently' (Vygotsky, 1998, p. 202). When the child faces a new crisis with new demands, the zone of proximal development alters. Vygotsky referred to this as the child entering a new age period. Thus, he saw age periods not in terms of years lived, but rather as the transitions of adapting to the new demands posed by crises in different times of life. Using this concept, I interpreted the crisis faced by the Haitians and Dominicans as one that would require a shift from 'life-before-the-earthquake' to 'life-after-the-earthquake'.

Activity settings and institutional practices

Hedegaard (2012) agrees with Bronfenbrenner's conceptualization of children's everyday life taking place in institutions such as families, kindergartens and schools, but argues that he did not address how children contribute to institutional practices. Hedegaard (2012) extends both Vygotsky's and Bronfenbrenner's theories by introducing institutional practice and activity settings as the conditions for the child's activities. Her emphasis is on the relationship of reciprocal demands that are created as the child participates in the different activity settings which constitute institutional practices. Using Vygotsky's concept of new demands stimulating development she stresses that these demands are dynamic and two way, between not only people but also the child and their environment. Hedegaard (2008) also draws on Elkonin (1999) who focused on the significance of social practice in different institutions and how these mark important changes in the child's development. Practice is understood as the approach taken by the institution over time. Thus, the concept of life periods in development is related to the different types of institutional practice and the activities the child participates in. For example, children go through marked development when they move from preschool to primary school and meet a whole new set of demands.

Hedegaard (2008) explains that children have to learn new competences at each period of development, and the efforts and motivation to learn are usually oriented towards successfully 'participating in the practice traditions of particular institutions' (p. 15). Activity settings are described as events that take place within an institutional practice that reflect societal traditions and with multiple participants (Hedegaard, 2012). Their participation in the activities is part of defining the meaning of the activity setting. The concept of activity setting is 'central for conceptualising how institutional practice and people's activities change historically both in the form of children's development and in the form of change of societal practice' (p. 132). She suggests that an activity setting, seen from a specific person's perspective, is their social situation. Different people in the same activity setting thus experience different social situations, each from their own perspectives. Hedegaard (2012) suggests analyses of activities in social situations require exploration of both the practice of the institution where the activity takes place and the activity from the child's perspective. I employed institutional practices and activity settings as analytic concepts to help understand the children's social situations of development after their transitions into the shelters, looking particularly at the relations between the child's activities and the family and shelter practices. Figure 10.2 shows how I adapted Hedegaard's (2012) model (see Chapter 1) to the context to show the Haitian child participated in activities and interactions with others in activity settings that reflect institutional practices.

However, these shelters were not established institutions with long-standing practices. Rather they could be seen as what Edwards terms 'sites of intersecting practices' (Edwards, 2010). The two practices to be found in the shelters were the practices that had a direct relationship to the Dominican way of life and the Haitian practices of the families within the shelters. Hedegaard (2012) proposes that to understand a child's social situation, we need to analyse the child's activity from the three planes indicated in Figure 10.2: the formal societal, general institutional and the specific settings of the persons (see Chapter 1). She explains that the formal societal plane reflects historically evolved cultural traditions that are formalized into laws and regulations as conditions for the existence of an institution. In this context, it was the cultural traditions of the Haitian society that influenced the conditions of the institutions of families and the cultural traditions of the Dominican Republic that laid the conditions for the existence of the shelters. The second is the general institutional plane that reflects traditions and demands in the form of practices, which in this case were related to the practices within the Haitian family units and practices of those running the specific shelters. These practices reflect the values embedded in and created by the Haitian and Dominican culture and traditions. The specific plane reflects the shared activity settings of persons in a situation. It is at this point that the two different practices intersect. Exploring interactions in activity settings can therefore help show the perspectives of the different participants. This enhances our understanding of their new demands and, by doing so, lays the groundwork for developing what Edwards terms 'common knowledge' (see Chapter 1, this volume; Edwards, 2010, 2017). In brief, common knowledge consists of what matters, the motives that shape the practices of potential collaborators. Common knowledge, knowledge of what matters in the practice of the other, may then become a resource, which can mediate collaboration across practice boundaries. It is, Edwards argues, built and deployed in sites of intersecting practices.

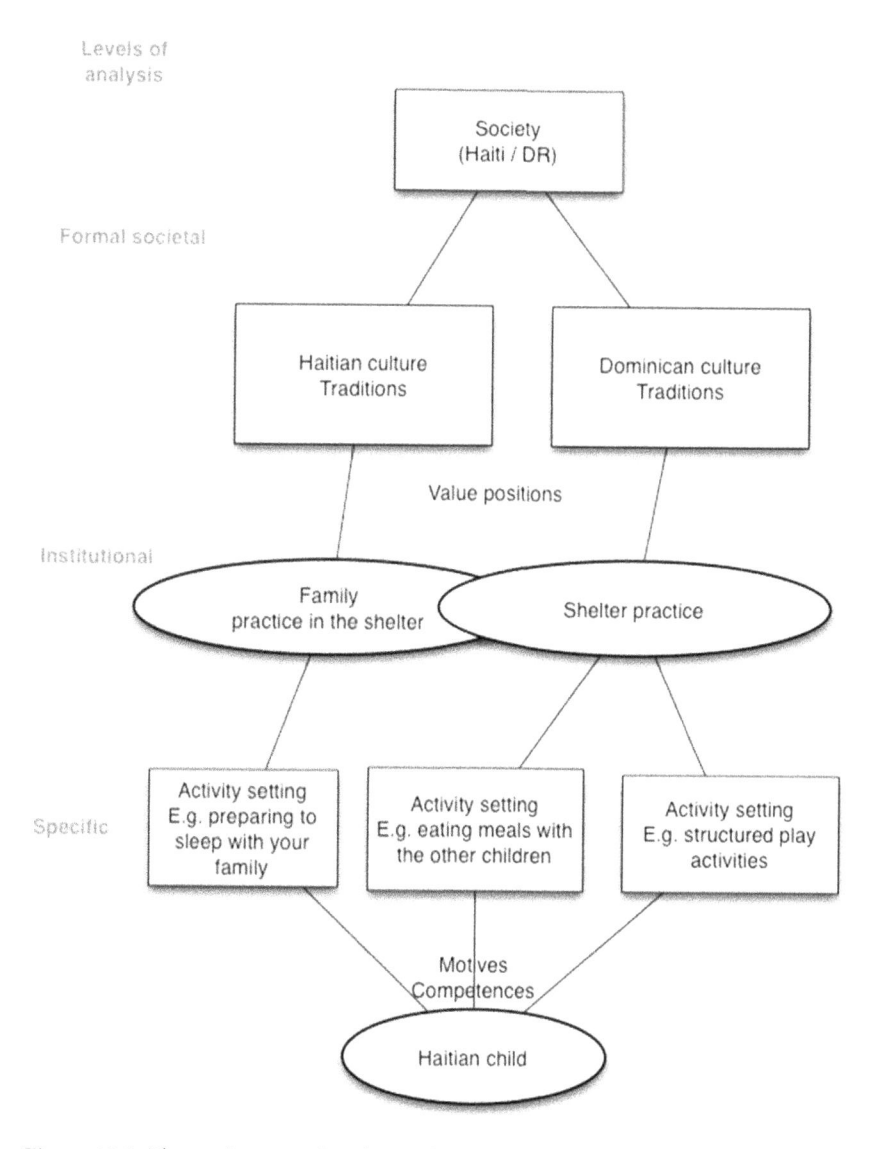

Figure 10.2 The application of Hedegaard's (2012) model to the research context.

Resilience and cultural-historical theory

Cultural-historical theory provides us with analytic concepts that enable an in-depth exploration of what takes place in a crisis situation in which a child is faced with new demands that call for development. The focus is not only on the child but also on the conditions for development (the institutional practices they encounter) and the interactions and relations the child participates in with others in activity settings. Emphasis is on the dialectic relationship between the social conditions and the child being able to shape those social conditions. With this perspective, resilience must be viewed as a capacity to contribute, as well as to use, resources in crisis situations and understood as development that takes place at individual and systemic levels simultaneously (Edwards and Apostolov, 2007). However, in sites of intersecting practices, children are particularly challenged if they want to influence and shape the activities in practices that are not the practices in which they have been raised – as we shall see when there is a need for a Haitian child to challenge the dietary tradition of Dominican culture.

Cross-cultural crisis response framework

Merging the application of Bronfenbrenner's model and cultural-historical theory concepts to make sense of my data, I created the cross-cultural crisis response framework shown below in Figure 10.3 and applied it to the research context. I suggest this model can be used to explore opportunities to promote resilience in a post-disaster setting with groups of people from different countries and/or cultures with different practice traditions. I will explain the use of the model using the case study of Ricardo at one of the shelters.

There are two sections to the model, A and B. Section A presents the historical context and relationship between the populations from two different countries. The focus is on relations in terms of politics, economic and ecological resources and cultural practices, explored through interactions and relations of research participants. It is similar to Bronfenbrenner's macro level of analysis and Hedegaard's formal societal plane of analysis, only with the added complexity of there being two groups, which calls for attention to the historical relationship between the two nations and how this impacts current relationships in sites of intersecting practices. The results of section A lay the foundation for what takes place in section B, which is the crisis situation encountered at the time of the research (illustrated as the large circle which section B is embedded in).

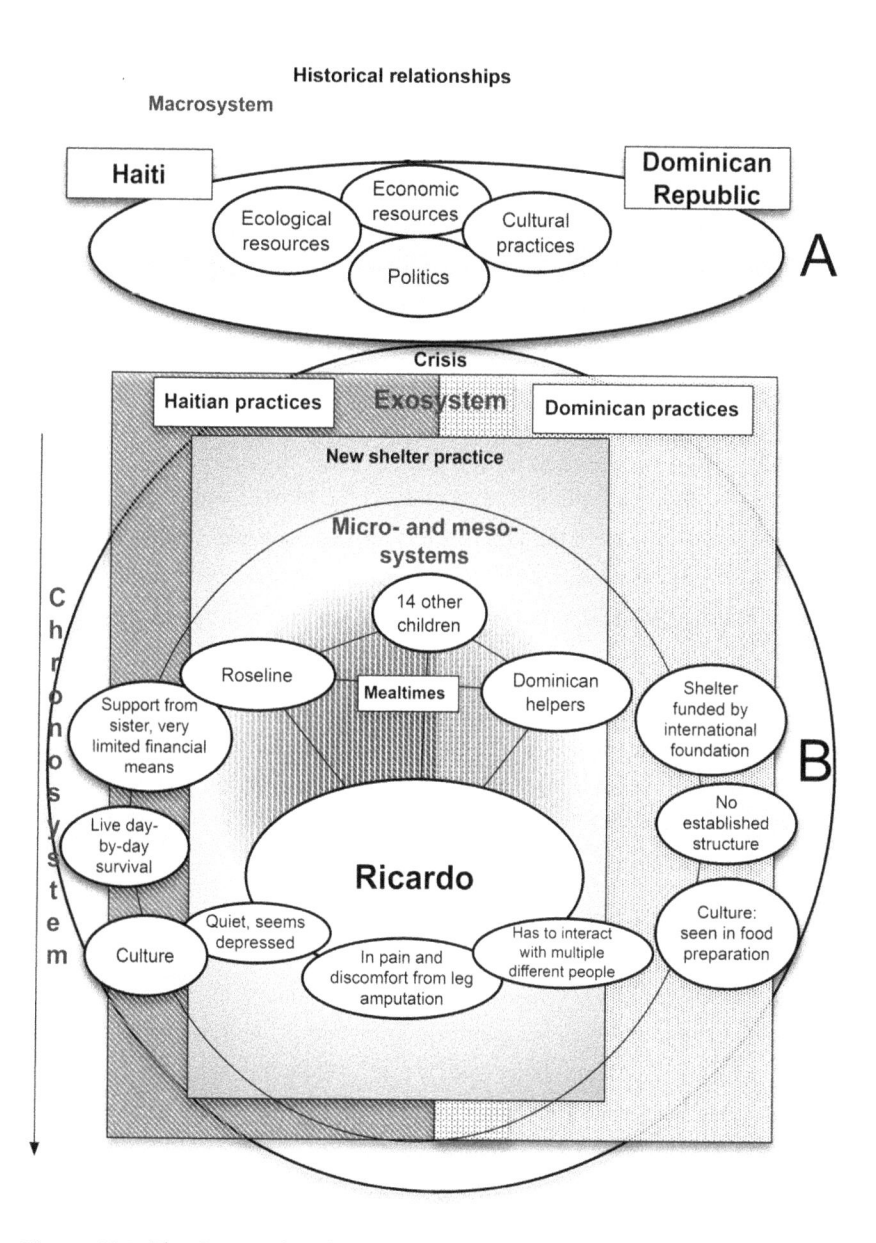

Helping Children in Cross-Cultural Post-Disaster Settings   207

Figure 10.3 The Cross-cultural crisis response framework (CCCRF) applied to the social situation of a Ricardo at a shelter in Santo Domingo in the Dominican Republic after the earthquake of 2010.

Section A: Past and current relations between Haiti and the Dominican Republic

Although they share the island of Hispaniola, striking social, cultural, economic, political and ecological differences divide the two nations. Brief periods of peace are overshadowed by strong memories of reciprocal acts of violence and retribution, which feeds a mutual sense of mistrust. Farmer (2010) states the Dominican Republic remains a country in which racism and dislike of all things Haitian are 'tolerated and condoned' (p. 506). At the time of the earthquake, Haiti ranked 145 of 187 countries in the UN Human Development Index, characterized as a low human developed country, compared to the Dominican Republic which ranked 88 and was ranked as a medium human developed country (United Nations Development Program, 2010). The economic disparity between the two nations meant that the injured Haitians who came to the Dominican Republic were wholly dependent on the Dominicans for their survival while there. This was not easy for the Haitians and influenced interactions between them and perceptions of each other. A translator for a mother in one of the shelters said:

> They [the Haitians] are receiving help, but the thing is that she feels like a beggar and sometimes things arrive for them and they are not really given the things that are donated for them. Actually, the people want them to come and ask all the time when they could just say that there is 'x' thing here that came for you guys if ever you need it. So, for her it is a struggle because she is not used to begging and asking.

The different histories and heritages have led to differing cultural traditions and practices. Take the example of religion: while Dominicans are predominantly Roman Catholic, Haiti's religions are more diverse and include Roman Catholicism, various Protestant traditions and Vodou. Vodou combines West African traditions and Catholicism and is practised by the majority of Haitians, often in combination with their Christian faith (World Health Organization, 2010). Two Dominican government representatives said:

> We still hear comments, … , some people say that they deserve it (the earthquake) because they used to praise the devil and, you know, and I was in shock, I was like, you know it's just two days after the earthquake … however, we cannot miss the reality that although we are in the same island, we are completely different, it's incredible, language, religion, traditions and habits, it's like we're very, very, very different.

Section A of the cross-cultural crisis response framework (CCCRF) provides invaluable information for understanding of the relations between the two nations. Their histories led to prejudiced attitudes and mutual fear and mistrust. Understanding these relations was important when exploring pathways to resilience, as they created the foundation for interactions and relations between two populations and affected opportunities for interventions.

Section B: The social situation of development for a Haitian child

Section B represents the crisis situation that has led to the social situation of development for Ricardo, a Haitian child, in a shelter in the Dominican Republic. There are direct and indirect links between Ricardo and others in his life: his mother, peers in the shelter, the other Haitians and the Dominican helpers, which are in his micro and meso-systems. It is in the micro-system that proximal processes take place in activity settings. It is interactions and relations between different people in activity settings that lead to new demands and the need to develop new competencies and skills. I suggest there is potential for the emergence of a new practice from efforts at collaboration made in relation to activity settings, such as meal times. A new practice would be influenced by the original practice of the shelter, which is part of the Dominican practice and way of life, and by the Haitian practice and way of life. The Haitians and the Dominicans who participate in the activity settings are influenced themselves by their respective nation's practices, resources, traditions and culture, as well as by the historical relations of the two nations as described in Section A. The chrono-system is integrated into the entire analysis, from the historical relationship between the two populations, to their experiences in the present. I propose that it is by exploring what happens in activity settings that practitioners involved in interventions can build and help build the common knowledge needed to promote resilience among both the displaced population and those supporting them.

Background information on Ricardo

Ricardo was 14 years old on the day of the earthquake. He was at home with his cousin when the house collapsed on top of them. Ricardo's left leg was crushed. His cousin died in his arms. When he was found, Ricardo was in critical condition. A medical crew with a helicopter took him to a hospital in Jimani. Roseline, his mother, did not have the correct papers to cross the border so she was not able to accompany him. It was difficult for both of them. Ricardo was afraid and unhappy without his mother, and Roseline knew he was in a bad state and needed help, and she could not be there. While he was recovering at the hospital from having his left leg amputated just above the knee, two Haitian volunteers visited him and helped take care of him. They made phone contact with his mother, for which Ricardo and Roseline were very grateful.

Roseline managed to get the necessary papers and came to Santo Domingo where she easily found Ricardo, because of her contact with the two volunteers. Ricardo and Roseline were then transferred to the shelter. As a single parent, Roseline's economic situation had been unstable before the earthquake and she was worried it would become worse. She was concerned about her son's new disability, and saw this as a new challenge as they waited for a prosthetic leg before returning to Haiti.

There were around fourteen other children in the shelter, aged from 4 to 14 years of age, with ten under 10 years old. Ricardo was the only child with a leg-amputation, and was thus unable to participate with the other children when they ran around. He loved to play football, but he knew that even with the awaited prosthetic leg, he would never play like he used to. Roseline told us Ricardo got on well with the other children. A child had teased him about his leg and then all the parents had a meeting and gave firm orders to the children that this must never happen again, and it had not.

Ricardo's social situation of development

Ricardo was an active and happy boy before the earthquake, playing football and spending time with friends, listening to music, drawing and reading and he was very close to his mother. The consequences of the earthquake led to Ricardo facing a life-changing crisis with multiple new demands. These included bodily changes that needed physical adaptation and learning to walk with a crutch, pain and itchiness in the amputated leg, reduced mobility leading to changes in activity, lifestyle and social interactions, having to cope with grief and loss of loved ones and feeling guilty for his cousin's death, being in a foreign country where he could not understand or speak the local language, staying in a shelter with about 29 other Haitians he did not know and a group of about 15 to 20 Dominican helpers he did not know, being in a group of 14 other children where he was the eldest, and the only one not able to run around, being served food he did not like, and experiencing strong and overwhelming emotional reactions every time someone mentioned anything to do with the earthquake.

In order to point to how people in this kind of situation may be helped, I take one simple example of an activity setting as a site of intersecting practices: mealtime. The administrator at the shelter asked that we speak to Ricardo and Roseline as she was worried about him as he sometimes went for days without eating, and had vomited a few times, yet there was nothing wrong with him medically. She described Ricardo as occasionally animated, but mostly depressed. Her perspective was that his not eating was a sign of depression and emotional distress and that he needed psychological help. His mother, on the other hand, attributed it to his dislike of the food. After more exploration, it was revealed all of the Haitians in the shelter disliked the food. In a focus group discussion with the parents, a mother said:

> The food is very smelly. The smell is bad. The children have many problems here because they cannot drink juice often, (or) milk often. The children are not satisfied, the food smells bad. They give food that has a bad smell. They give the food. But it is not us cooking the food.

This short excerpt highlights three key points that impacted the situation Ricardo was in. First, there were cultural difference in practices of cooking and activity settings of preparing and eating food; second, the parents were concerned about their children's well-being; and, third, there were unequal power relations between the two groups. The new demands faced by Ricardo – of being served food he did not like – both affected and were affected by interactions and relations with others, in the micro-system and meso-system of his situation of development. The situation illustrates how new demands faced by one person are interrelated with the new demands faced by others. In this example, the parents faced new demands while in complete dependency on others with whom they were not able to communicate directly, suffered from physical injuries and did not have control over their own lives to, for example, give the children the food they want to. The Dominican helpers faced new demands in caring for a group of people from a country with different cultures and practice traditions who did not speak their language, and who did not like their food (*my interpretation*: and therefore seemed ungrateful). Considering pathways to resilience and negotiating for health-sustaining resources, in this particular situation, it was not possible for Ricardo to impact on the Dominican practice of food preparation and change the food, so he instead changed his behaviour to stop eating the food that made him sick. One might, at first, argue that not eating is not a demonstration of resilience as if this behaviour and reaction continues it will lead to ill health. However, I suggest Ricardo navigated to an experience of personal resilience in consideration of the resources that were available to him. He adapted to the new demand of not liking the food by not eating.

The role of institutional practices in developing common knowledge to address problems

The differences in food preparation and preferences were mentioned in interviews in all three shelters in the case study research. It was an issue that led to tension in each of the shelters, but was tackled in different ways. The shelter where Ricardo lived was the newest of the three institutions and had been established in direct response to the earthquake. It was funded by an international foundation with headquarters in Nicaragua and was obliged to follow specific operational practices and methods of providing care that represented the ethos and culture of the foundation. The potential for a new practice in this shelter differed from the other shelters as it was influenced by the Haitians, the Dominicans working in the shelters and by the policies and rules of an external institution based in a third country. In this sense, it was a potential site of intersecting practices, where common knowledge about what mattered in each practice might be built and used and indeed a new practice eventually arise.

The administrator, however, shared that she was frustrated and challenged by the numerous foreign representatives from the foundation visiting the shelter and demanding changes in the management operations and procedures. This, together with a constantly changing Haitian population, had made it difficult to create a stable structure of activities and responsibilities in the shelter, where common knowledge might be built and used as a way of mediating cross-practice differences. Of the three shelters, this was the one we heard most accounts of mistrust and miscommunication between the Haitians and Dominicans. The food issue was not resolved in this shelter, and Ricardo was served food that made him feel nauseous till the day he left. The shelter closed down the same week Ricardo and Roseline returned to Haiti.

In the other two shelters, however, the food issue was resolved, and in similar ways. Both shelters were run by the same church and had teams of administrators and staff who were used to working together in caring for others. One of the shelters normally housed unmarried pregnant women and the other, people living with disabilities. Both shelters had adapted the homes to house and care for the injured Haitians. Each of the institutions had a psychologist working full-time to support the Haitians and the Dominicans. The psychologists, working with translators, bridged a gap in communication between the administrators and the injured Haitians, enabling the development of common knowledge that led to collaboration in addressing the food issue. After working there for some weeks, it was clear to the Haitians that the psychologists' motives were to provide emotional support and psychological first aid and help them to find possible solutions to their problems. The Haitians in these two shelters were in the same situation of dependency as in Ricardo's shelter and also afraid to complain about anything directly to the administrators of the shelters. However, they trusted the psychologists and shared their grievances with them about the food and that they were bored and distressed with too much time and nothing to do except worry about their families back home and the future. During this same time period, the Dominican cooks had noticed the Haitians did not eat the food, which offended them and led to enhanced feelings of resentment towards the Haitians who they described as 'lazy'. The cooks shared their feelings with the psychologists as they, too, trusted them.

I suggest that in this example it was the psychologists' ability to listen to, recognize and engage with the values and motives of others, emphasized by Edwards (2017) as an important condition for building the common knowledge, which enabled the collaboration needed between the Haitians and the Dominicans to resolve the food issue. The psychologists discussed what mattered to the two different groups regarding the same activity setting – preparation of the food, with each of the groups separately, and then facilitated joint discussion with representatives from both groups to find ways to address the problem. In both shelters, detailed plans were drawn up to share the cooking, cleaning and maintenance chores in the shelters between the Haitian men and women who were physically able. This had multiple positive results. It gave the Haitians meaningful activities to do, made them active and helped to promote a sense of coping and functioning, and enabled them to eat food they liked and needed for emotional and physical recovery. It also reduced the workload on the Dominicans who were exhausted from working for weeks without much rest, allowing them to recharge their own resilience in the face of the challenges that they faced daily.

Conclusion

In this chapter, I have regarded resilience as a form of development arising in response to crises, when people are enabled to take action in response. I merged concepts from Bronfenbrenner and Morris's (2006) bioecological model of development with concepts from Vygotsky and Hedegaard's cultural-historical theories to create a framework that I suggest is useful for exploring pathways to resilience in this cross-cultural situation. The different levels of analysis based on Bronfenbrenner's model gave rich insight into the impact of relations and interactions with other people, symbols and objects on the child's situation of development – both directly (micro-systems) and indirectly (meso-, exo-, macro- and chrono-systems). The chrono-systemic level of analysis called for an exploration of historical relations, which helped explain the animosity and mistrust expressed and shown between the two groups.

The focus on Vygotsky's concepts of new demands and reactions to new demands gave insight into what motivated participation in proximal processes in activity settings. The focus on Hedegaard's concepts of institutional practices provided an understanding of what the conditions were for the activity settings and reflected the traditions, values of the institutions and the people within them. The institutional practices can be said to have 'allowed and enabled' development in one specific way, or in another way.

I have exemplified the use of the CCCRF with the case of Ricardo's social situation of development, where he was faced with the new demand of having to eat food he did not like. Exploring Ricardo's situation with this model helped provide an understanding of what mattered from his perspective and that of his mother and the Dominican helpers. Eliciting and respecting what matters for others in sites of intersecting practices can produce common knowledge between different groups. When this common knowledge is employed as a resource for collaboration, it can identify what forms of collaboration are needed for meaningful and effective interventions. This was shown in the example of the activity setting of food preparation. I suggest that the lack of established practices and professional resources, particularly a full-time psychologist, in

Ricardo's shelter reduced the opportunity for building the common knowledge needed to address the problem and, therefore, impacted the opportunities for Ricardo in negotiating successful pathways to resilience.

While the primary focus in the CCCRF is on the child, the model provides structure for an expanded focus beyond just the child, including the child's relations with others, relations between the others in the child's world, relations between people and institutional practices, and to the history and prior relations of the two different population groups. All of this information gives us detailed insight into what the situation is, what the child experiences, if possible from the child's own perspective, what others around the child experience, how the child and others influence each other, and, ultimately, what opportunities there are for helpful interventions. Viewing a disaster response using the CCCRF urges responsibility for those planning interventions and emergency responses to carefully consider the roles of all involved in a child's life and not to confer sole responsibility on, for example, only the child, parents or the institution where the child is. This model seeks to show that growth is facilitated by how well parents or caregivers can support an alignment between the demands of the child and the child's demands on his or her environment.

To align the demands, common knowledge may be built through the efforts of the psychologists as it happens in the two shelters who listened carefully to what mattered in each of the potentially opposing practices and who then deployed the common knowledge as a mediating resource to enable active collaboration across the practice boundaries. By adding this to their professional repertoires they were also able to enable people in both institutional practices, Haitian and Dominican, to respond to the difficulties they were facing and to create pathways to resilience which were linked through the efforts of individuals, families and communities while facing the extreme challenges of a potentially traumatic transition.

References

Belfer, M. L. (2006). Caring for children and adolescents in the aftermath of natural disasters. *International Review of Psychiatry, 18*(6), 523–8.

Bisson, J. I., Ehlers, A., Matthews, R., Pilling, S., Richards, D., and Turner, S. (2007). Psychological treatments for chronic post-traumatic stress disorder. Systematic review and meta analysis. *British Journal of Psychiatry, 190*, 97–104.

Bronfenbrenner, U. (1979). *The ecology of human development: Experiments by nature and design*. Cambridge, MA: Harvard University Press.

Bronfenbrenner, U. (2005). *Making human beings human*. Thousand Oaks, CA: Sage.

Bronfenbrenner, U., and Morris, P. A. (2006). The bioecological model of human development. In R. M. Lerner and W. E. Damon (Eds), *Handbook of child psychology: Vol 1, Theoretical models of human development* (6th edn, pp. 793–828). Chichester: John Wiley and Sons.

Boon, H. J., Cottrell, A., King, D., Stevenson, R. B., and Millar, J. (2012). Bronfenbrenner's bioecological theory for modelling community resilience to natural disasters. *Natural Hazards, 60*, 381–408.

Edwards, A. (2010). *Being an expert professional practitioner: The relational turn in expertise*. Dordrecht: Springer.

Edwards, A. (Ed.). (2017). *Working relationally in and across practices – A cultural-historical approach to collaboration*. New York: Cambridge University Press.

Edwards, A., and Apostovlov, A. (2007). A cultural-historical interpretation of resilience: The implications for practice. *Critical Social Studies, 1*, 70–84.

Elkonin, D. B. (1999). The development of play in preschoolers. *Journal of Russian and East European Psychology, 37*(6), 31–70.

Farmer, P. (2010) Never again? Reflections on Human Values and Human Rights (2005). In H. Saussy (Ed.), *Partner to the poor. A Paul Farmer reader* (pp. 487–527). Berkeley: University of California Press.

Galea, S., Nandi, A., and Vlahov, D. (2005). The epidemiology of post-traumatic stress disorder after disasters. *Epidemiologic Reviews, 27*, 78–91.

Goldstein, S., and Brooks, R. B. (2005). *Handbook of resilience in children*. New York: Springer.

Hedegaard, M. (2008). A cultural-historical theory of children's development. In M. Hedegaard and M. Fleer (Eds), *Studying children: A cultural-historical approach* (pp. 10–29). Berkshire: Open University Press.

Hedegaard, M. (2012). Analyzing children's earning and development in everyday settings from a cultural-historical wholeness approach. *Mind, Culture, and Activity, 19*(2), 127–38.

Keys, H. M., Kaiser, B. N., Foster, J. W., Burgos Minaya, R. Y., and Kohrt, B. A. (2015). Perceived discrimination, humiliation, and mental health: A mixed-methods study among Haitian migrants in the Dominican Republic. *Ethnicity and Health, 20*(3), 219–40.

Komesaroff, P. A., and Sundram, S. (2006). Challenges of post tsunami reconstruction in Sri Lanka: Health care aid and the Health Alliance. *Medical Journal of Australia, 184*, 23–6.

La Greca, A. M., Lai, B. S., Llabre, M. M., Silverman, W. K., Vernberg, E. M., and Prinstein, M. J. (2013). Children's post disaster trajectories of PTS symptoms: Predicting chronic distress. *Child Youth Care Forum, 42*(4), 351–69.

Liebenberg, L., and Ungar, M. (Eds). (2009). *Researching resilience*. Toronto: University of Toronto Press.

Margolin, G., Ramos, M. C., and Guran, E. L. (2010). Earthquakes and children: The role of psychologists with families and communities. *Professional Psychology: Research and Practice, 41*(1), 1–9.

Masten, A. S., and Obradovic, J. (2008). Disaster preparation and recovery: Lessons from research on resilience in human development. *Ecology and Society, 13*(1), 9.

Norris, F. H., Stevens, S. P., Pfefferbaum, B., Wyche, K. F., and Pfefferbaum, R. L. (2008). Community resilience as a metaphor, theory, set of capacities, and strategy for disaster readiness. *American Journal of Community Psychology, 41*, 127–50.

Raviola, G., Eustache, E., Oswald, C., and Belkin, G. S. (2012). Mental health response in Haiti in the aftermath of the 2010 earthquake: A case study for building long-term solutions. *Harvard Review of Psychiatry, 20*(1), 68–77.

Scribner, S. (1997). A sociocultural approach to the study of mind. In E. Toback, R. J. Flamagne, M. B. Parlee, L. M. W. Evens and A. S. Kapelman (Eds), *Mind and social practice: Selected writings of Sylvia Scribner* (pp. 266–80). New York: Cambridge University Press.

Skovdal, M., and Daniel, M. (2012). Resilience and coping strategies of HIV-affected children in sub-Saharan Africa. *African Journal of AIDS Research, 11*(3), 153–293.

Summerfield, D. (2001). The invention of post-traumatic stress disorder and the social usefulness of a psychiatric category. *BMJ, 322*, 95–8.

Ungar, M. (Ed.). (2005). *Handbook for working with children and youth: Pathways to resilience across cultures and contexts*. Thousand Oaks, CA: Sage Publications.

Ungar, M. (2011). The social ecology of resilience. Addressing contextual and cultural ambiguity of a nascent construct. *American Journal of Orthopsychiatry, 81*, 1–17.

Ungar, M. (2012). Social ecologies and their contribution to resilience. In M. Ungar (Ed.), *The social ecology of resilience: A handbook of theory and practice* (pp. 13–31). New York: Springer.

United Nations Development Programme. (2010). *Human Development Report 2010. 20th Anniversary Edition. The Real Wealth of Nations: Pathways to Human Development*. United Nations Development Programme.

UNICEF. (2011). *Children in Haiti. One year after – The long road from relief to recovery*.

Vygotsky, L. S. (1998). *The collected works of L. S. Vygotsky: Vol. 5. Child psychology*. New York: Plenum Press.

Walsh, F. (2012). Facilitating family resilience: Relational resources for positive youth development in conditions of adversity. In M. Ungar (Ed.), *The social ecology of resilience: A handbook of theory and practice* (pp. 173–85). New York: Springer.

Weiss, M. G., Saraceno, B., Saxena, S., and van Ommeren, S. (2003). Mental health in the aftermath of disasters: Consensus and controversy. *Journal of Nervous Mental Disease, 191*, 611–15.

Wertsch, J. V., del Río, P., and Alvarez, A. (1995). Sociocultural studies: History, action, and mediation. In J. V. Wertsch, P. del Río and A. Alvarez (Eds), *Sociocultural studies of mind* (pp. 1–34). Cambridge: Cambridge University Press.

World Health Organization. (2010). *World health statistics 2010*. Geneva: World Health Organization.

Yamagata-Lynch, L. C. (2010). *Activity systems analysis methods: Understanding. Complex Learning Environments*. New York: Springer.

Part Three

Supporting the Agency of Children and Young People in Transitions

When Young Adulthood Presents a Double Challenge: Mental Illness, Disconnected Activities and Relational Agency

Sofie Pedersen

Introduction

Young adulthood is often imbued with fundamental existential questions of 'Who am I?' and 'Who am I supposed to be?'. This existential uncertainty is accentuated when everyday life is burdened by massive psychosocial or psychiatric problems and lived in an institutional setting within the frame of social-psychiatry. Young people living with severe psychiatric problems such as paranoid schizophrenia or personality disorders have to face not only general developmental tasks and challenges but also severe and bothersome symptoms, considerable side effects of medicine, and, not least, the social isolation in the wake of living with mental illness.

These young adults are thus faced with a continuous double challenge: they find themselves in the midst of the general challenge of building and mastering what we call young adulthood, developing an independent stance in life, building competences to meet the demands of this increasingly independent lifestyle, starting or completing an education or making the transition to adult work life, all the while building lasting relationships outside a family setting. At the same time, these young adults must cope with the extraordinary challenges that follow from dealing with severe mental illness. Often these challenges are so pervasive that a life outside the institutional setting appears impossible to participate in. This implies that the activities that are shared by their peers are often perceived as out of reach, which in turn may lead to further isolation or the feeling of living life on the edge of normality. In addition, self-understanding, along with the motive orientation, is often shaped by a strong psychiatric discourse and an everyday life within various institutional settings, which in turn may hinder the very development that is being sought.

Treatment options are primarily organized within the realm of psychiatry and are often highly individualized. Despite this being helpful to a majority of young adults who are able to organize and manage their everyday life with mental illness with the help of a traditional psychiatric approach, it is not sufficient (or relevant) for others. It is this group of 'others' that this chapter concerns.

At a private social-psychiatric living facility in Copenhagen, a different approach is taken to life with mental illness with an emphasis on community, meaningfulness and what we could call reconnecting with others via joint activities. Treatment focus is turned upside down in the sense that what would be the focus in the psychiatric system, namely managing symptoms, taking medication on time and so on, is deemed less relevant and not put to the fore. Rather, everyday life is lived – and built – around *doing* things together and developing new motives for participation and engagements with and in the world. This approach draws heavily on cultural-historical activity theory and implies an alternative conceptualization of mental illness, as well as emphasizing the importance of building 'relational agency', as termed by Edwards (2005).

This chapter will propose an understanding of the young adults' problems as *disconnected activities* rather than mental illness and discuss the difference this conceptualization entails in relation to the concrete social-psychiatric practice. The ambition is to present a practical example of how to concurrently co-explore what matters to the young adults and co-create a mutually meaningful community through which motive orientations and capabilities to meet the demands of young adulthood can be developed.

Social-psychiatry: An institutional setting of developmental possibilities and impediments

To frame the social-psychiatric practice in question, I shall briefly give an account of the structure of the Danish psychiatric system. The system comprises three independent organizational units that are all part of the public welfare system, albeit with different organizational anchorage. Psychiatric hospitals and outpatient psychiatry are part of the health care system and organizationally connected. In addition, we have social-psychiatry, which is organized under the social system. Social-psychiatry grew out of a tradition of social work and hence has a focus on building competences for everyday life, outside of a hospital setting. Social-psychiatric living and treatment facilities may be public or private but all adhere to the same regulations for the area, and residency is financially covered by the municipality, as part of the social welfare system.

Social-psychiatric work centres around the challenges of everyday life with mental illness. This implies that the work effort is concurrently aimed at the residents' managing of symptoms of mental illness, as well as supporting them in building a meaningful everyday life for themselves – with the inbuilt imperative of moving towards an increasingly independent lifestyle. This is especially emphasized in the case of young adults, which this chapter will specifically discuss. In many ways, the fundamental imperative behind social-psychiatric institutions is thus developmental; people are assigned a stay with the specific goal of developing skills and competences for an increasingly independent life. In this way, we can consider the social-psychiatric living and treatment facility a developmental possibility in its own right.

At the same time, however, the way the institutional practice is organized means that it may also become an impediment for the very same development that it is supposed to support and facilitate. Allow me to briefly clarify this point: Because of the financial dependency on the social system, young adults are only granted a stay at a social-psychiatric living facility for six months at a time, which may then be prolonged. However, measures of progress and development are mandatory, which means that the social work carried out needs to be translated into concrete measurements of improvement. As a practical consequence, mental illness symptoms frequently become the pivotal point of conversations or work effort, as these are easily measured, and they become a conspicuous part of the institutional culture. Though repeated conversations about mental illness may be an important part of recovering or regaining a sense of control over one's life situation, it may at the same time foster an activity structure around having a mental illness, which in turn implies a possible self-understanding tied to seeing oneself as mentally ill.

A stay at a social-psychiatric living facility is often preceded by encounters with the psychiatric hospitals, and often the young adults have already had what we could refer to as a considerable psychiatric career. This is strongly reflected in the young adults' self-understandings and therefore also in their motive orientation and their perspectives for life. Few are able to formulate what they are directed towards or what they dream of – instead, they rely heavily on their psychiatric diagnosis as both an explanation for their current life situation and predictor of their future. In addition, they experience the demands that they are faced with, if they want to participate in life outside the institutional setting, as too complex or out of reach. The result of this is a tendency to be resigned to or maintain a motive orientation that does not foster much newness.

Psychiatric diagnoses are often brought up as one of the first things, as a concurrent attempt to explain their current situation and an expression of a deep desire to be understood – or maybe even a way of disclaiming responsibility. As an illustration, one of the residents, Andrew, has adopted a self-understanding of being bipolar, which to him implies a life with certain restrictions, in the sense that all kinds of bodily arousal should be avoided. This implies alcohol and drugs, but also intimate connections with the opposite sex, especially if this involves strong feelings such as falling in love. His motive orientation is therefore deeply imbedded in a psychiatric self-understanding related to the avoidance of future manic episodes. As understandable as this may be, it may simultaneously prevent the development of a meaningful everyday life. We shall return to Andrew later.

The strong psychiatric discourse, the illness-framed self-understandings, the resignation and social isolation, along with motive orientations not meeting the general societal demands for an independent lifestyle, are among the core challenges we encounter in social-psychiatry. In addition, problems are individualized, both by the young adults and by the case workers with whom we collaborate, leaving limited space for reconfiguring the life trajectory of the young adult.

Reformulating the problem: From individualized to relational problem conceptualizations

The young adults we encounter in social-psychiatry often carry with them experiences of being labelled or even stigmatized, as problematic, difficult or mentally ill. This entails a rather unfortunate misconception: that the problem, in whatever shape it may appear, belongs to the individual. In turn, this conveys a deep insecurity in relation to their own sense of direction, of motives and basically of ontology: who am I and where am I going? Often previous meetings with the psychiatric system have led to augmented psychiatrically informed self-understandings, which may have the advantage of supporting a compliant collaboration with the psychiatric system. Concurrently, however, this augmented psychiatric self-understanding often carries the disadvantage, in terms of development, of projecting a life in psychiatric terms – needless to say that this is neither inspirational nor stimulating for the motive orientation of the young adults.

To account for how we work to circumvent this challenge of individualized problem attributions, there are two issues that need to be addressed: the first pertains to the relational dimension of mental illness and the second to the role of motives.

The relational aspect of mental illness

I have no intention of providing an account of the history of mental illness, nor the diagnostic understanding of specific illnesses. Rather I will discuss the need to rethink our understanding and conceptualization of mental illness, in the light of a cultural-historical approach. The emphasis will therefore be on the possibilities offered by embracing this theoretical stance and the criticism that could be conveyed towards more traditional perspectives on mental illness will not be directly addressed. General conceptualizations of mental illness imply that it is *the person* (in the singular) who requires treatment, and the social or relational aspect that is inevitably inherent is most often obscured. By emphasizing a *relational aspect* as inherent, I simply wish to point to the fact that human lives are lived interdependently, as dialectically entwined, and mental illness must be comprehended accordingly. The idea of mental illness as a relational matter is not new and draws references to the work of Ronald Laing (2010), and more explicitly that of Erik Wulff (2013); Wulff theorized that schizophrenia was not an illness residing *within* the person but rather a manifestation of defective social relations (for an elaboration, see Holmboe and Risdorf, 2013).

Mental illness as disconnected activity: An attempt at reconceptualization

The idea of mental illness as a relational problem resonates with the work of Karpatschof (1989), who proposes to understand mental illness as *disconnected activities*. I shall briefly present his work as it provides a conceptualization of mental illness that has proved productive in relation to working with the young adults. Drawing on Leontjev's notion of activities (Leontjev, 2002), Karpatschof argues that mental illness can be understood as *disconnection* from the activities that constitute personality: personality is anchored in the ontogenetically developed activity structure, thereby reflecting participation in a myriad of practices and intersubjective relations. Here, Karpatschof employs the concept of *integrated activities* to reflect the embeddedness of people's activities in a shared social meaningfulness, thus emphasizing the inherent intersubjectivity of the human lifeworld.

An integrated activity structure is neither a given nor a permanent condition, but rather something that must continuously be created and recreated – and its meaning renegotiated – in relation to the concrete challenges and dilemmas that life inevitably presents. The notion of *disconnected activities* describes the situation where the psychological pressure on the person has become so intense that it is no longer possible to maintain the activity structure in a personally meaningful way. Here, ontogenetic differences become evident as some people have less well-established social networks to draw on in times of adversity. A well-integrated activity structure allows for being momentarily thrown off-course by life events; however, for some people this may not be the case for two reasons: (a) the strength of the potentially traumatic life event may be too hard to handle based on the current activity structure and (b) the activity structure may be grounded in intersubjective relations and practices that may in themselves have been challenging, for example, growing up with sexual or physical abuse, severe bullying, poverty or parents' substance abuse. The people we encounter in social-psychiatry often present an unfortunate but very understandable combination of both, thus presenting ontogenetic histories of violence, abuse or emotional neglect, combined with social exclusion, drug abuse and futile friendships. This in itself does not *cause* mental illness, but it presents a risk, in the sense of contributing to a potentially fragile foundation for the personality.

To follow Karpatschof's argument, it is paramount to emphasize the foundational intentional or motive-driven aspect of the human lifeworld (see also Engelsted, 1995; Hedegaard, 2003, 2012); people are always being directed towards something in the world – towards building some sort of meaningfulness. In situations where that *something* can no longer be achieved (as the direction of the former integrated activities), new actions and activities are sought out to replace the meaningfulness that is no longer available. To exemplify, these could be attempts to cope with emotional fluctuations through various kinds of self-harm, such as cutting, self-induced vomiting, bashing one's head against the wall repeatedly or via the development of a large consumption of alcohol or drugs (exceeding recreational use), just as it may manifest as obsessive or paranoid thoughts and actions, auditory hallucinations or a distorted sense of reality. This is what Karpatschof terms *disconnection*. Thus, he uses the same psychological dynamic – the foundational human directedness – to explain both the process of establishing integrated and disconnected activities.

Paradoxically, the process of disconnection is an attempt to *maintain* a connection to something meaningful and recognizable – an attempt to maintain the foundation for the personality. The dissolution of the personality structure equals a psychotic state of mind, where the grounding in a shared reality is left behind, and where disintegration of the self is ubiquitous.

Karpatschof's proposition to regard mental illness as disconnection is constructive in the sense that it does not reduce mental illness to either childhood trauma or unbalanced neurotransmitters, but instead insists on explaining mental illness with the same psychological dynamics as are involved in life in general and, thus, not as something qualitative different. A normative reading, however, may suggest that there is a sharp divide between a connected and a disconnected activity, which poses the question of who is to judge the quality or status of an activity – here I see an inherent risk of introducing a normativity in categorizing activities as either or.

To circumvent this potential issue, rather than adopting Karpatschof's terminology, I would propose the more dynamic formulation of *disconnecting* – thus replacing the adjective *disconnected* with the present participle *disconnecting* – to emphasize the active and dynamic process that is referred to. A *process of disconnection* serves to explain the manner in which the young adults describe *processes of disengaging* in shared meaningful activities, the *lack of motives* and a *general loss of meaningfulness* in their lives. So as to not lose their sense of self, and because they were unable to reconnect or re-establish their sense of connection with prior engagements, alternative actions arose that over time turned into activities, such as intensive (and perhaps excessive) marijuana use, obsessive-compulsive thought patterns or self-mutilating behaviour. It is neither pivotal nor therapeutically interesting to establish at what point in time these actions turned into activities and became all-encompassing in terms of the person's motive orientation. Rather, we need a terminology by which to understand this process in a way that opens up to ways of *reconnecting*. The notion of *disconnecting* presents a potential as it allows for a processual grip on a person's trajectory, without normative categorization.

Adopting Karpatschof's understanding of mental illness as a process of disconnecting thus creates openings in terms of treatment that transcends the focus on merely alleviating or removing symptoms or changing behaviour, by emphasizing the need for developing new directedness or motive orientation for connecting with the world.

Motive development and co-creative processes in psychosocial work

The pertinent question of *who one is* and desires to become is central to working with young adults with psychosocial problems. This is so not because they have problems, but rather because this is a *general* question that many young adults are struggling with – and it thus presents a productive vantage point for collaboration. What are the motives for participation in different kinds of practices, or perhaps even the motives for the future? And if these are unclear, fickle or futile, as they often appear to be, then how can the development of motives be supported and nurtured through shared processes of co-creation?

Commencing collaboration with questions relating to interests, hopes and dreams transgresses the normative evaluation of the person and creates a space of possibilities for potential new actions, activities and, most importantly, meaningfulness. It allows us to emphasize the importance of creating or building something with one another – more so than engaging in mutually objectifying processes by making the other person the object of our work effort. Here, I draw references to psychosocial practices established by, for example, Vianna and Stetsenko (2011), Nissen (2006, 2012), Mørch and Nissen (2001), as well as Minken (2002). I will briefly touch upon a few examples, the first being Minken's work in Norway. Minken (2002) established a successful intervention project, where he organized therapeutic work around a joint interest in motorsports. This entailed an open-ended process perspective where the overall goal was to develop new motives for participation and, through this new activity, structures. Minken's approach emphasized psychosocial treatment as a goal-oriented activity *contributing to change* in a person's life; this implies that the person seeking treatment was not rendered an object for the professional's work effort, but rather that the person was *invited to participate* in activities that were continuously co-created and co-developed by the person, other young people and the professionals in relation to a shared interest in motorsport. Thereby, the young person could concurrently maintain and build agency and could thus become (or remain) the central agent in his or her own life. Through joint collaborations on fixing bikes, practising driving skills and cleaning bike engines, the young people not only acquired isolated technical skills but also became engaged in friendships and mutual dependencies in teamwork; learnt (meaningful) discipline; and developed new zones of proximal development by continuously expanding their skills and developing new motive structures. A shared interest in motorsport was thus made the catalyst for a collaborative project that opened up new possibilities for action and participation through which the participants could negotiate and develop new meaning sets – in relation to themselves, to others and to the world. To draw on Schutz's (2005) distinction between different kinds of motives, Minken's project facilitated motives that were *forward-directed* (rather than directed by the past) and thus aimed at building (and achieving) goals for the future.

Minken's approach underlines the need to co-construct new joint activities through which the young people can develop new motives, activity structures and self-understandings. Similar points are found in Stetsenko's proposition for adopting what she terms a 'transformative activist stance' in psychosocial work which emphasizes the co-creative, emancipatory and relational aspect of human development (2008, 2012; concrete examples are provided by, for example, Vianna and Stetsenko, 2011).

Another example originates in my own prior work (Borup and Pedersen, 2010a, b), where the co-creation of a joint home became the collaborative project in a social-psychiatric living facility for young adults. Here, the gradual transformative processes of changing what to some residents felt like a waiting room into a place they could call home implied new ways of relating to one another along with new ways of participating. This in turn altered the ways in which the residents perceived not only each other but also themselves, and it gave way to new needs and motives that were impossible for either of the involved parties to conceive before we started out these transformative processes of co-constructing a home.

There are two important points here that resonate well with the work carried out with the young adults in Copenhagen: the first relates to an emphasis on the process itself more so than the end goal or result; it is through processes of co-creating something and relating to one another that new needs and motives arise, new activities are formed, and thus, in the longer perspective, new ways of being in the world and understanding oneself emerge. The second point is that to obtain good therapeutic results, one need not engage in ambitious activities, such as running a marathon or climbing Mt Everest. On the contrary, the transformative processes can be meaningfully found and co-created in everyday life settings, as I will now try to describe when turning to the concrete social-psychiatric practice in Copenhagen.

Supporting processes of *re-connection*

Young adulthood is full of contradictory invitations, demands and possibilities of whom to become and what to make of oneself, and carries an implicit expectation of individual responsibility for creating a meaningful path in life – especially in a time with a strong discourse of possibilities being endless (see also Pedersen, 2015). A majority of the challenges that young adults are facing relates to *how* to approach and act in such a space of possibilities and contradictions. Their future lies somewhere outside the institutional setting, which requires for them to develop both a motive orientation and the capabilities to handle a more independent lifeform and the inherent demands. Therefore, we need to support and create a zone of proximal development (Vygotsky, 1978) that allow for a young adult to relate to and approach the demands of the world outside the institutional setting. For some this implies developing a motive orientation enabling them to actually recognize and relate to these demands in a sensible manner, and for others it becomes a matter of developing specific capabilities to address the needs and demands they are experiencing. Should the social-psychiatric institution fail in relating to more general societal demands for young adulthood, the institutional setting in itself risks becoming an impediment for further development in that it creates a likelihood for the young adults to linger in what we could call a parallel society – a point also voiced by Bauman (2005).

Our work with the young adults is grounded in the conceptualization of mental illness as presented by Karpatschof, which implies an emphasis on supporting *processes of re-connection*: Re-connection to meaningful practices in which they can expand or build new self-understandings that allows for them to be *young adults*, and not primarily mentally ill. This endeavour is first and foremost facilitated and supported through the co-creation of a strong *sense of community* at the living facility, which theoretically reflects our grounding in CHAT and thus emphasizes the importance of the collective or the social in relation to facilitating individual development (see Vygotsky, 1978; Makarenko, 1974). On a practical level, establishing a sense of community is an attempt to model an ordinary shared housing arrangement among young adults, which implies having to coordinate and share the responsibility for indispensable everyday life tasks such as grocery shopping, cooking and cleaning. These activities are coordinated on the weekly house meeting, where the week is planned, and other joint activities are discussed and coordinated, such as trips, concerts, going to the movies or organizing a joint bicycle repair day. Besides these practical coordinating tasks, the house meeting also serves as the venue to handle conflicts and to share and align hopes and dreams for what a shared future looks like; this is where the young adults, assisted by the staff, build *common knowledge* (Edwards, 2011, 2017, and Chapter 1 of this volume) of what matters in what we are doing with one another and how this micro-community is or becomes meaningful to all. I here take common knowledge as something to not only develop among professionals but also among the young adults and members of the staff – eventually also including the municipal case worker assigned to the case. Evidently, this is an ongoing and demanding task that is continuously challenged by the various backgrounds and experiences that the young adults bring to the table, and the fact that occasionally new people move in (and others out). Despite the difficulties that our insisting on a community in the house may bring, we recognize how the young adults share a directedness and desire to be part of a community, to feel at home and to have a place and a group of people to contribute to. A desire that is often disregarded when trying to understand the motives of people in social-psychiatry or other marginalized positions.

In our experience, the weekly house meetings serve as grounds for establishing relations between the young adults and even relational agency. The relational agency (Edwards, 2005) among the participants arises when they experience how it is possible to discuss and solve conflicts on a collective level, by sharing their perspectives and hopes with one another and in realizing that they may have more in common than what separates them. Or, in Edwards's words, it is the 'capacity to align one's thoughts and actions with those of others in order to interpret problems of practice and to respond to those interpretations' (Edwards, 2005, pp. 169–70). This fosters an enormous sense of belonging and a capability that not only adds positively to the individual self-understanding but at the same time supports relations *between* the young adults and helps form social connectivity.

In addition to the continuous focus on building and supporting the social connections through the emphasis on community in relation to a shared housing arrangement, there is a myriad of individual challenges and interests to meet. I will exemplify in the following pages.

Cheesecake therapy as means of building relations

When Karen moved into the house she had a hard time relating to the other residents; she preferred close and rather exclusive relations with members of the staff, which was partly good in that it allowed for some relations to form and partly presented an enormous challenge in that the relations were so exclusive. At the same time, Karen had a very strong narrative of being severely personality disturbed, and she could explain all her actions by this reference. It so happened that Karen enjoyed baking cakes, which was a passion she and I shared. We therefore started spending quite a lot of time planning which cakes to make, baking them and serving them to the rest of the residents. It was thus a shared interest that could be used as a starting point for building relations – not only Karen's and mine but also relations between Karen and the other residents (who loved cakes and the fact that someone was willing to bake them). On top of this, our shared interest in baking was a way to co-develop our skills; I learnt a lot about experimenting with cheesecake flavours from Karen, whereas she learnt that a big part of baking cakes was the feeling of joy from contributing to the small community in the house. For her, our shared baking practice came to serve as a way into the house, as a way of becoming a member of the community as it granted her a position from where she could participate. Participation presented an immense challenge for her and was something where she needed to develop some skills in relating to others if she were to meet the demands of being part of the community. The interesting point here is that this development was possible because it built on Karen's already-existing motive orientation (baking cakes and relating to members of the staff), which meant that it did not feel like either an imperative or a criticism of her actions or lack of interest in the other residents. For some time, it was therefore more constructive, in a therapeutic sense, to spend my time with Karen collaborating on cake production in the kitchen, rather than having exclusive therapy sessions in the office.

Running shoes versus resignation

The experience of being faced with imperatives, criticism or demands that were difficult to meet were David's (one of the other residents) biggest challenges. Over time, this had led to an immense reluctance to do anything, a resistance towards what he experienced as an imperative to *change* and leave his self-understanding behind. David had long periods of time where he basically gave up on things, spent all of his time playing online games or programming stuff on the computer, as a repetitive action pattern that did not appear to lead anywhere. Various attempts to get him back to school had proved fruitless, and for every attempt he seemed even more resigned and often tried to sleep his day away – mostly to be out of the way of the staff, whom he felt were nagging him. David had two main interests, one being computers and programming and the other being parkour. Parkour is an outdoor training discipline where movement in urban spaces is expanded to include running, climbing, swinging, vaulting, jumping, rolling, quadrupedal movement and so on, depending on what the situation or the environment allows for. It is a rather physically demanding sport, and David had thus refrained from actively practising it for quite some time, although he would often refer to it as something he longed to resume.

Over time, we managed to engage David in going running once a week, in a small running club consisting of him and me (or another member of the staff). He was in rather bad shape, but motivation could be found in relating it to his desire to pick up parkour practice again, for which he needed to be a bit more fit. The running sessions turned out to be excellent occasions for deep and meaningful conversations – about life, challenges, the meaninglessness of his current situation and how far away he felt from living the life he wanted. There was something about both of us wearing running clothes and being physically challenged that made an interesting break with the therapeutic set-up we were able to master back at the house. At the house we were always locked in our formal positions of psychologist and resident, whereas, when out running together these positions were not important; it was more important who could first make it to the next lightning pole or who could challenge the other person to run faster. During our runs, we would not so much talk about formal stuff, but more about music, concerts and dreams for the future. At times, we would walk rather than run because there was so much to talk about, or because one of us was out of breath. Eventually it evolved into a walking practice, where we would do long walks and reflect on life and the challenges that David was facing. The turn to the walking practice coincided with David starting an internship at a computer repair shop where he soon thrived and started perceiving himself as a valuable worker. This led to him regaining enough confidence to restart an education and stick with it. Our conversations then served as a joint reflection space of the challenges that were inevitably part of engaging in new practices, such as education, which was something we could both relate to.

As the brief examples with Karen and David demonstrate, it is not necessarily the bigger questions in life that need to be addressed in order to engage the young adults in developing their motive orientations, but more so it is often the minor aspects of everyday life that may serve as generative starting points for collaboration and the development of relational agency. It is in these small pockets of everyday life where we manage to find space for personal interests that motives for participation exceeding the current situation arise, and where the foundation for new needs and motives can be built. In such relational encounters, agency is developed contributing productively to the activity structure, by ways of constructing or expanding it. Over time, this leads to new ways of participating, new relational embeddedness and meaningfulness, in other words, *re-connection*. This re-connection served to resolve the prior state of dis-connectedness that constituted the mental illness. For various reasons, Karen and David did not display explicit motives to participate in the social community at the house or to pursue an education. However, when their hobby-like interests enabled their building relations so that new ways of participating became possible, new motives for further participation emerged. And though this may seem banal, it targets the tendency to expect young adults in the social-psychiatric system to have clear motives for recovery, an education, a job – in other words, a normative lifestyle. And when they do not display clear motives there is a tendency to find them unwilling to cooperate, or impossible to work with *as* they do not present as *motivated* for development. We tend to forget that the societal demands required to handle an independent lifestyle outside the institutional setting may appear too enormous or out of reach – and the motive orientation to meet them needs to grow, at its own pace, from interests or joyful activities that are already present, in order to be meaningful.

Regaining a grip on youth life: New activities and self-understandings

A developmental challenge that presents itself when living with mental illness is tied to the prevalent psychiatric discourse. Evidently, the psychiatric discourse in itself is not the most prominent problem; however, it is an unanticipated developmental challenge that often proves difficult to overcome. The case of Andrew serves to illustrate this point.

Andrew had lived at the social-psychiatric living facility for a few years. In his late teens and early twenties, he had extensively used marijuana and he had been involved in various sorts of petty crime. Following an arrest and a trial, this lifestyle stopped abruptly. Andrew received a treatment sentence and was admitted to a psychiatric hospital. Here he was diagnosed with bipolar disorder, and over the course of two years at the psychiatric hospital he learnt to perceive himself as *vulnerable*. The logical consequence being that any kind of excitement or arousal should be avoided to avoid future manic episodes. Passivity and a general hesitant attitude followed and became Andrew's prominent mode of being. This led to an array of existential questions for him in relation to the quality and form of life that he could envision for himself.

An intense search for new possibilities began and Andrew's passion for photography became the lever to engage in new activities: He started an internship as a photographer's assistant, which slowly allowed him to develop a motivation of his own to get up in the morning. Over time, the internship developed into an actual job, and gradually Andrew's self-understanding changed into seeing himself as more and other than mentally ill. However, the mental illness narrative, reflecting a strong psychiatric discourse, persisted in relation to a specific part of his life: that pertaining to intimacy and relationships. Andrew was determined not to become manic again so the idea of falling in love was a very remote dream and something that he had accepted was not in the cards for him, given his illness. Over time, as he regained a grip on his everyday life, this idea grew into a contradiction for him as he felt a growing desire to relate to the opposite sex. But he was scared, mainly because he was doing so well and did not want to jeopardize the sense of control that he had.

Instead of having our weekly session in the office, Andrew and I developed a practice of taking long walks and visiting different coffee shops in the city, while exploring the city by foot. It allowed Andrew to smoke without annoying me, and it allowed for the conversation to flow freely between us. We found that this sort of fluid reflection space afforded a more relaxed setting for reflecting on life's challenges together, than a traditional therapeutic session could have. Concurrently, it permitted an approximation of more general ways of talking about problems, thus, moving away from a psychiatric discourse and framework for life in general. In addition, it served to transgress a tendency to objectify each other as fixed positions (as therapist and client) and allowed for us to be two people sharing thoughts on life, albeit from different perspectives.

To return to Andrew's challenges in relation to relating to the opposite sex, it so happened that I was also dating at the time, and I used this as an opening for Andrew to relate to a world that he felt very disconnected from, by sharing some of my own observations and experiences. Gradually, he became motivated for actively engaging in dating, installing a dating app on his phone and relating to the girls with whom he connected. As with other challenges he met in his everyday life, Andrew would share his concerns and insecurities with me, and in relation to his newfound dating activity we would discuss the wording of concrete messages and answers. When messages consecutively turned into dates, we would discuss good venues, things to do and how to work around the fact that he was still living at a social-psychiatric living facility. As for most people, the world of dating is full of ups and downs, and so it was for both Andrew and me; this we were able to share and use each other's input constructively in a joint exploration of and reflection on being part of the dating world.

What the case of Andrew serves to illustrate is that through our continuous walking and coffee-drinking sessions, Andrew and I developed a relational agency that allowed for Andrew to act on a motive orientation that before had appeared impossible to meet, given his rigid self-understanding as bipolar. In this gradual approximation of new activities, Andrew developed his motive orientation further and was able to leave behind what he referred to as a *disabled youth life*. The conversational space that was created between us offered a place for reflection and joint exploration of the challenges that Andrew – and to some extent I – was facing in the course of conducting our everyday life, in relation to work, establishing friendships and potential relationships, and also emancipating the barrier that a mental illness narrative had resulted in for Andrew. The example illustrates that putting an emphasis on rebuilding strong connections with other people and regaining a firm grip on everyday life is a very effective response to not only dealing with mental illness but also how a mental illness discourse may linger on and serve to prevent further engagements in young adulthood. It points to the requirements of the presence of other people to engage in relations with – relations through which concrete spaces for developing new stances in life are co-created that ultimately give way to new self-understandings. Concurrently, it underlines the importance of co-creating meaningfulness and content in life; this cannot be dictated from a position of superiority or knowing-better. Rather, it must be developed as a shared knowledge through the joint exploration of life's opportunities, conditions and demands, and through shared openness and a genuine interest in the other person.

Meeting the double challenge of young adulthood

The young adults we encounter in social-psychiatry are struggling to build a meaningful everyday life in liminal positions in between the challenges and opportunities of young adulthood, on the one hand, and a formal social system, on the other hand, that tend to narrowly label them as mentally ill, or primarily see their *functional* needs and abilities. This presents a challenge of how to best support their development, and ultimately their transition, from a life of narrow institutional dependency to a life of increased social participation and interdependency, and psychological well-being.

I would argue that there are no simple solutions to this, but that we need to emphasize the *processual aspect* of co-creating new possibilities for becoming as open-ended movements and not the implementation of a one-size-fits-all model. The human psyche is dynamic, closely related to the practices in which we participate, and our concrete and situated possibilities for action. Therefore, we need to co-create spaces for participation with one another, to facilitate the development of meaningfulness and agency. In dealing with mental illness, we need to assume a wholeness perspective rather than single out the aspects pertaining to mental illness, detached from everyday life practices. When succeeding in this endeavour, we see how young people (e.g. Andrew and David) manage to develop new ways of integrating their activities and establish new meaningfulness and purpose in life.

Narrowly focusing on mental illness symptoms, for example, by attempting to make the young adults discontinue their self-mutilating behaviour, doing drugs or repeatedly telling them that what they are thinking or experiencing is wrong, may very well spur resistance to collaborate, as these well-intended attempts to help are often experienced as attempts to remove or undermine a person's self-understanding – such attempts are thus often ineffective. When one feels under attack, a considerable effort may be exerted to maintain a recognizable image of oneself and the world however dysfunctional this may be. This was one of the predominant dynamics displayed by Karen when she first moved in. Building a new self-understanding is a long process of trials, negotiations and consolidation – it takes time to recognize yourself anew. The resistance and the conflicts that may arise are not dangerous or to be avoided; rather they should be seen as the main generators of development, because this is where new spaces for becoming arise. This is in line with key understandings of developmental dynamics within the cultural-historical framework (see, for example, Riegel, 1975; Hedegaard, 2003, 2009, 2012).

At the social-psychiatric living facility in Copenhagen, we try to support these developmental processes in relation to motive orientation, new activity structures and self-understandings that reflect being a young adult rather than mentally ill. In our concrete practice, these processes are facilitated and supported mainly by way of two central and interrelated agendas: (1) the continuous focus on building a sense of community and (2) building relational agency around motives or interests that are already present and using these as starting points from which to develop directedness towards and engagement with the world, and more specifically in relation to the demands that the young adults are facing in handling young adulthood.

Processes of re-connection are not an individual matter; they require the presence of other people, of concrete activities to connect to and engage with and a general feeling of belonging somewhere. The joint reflections with Andrew or David, or the cheesecake baking with Karen, would not matter in terms of individual development if taken out of the context of the community. And although the community that we co-create at the living facility may appear unambitious in its focus on basic reproductive tasks, it provides an important arena for developing social relations and acquiring some of the capabilities that are needed to handle general demands for young adulthood. This analysis underlines how developing individual agency in double-challenged young adulthood can be supported and accomplished through the building of shared or relational agency. Furthermore, it is worth remembering that a fair share of the young adults come with personal histories of emotional neglect or abuse and have a hard time relating to other people; acquiring such capabilities is certainly important groundwork for further development and is difficult to achieve without a community to relate to. In that sense, it is the *relational meeting* that is the essence of our work, and building meaningful everyday lives is our shared point of interest, addressing general challenges of young adulthood and its transitions together.

Mental illness may, in clinical terms, linger as a travel companion throughout life but it need not be an obstacle for building and living a full and meaningful life. What we find to be productive in embarking on this process of *reconnecting* with the young adults is for mental illness to lose its status as the primary descriptor of *who the young people are* and *what they can do* in life. Through joint processes of reflection on what constitutes community and what everyday life *could* and *should* look like for us, that very same community is developed and common knowledge of how to understand the concrete struggles, stories and symptoms of the young adults is co-created, contributing to a development of both individual agency and our shared practice.

Through engagements in shared activities and the building of relational agency, it is possible to overcome severe manifestations of mental illness. Methodologically, this points towards increased therapeutic emphasis on collective everyday tasks and on building relations around shared interests, questions and challenges. To employ a theoretical stance of regarding psychological difficulties as disconnecting activities rather than mental illness creates a space of possibilities; both therapeutically and practically. However, there is an inherent and continuous ethical challenge when working with development and motive orientations as it includes the risk of construing a forced motivational project. This accentuates the need to engage in continuous and open co-explorations and reflections with the young adults on *what matters* and how to best ensure that our time together is meaningful.

Acknowledgements

I am thankful to David Brian Borup for contributing to earlier versions of the text, through joint reflections and co-explorations of the social-psychiatric practice.

References

Bauman, Z. (2005). *Forspildte liv. Moderniteten og dens udstødte*, 1. eds., 1. issue. Copenhagen: Reitzels.
Borup, D. B., and Pedersen, S. (2010a). Er udvikling overhovedet meningen? *Nordiske Udkast*, 38(1–2), 104–23.
Borup, D. B., and Pedersen, S. (2010b). Træk tempoet ud af det sociale samvær and Erfaringer med indarbejdningen af den antropologiske psykologis grundmodel. In P. Bertelsen (Ed.), *Aktør i eget liv* (pp. 175–216). Copenhagen: Frydenlund.
Edwards, A. (2005). Relational agency: Learning to be a resourceful practitioner. *International Journal of Educational Research*, 43(3), 168–182.
Edwards, A. (2011). Building common knowledge at the boundaries between professional practices: Relational agency and relational expertise in systems of distributed expertise. *International Journal of Educational Research*, 50(1), 33–39.
Edwards, A. (2017). Revealing relational work. In A. Edwards (Ed.), *Working relationally in and across practices: Cultural-historical approaches to collaboration* (pp. 1–21). New York: Cambridge University Press.
Engelsted, N. (1995). *Personlighedens almene grundlag del I og II. En teoretisk ekskursion i psykologiens historie*. 2. eds., 2. issue. Aarhus: Aarhus University Press.
Hedegaard, M. (2003). Børn og unges udvikling diskuteret ud fra et kulturhistorisk perspektiv. *Nordiske Udkast* 31(1), 27–45.
Hedegaard, M. (2009). Children's development from a cultural-historical approach: Children activity in everyday local settings as foundation for their development. *Mind, Culture and Activity*, 16(1), 64–82.
Hedegaard, M. (2012). Analyzing children's learning and development in everyday settings from a cultural-historical wholeness approach. *Mind, Culture, and Activity*, 19(2), 127–38.

Holmboe, A., and Risdorf, H. (2013). Introduktion til Erich Wulffs fænomenologiske og kritisk-psykologiske analyse af det skizofrene vanvid. *Nordiske Udkast 41*(2), 24–36.

Karpatschof, B. (1989). Galskaben, psykiatrien og virksomhedsteorien. In M. Hedegaard, V. R. Hansen and S. Thyssen (Eds), *Et virksomt liv – udforskning af virksomhedsteoriens praksis* (pp. 104–20). Aarhus: Aarhus University Press.

Laing, R. (2010). *The divided self: An existential study in sanity and madness.* London: Penguin.

Leontjev, A. N. (2002). *Virksomhed, bevidsthed, personlighed.* Copenhagen: Hans Reitzels.

Makarenko, A. (1974). *Vejen til livet: En fortælling om opdragelse.* København: Forlaget Tiden.

Minken, A. (2002). *Alvorlig Moro. Idé og Virksomhet ved Motorsportstiltaket.* 2. ed. Oslo: Oslo Kommune, Rusmiddeletaten.

Mørck, L. L., and Nissen, M. (2001). Vilde forskningsprocesser: kritik, metoder og læring i socialt arbejde. *Nordiske Udkast, 29*(1), 33–60.

Nissen, M. (2006). Pædagogisk psykologi – et bud på en positiv bestemmelse. In B. Elle, K. Nielsen and M. Nissen (Eds), *Pædagogisk psykologi – positioner og perspektiver* (pp. 61–81). Roskilde: Roskilde University Press.

Nissen, M. (2012). *The subjectivity of participation: Articulating social work practice with youth in Copenhagen.* Houndmills, Basingstoke: Palgrave Macmillan.

Pedersen, S. (2015). The ought to be, how to be, or not to be – A study of standards and subjectification processes in high school. PhD dissertation, Copenhagen University, Department of Psychology. ISBN 978-87-7611-924-9.

Riegel, K. F. (1975). Toward a dialectical theory of development. *Human Development, 18*(1–2), 50–64.

Schutz, A. (2005): *Hverdagslivets sociologi.* Copenhagen: Reitzels.

Stetsenko, A. (2008). From relational ontology to transformative activist stance on development and learning: Expanding Vygotsky's (CHAT) project. *Cultural Studies of Science Education, 3*(2), 471–91.

Stetsenko, A. (2012). Personhood: An activist project of historical becoming through collaborative pursuits of social transformation. *New Ideas in Psychology, 30*(1), 144–53.

Vianna, E., and Stetsenko, A. (2011). Connecting learning and identity development through a transformative activist stance: Application in adolescent development in a child welfare program. *Human Development, 54*(5), 313–38.

Vygotsky, L. (1978). *Mind in Society. The Development of Higher Psychological Processes.* Cambridge, MA and London: Harvard University Press.

Wulff, E. (2013). Om konstitutionen af den skizofrene uforståelighed. Bidrag til en subjektkonstruktivistisk teori om 'vanviddet'. *Nordiske Udkast, 41*(2), 37–54.

ID
Children with Disabilities Growing Up and Becoming Adults: Sociocultural Challenges around the Transition to Adulthood

Louise Bøttcher

Introduction

Transitions are changes from one practice to another, each consisting of several activity settings (Hedegaard and Edwards, 2014). In a cultural-historical perspective, transitions can spark a developmental crisis as the child moves from one institutional setting to another (Winther-Lindqvist, 2019). The transition interrupts established relations between the child and its social settings and creates opportunities for new forms of social relations. When the child is anticipating or confronted with tasks that challenge existing ways of thinking and acting, it places new demands on the child's way of participating and stimulates the development of new motives. The child develops new ways of understanding through new ways of participating in social interaction. As the child become a more skilled social participant in the new setting, he or she can participate in activities in new ways and the requirements for participation become more advanced.

Research in disability and transition is mainly positioned within *the social model of disability*. The social model accentuates the central role of legal, societal and social factors and how they cause barriers to equal social participation of children and adults with disabilities, both within and across social institutions (Shakespeare, 2006). This research, taking parents' perspective, has highlighted several problems in the transition process: (1) when young adults with disability finish compulsory school, there is often a limited set of opportunities for them and (2) the institutionalized support to the transition process is full of uncertainties and flaws (Pallisera, Fullana, Puyaltó and Vilà, 2016; Winn and Hay, 2009).

Parents feel that the transition requires extensive work in order to create a stable adult life for their child, both with regard to employment and to general social participation (Dyke, Bourke, Llewellyn and Leonard, 2013). Furthermore, Bele and Kvalsund (2016), using a life course approach in their study of a group of young adults who had been identified as students with special needs during compulsory school, found that the students who had been in special class units had a greater risk of having restricted social networks in their early twenties. The way the students had been supported in mainstream school had long-term repercussions on their transition to adult life.

In understanding institutional transitions, I will draw on a cultural-historical model of transition (Winther-Lindqvist, 2019). The model stresses how institutional transitions commence with a time of preparation both socially and personally. The child might envisage themselves in the new setting. Institutionally, it is made clear that the child is about to move to and be welcomed at the new setting. The crisis of the transition is followed by integration or disintegration in the new setting, depending on how the child settles in and reorients according to the new institutional values and activities (Winther-Lindqvist, 2019). I will use the processual elements from the model to analyse the transition from child to adult, even though this transition is only partly an institutional transition. The shift from child to adult is less clear-cut than the institutional shifts even though it can involve an institutional shift. Nonetheless, the model provides an analytical structure for understanding transitional processes connected with institutional shifts in a larger sense, such as the shift from child within a family to adult within adult institutional settings.

The aim of this chapter will be to outline important challenges associated with the transition to adulthood for young people with disabilities. Children and youth with severe disabilities are in a zone of social concern, because their development is often more complicated than the development of typically developing children and youth. Society is organized according to typical development – for example as age-graded expectations – and thus children and youth with disabilities, and their families, experience repeated mismatches between societal expectations and the individual skills and competences of the child. The transition to adulthood is a good example. Around this time, mandatory school comes to an end based on the assumption that the young people have learnt the necessary skills for life as an adult, typically skills for further education, employment and participation in society more generally. The societal demands and institutional objectives shift from fundamental learning of cultural skills and knowledge to self-organized life as an adult, for example, seen in the choice between a vast array of educational and vocational possibilities for typically developing young people. Societal assumptions that a child at 18 years of age no longer needs parents to take care of him or her can be seen; for example, as the child turns 18, Danish welfare terminates the compensation offered for parents of children with disabilities for loss of income due to the child's increased need for care. This assumption is challenged in relation to many young adults with severe disabilities. Education, ongoing monitoring and/or practical help might continue to be of importance even after the years of mandatory school (Winn and Hay, 2009). Examples from a multiple case study of eight young adults with severe disabilities and their transition process will be used to draw out the sociocultural challenges in the transition to adulthood.

A cultural-historical and dialectical understanding of disability

In Lev Vygotsky's theoretical work *Defectology* (Vygotsky, 1993), the psychological development of children born with a disability is understood within his general frame of child development and how development arises from the child's social situation of development shaped by the cultural-historical development of the society. Vygotsky outlined development as made up of two lines. The first is the *natural line of development*, which is the individual biological maturation. The second is the *cultural line of development*, understood as the socialization process, whereby the child acquires knowledge of and the ability to use cultural tools through his or her participation in social practices. Under normal circumstances, the natural and the cultural line of child development support each other. In their everyday settings, children encounter and participate in activity settings organized according to the cultural expectations to what children at that age level are able to do – or able to do given the support that is also part of the activity setting. The demands and support are built into the organization of the activity settings as age-graded zones of proximal development and are apparent as typical taken-for-granted ways of organizing children's and young people's everyday life within a particular cultural-historical setting.

The situation is quite different if the child has an impairment. The cultural-historical institutionalized demands in mainstream settings do not support and accommodate the development of children with atypical psychophysical constitutions the same way they do with children without impairment. When the fusion between the natural and cultural lines of development functions sub-optimally or breaks down due to this developmental incongruence, it often becomes expressed as *developmental delay*, meaning the child's developmental level as a whole is different and often behind what is typically expected in relation to the chronological age of the child (Bøttcher and Dammeyer, 2016). Many types of disabilities are associated with developmental delay; some impairment slow down biological maturation, others mainly impact through the difficulties the child experiences with participation, impacting on the child's possibilities for developing higher mental functions and relevant social skills.

The zone of social concern arises, because asynchrony with normal age-graded expectations and support increases the risk of cultural deprivation. Values about appropriate developmental skills are inbuilt in activity settings, along with cultural age-standards, as *social developmental windows* (Bøttcher and Dammeyer, 2016). During the opening of a social developmental window, development towards a particular developmental skill is supported through the institutional organization. Specific age periods are associated with an abundance of social opportunities that are related to current cultural-historical ideas about age appropriateness. When the age period ends, specific social opportunities disappear or are at least strongly reduced. As long as the child is able to develop along the typical developmental trajectory, the cultural-historical opening and closing of social developmental windows provide the child with relevant demands and opportunities. However, for the child following an alternative developmental trajectory, out of sync with social developmental windows, relevant peers and activities might not be as readily available. To exemplify, students with disabilities in the Western part of the world are all included in mandatory school providing them with activities, teaching them essential knowledge and skills, adult monitoring and a social group to belong to. However, the time after mandatory school is often associated with a decrease in social institutionalized support. The young adults with disability might participate in, for example, community day programmes, but contrary to young adults without disability, they might still need help and supervision in their leisure time (Davies and Beamish, 2009). Young people who had gone to special schools often lack a social network after the end of mandatory school (Pallisera et al., 2016; Winn and Hay, 2009). Furthermore, the level of funding after mandatory school is experienced as insufficient to support the continued education of young people with developmental delay (Davies and Beamish, 2009). Thus, across studies, we see a mismatch between the continued need for supported learning and a societal withdrawal of institutional support and financial resources that accentuates the disability not only in the present but also in the future as the development of the young adult is not supported in an optimal way.

However, developmental trajectories are never inevitable but are actively created by children, parents and professionals. In cases of more profound or multiple disabilities, overcoming the incongruence needs to be managed through the creation of alternative institutional trajectories, either as individualized adaptations within a mainstream setting or by placement in specialized institutional settings. Managing transitions and creating alternative developmental trajectories often requires a lot of work from parents and professionals (Dammeyer, 2010; Davies and Beamish, 2009; Dyke et al., 2013).

Methodology: Transition and disability

The design of the present study was inspired by themes from the existing research in the area of disability and transitions, but took another theoretical approach. The point of departure is the dialectical disability approach outlined above. According to a cultural-historical methodology, the social conditions are only one side of the developmental process associated with the transition to adulthood. The other side is the young adult, his or her intentions and way of participating in his or her everyday social situations (Hedegaard and Fleer, 2008; Hedegaard, 2008). It is only through understanding the person's participation in the institutional practices and her or his involvement towards relevant goals in the practice that we can begin to understand the development in competences and motives that is at the heart of a successful transition. The methodological consequence is a design that makes it possible to include data on the particular social situation, including impairment, and locally established demands and support in order to understand the congruence or incongruence with demands and support in the new practices and how they create the challenges associated with transitions.

Another methodological inspiration is the life course perspective. The life course methodology emphasizes the complex cumulative developmental impact of earlier experiences. Furthermore, it embraces the idea that the developmental trajectory of a person is linked with other persons and general cultural-historical constraints and opportunities in specific time periods. Recognizing the importance of the life course perspective, this study focuses on how motives, competences and conditions in the transition process are related to earlier demands and opportunities and projects towards the future.

Design

The practice settings of children and young people with severe disabilities in Denmark are guided by the Salamanca Declaration (1997) and societal value positions about inclusion. The welfare system and the municipality have the obligation to ensure that families with children with disabilities and people with disabilities have equal opportunities for social participation (for example legalization on social service no. 369 from 18 April 2017).[1] I interviewed eight young people and their parents about their previous and current life situation and dreams about the future. All eight participants had severe cerebral palsy (CP) and severe difficulties in developing verbal speech. Despite the similarity in impairment, their life situations differed a lot, from Emilia attending mainstream high school to Susan and Frederick with substantial developmental delay in emotional, cognitive and/or communicational abilities. The young participants were between 15 and 26 years of age and all in the middle of the transition process towards life as an adult.

The study used a combination of interviews with the young participants and interviews with their parents. All participants were interviewed twice. The first set of interviews focused on the life history of the young participant and the family. The second set of interviews a year later were follow-up interviews, exploring what had happened in the past year and in regard to the transitional challenges identified in the first interviews. The interviews were individually tailored to accommodate the communicational preferences of each of the young participants. Susan and Frederick found the interview situation too cognitively or emotionally demanding, and interviews were substituted with discussions about their communication with them and their pedagogue and language therapist instead. The case of Susan was supplemented with an interview with her music therapist when it turned out she had had an important role during Susan's transition process.

References in parentheses refer to statement numbers in the interview material.

Table 12.1 Characteristics of the young participants

Participant	Age	Current communication and transportation means	Social situation
Susan	26	Communication board, some words, body language. Walks in low manual wheelchair.	Finished adapted youth education. Temporary living unit. Waiting for opening at chosen institution for permanent living.
Sarah	22	Helper translates verbal language, letter sheet for spelling. Uses power wheelchair.	Finished adapted youth education. Own flat with UPA.
William	21	Helper translates verbal language, yes/no with eyes. Uses manual wheelchair.	Adapted youth education, technical music production line. Live at home with UPA.
Frederick	20	Communicates yes/no with eyes, uses communication book. Uses manual wheelchair.	Adapted youth education at boarding school. Headed for institutional living.
Jonathan	19	Uses gaze-controlled voice-output system (Tobii), yes/no with eyes. Uses manual wheelchair.	Specialized youth education at boarding school/Egmont. Headed for UPA and own flat.
Emilia	16	Uses gaze-controlled voice-output system (Tobii), helper talks/elaborates, yes/no with eyes. Uses power wheelchair.	At home. Attends local high school with practical helpers. Headed for UPA, university and independent living.
Freya	15	Uses hand- and gaze-controlled voice-output system (Tobii), iPad with communication programme, yes/no with words/mimic. Uses power wheelchair.	At home. Attends local school with practical helper. Headed for high school, UPA and independent living.
Magnus	15	Helper/teacher translates verbal language, iPad with communication programme. Uses power wheelchair.	At home. Attends local school, self-constrained special class. Headed for 'Efterskole' and afterwards adapted youth education.

Findings

Transition from mandatory school to youth education: Motives and uncertainties

School transitions are prepared for socially, collectively and subjectively. While Winther-Lindqvist (2019) focuses on the transition from kindergarten to reception class, the social preparation also goes for the transition to further education. The educational policy in Denmark has stressed the need for all young people to complete a youth education[2]. In Denmark, 'youth education', as a term, refers to all post-secondary education that does not qualify for a vocation in itself, but qualifies for further education at universities or university colleges or further vocational training. 'Youth education' may be high school or school aimed at vocational training. To support this policy, municipalities have specific young people's education counsellors with responsibilities for organizing information meetings with parents and students several times during the last two years of mandatory school and discussing future plans with students. Thus, the phase of anticipation and preparation described in relation to school start also applies to the transition to youth education. The difference is the possibility of choice. Young people have to consider which youth education to choose (e.g. high school versus school for vocational training). Thus, this institutional transition is interwoven with considerations about what one would like to do afterwards, what kind of adult life the young person envisions for him or herself.

The educational trajectory for young people with disabilities after compulsory school contains two main possibilities. They can attend mainstream education, for example, high school, similar to young people without disabilities. However, in 2007, a new law entitled young people with disabilities, who are unable to partake in mainstream youth education, to three years of adapted youth education.

The preparation phase is important because it allows the young people to mentally engage with expected core activities in the future practice and initiates the neo-formation of new motives. However, for several of the participants, the preparation for the transition from mandatory school to youth education was a period of uncertainty rather than anticipation. Contrary to students without disabilities, the young people in the study had fewer options. Unless the family lived in an urban area, there may be one local option only for adapted youth education. Jonathan and his parents found that the place he was offered was far from what he needed.

> Jonathan's father: I visited the place. It was an old school building they had converted into an adapted youth education unit. I was really negative, when I came home.
> Interviewer: Why?
> Jonathan's mother: There were stairs everywhere.
> Jonathan's father: It was on the first floor. And there were stairs. The bathroom was downstairs and no guarding on the stairs. We could just image him in his wheelchair, going over the top.
> Jonathan's mother: There was no physiotherapy at the school, he would have to go by bus to somewhere else. ... And the teachers, they had no knowledge about communication at all. (Jonathan parents interview 1, statement 301–16)

The anticipation took the shape of dread. Jonathan needed teachers and professionals who knew how to support his further development of augmentative and alternative communication (AAC). The negative impression was related to the suspicion that the institutional objectives and demands and support in the practice settings were poorly related to Jonathan's current needs and future desired type of life. Jonathan had applied for another (more expensive) adapted youth education that specialized in young people with physical and communicational impairment, organized as a boarding school, but his application had been declined. Thus, there was a mismatch between the place Jonathan and his parents were motivated towards and the place they had to prepare for.

Another of the participants for whom the preparation of the transition from mandatory school to youth education turned out to be uncertain was Emilia. Emilia and her family had always had the dominating motive that Emilia should participate in mainstream settings as much as possible and live a life as close to her peers as possible (Emilia parents1, 95). Emilia had attended mainstream school all along. Her goal was to become a researcher in science and thus she needed her high school examination to continue to university. Based on these two motives, the idea was that Emilia should attend a local mainstream high school. Emilia was an extremely competent communicator with her gaze-controlled voice-output computer and was mainly challenged by her more strenuous and time-consuming work processes. The idea was for her to take fewer subjects each year and finish in five years instead of the typical three years. Emilia felt prepared: 'I had the necessary grades' (Emilia1, 55). However, the young people's education counsellor declared her 'unsuited' for high school and the head of the local high school rejected Emilia's application despite her having the required grades:

> Emilia's mother: These people, they hold such power over the future of young people. They wanted her to take her high school exam as single subjects and it takes forever. Like, this was their idea about Emilia's future. While we thought she should have a life as close to a normal youth life as possible. (Emilia mother1, 95)

Similar to Jonathan, Emilia and her family felt that the institutional objectives and demands and support in the suggested practice setting were poorly related to her future desired type of life. Luckily, the town had two high schools and the head of the other high school accepted Emilia as a five-year student without further ado.

A third participant who experienced uncertainty in the transition from mandatory school to a new place was Freya. She and her family wanted her to do what many of her peers do to: spend an extra year at an 'Efterskole'. An 'Efterskole' is a boarding school where students follow mandatory school subjects often along with other subjects in relation to particular interests such as art or outdoor life. All families are required to pay part of the expenses themselves, while the state pays the rest. Freya had known for a long time she wanted to go and they had visited the particular school which had experience with including students with disabilities (Freya parent1, 89). However, due to Freya's need for assistance, the municipality would need to add additional funding. Her municipality resisted providing the necessary funding, which made the preparation for the transition full of uncertainty:

> Freya's mother: So right now we're kind of panicking in case it fails with the boarding school, both because we think it is unfair, Freya really wants to go, but also, what's the alternative? (Freya parents1, 95)

Across all three examples, the young people were individually preparing themselves for the transition by imagining how they would like to participate in the desired institution. However, their time of preparation was also a time of social resistance and uncertainty rather than socially supported preparation for the transition that is the societal policy. The parents of Susan, William and Frederick also described elaborate negotiations with the municipality before they managed to secure the transition to a desired education unit (Susan parents1, 221; William parents1, 219; Frederick parents1, 69). The problem was located in the transition process and the lack of societal backup for the young person with disability's institutional transition to youth education – very much in contrast to societal goals in relation to young people without disabilities.

The time after the transition to the desired place – all three were successful in the end – was much more straightforward. Even though the new activity settings contained many new demands, the receiving institutions were experienced as welcoming and competent in accommodating their practice to the young persons and supporting their participation and appropriation of new competences.

The impact of individual capacities in the time after the transition

For some of the participants, the move to youth education was at the same time a transition to move out of their childhood home. The pressure for a move around the same time as typically developing peers was partly based on sociocultural ideas such as 'after eighteen, then you need to try to be on your own. You shouldn't continue to live at home' (Susan parents1, 208) and – in the case of Jonathan and Frederick – an institutional necessity to move to a boarding school to attend an adapted youth education accommodated to their needs for AAC. Several of the participants found the time after the transition very difficult. Starting with Susan, her parents had tried to prepare her for the move out of home to a boarding school. They had talked about it and bought furniture and she had participated in assembling her new furniture. Still, at the time of the parting she became extremely upset and she continued to find it very difficult to live away from home. She was mainly non-verbal and communicated by pointing to symbols at her communication table. However, the challenge in the new situation was not just a matter of lacking the right symbols, but rather the continuation of a life-long experience of being overwhelmed by her emotions:

> Music therapist: This whole long process. The starting point was Susan's huge longing for her parents. To say goodbye. She has had it like this since kindergarten, really longing and really … painful. … We could talk about it, but it was as if words weren't enough. … She could handle it in a song called 'Lasse Lasse Little'. Then I ask, Susan, I wonder, when you say goodbye, does the world get very big for you too [The song goes 'The world is so big, so big, Lasse Lasse little']? And then she pointed [to express non-verbally], 'the universe get so big and I get so small'. (Music therapist, 5)

The crisis was connected with the demand of living away from home and her parents that set forth emotions she did not have the competences to handle. The music therapist supported Susan through a combination of songs that contained and expressed the difficult emotions. In parallel to the songs, Susan worked with the inclusion of new symbols for her emotions on her communication table. Together, these activities supported Susan's development of higher mental functions in relation to her emotions and the neo-formation of a motive to share and further handle her emotions with the professionals and her parents through communication:

> Susan's father: She needs to learn to handle emotions. What are these emotions I feel whelming up inside, right now?
> Interviewer: Does she talk more about emotions?
> Susan's mother: There was a period [after the move] where it was very important for her. (Susan parents1, 331-3)

Susan's parents experienced her new motive for sharing and understanding emotions in the time after the transition. Thus, we can hypothesize that even though Susan was engaged in collective preparation for the transition to life away from her childhood home and parents, the subjective process of anticipating herself in the new setting required her to mentally and symbolically engage with ideas of the future and this was beyond her ability at that time. Thus the difficult transition was connected to Susan's lack of higher mental functions to reflect and handle her emotions at the time of the transition, both during the preparation phase in which Susan was unable or unwilling to engage with the imagination of a future living away from her parents and the realization phase, where the new situation elicited strong emotions in Susan. For Susan, the state of crisis following the transition took several years while she slowly began to integrate into her new social situation.

Frederick is another of the participants for whom the transition was very difficult. Frederick had no formal communication system at the time he started at the boarding school. At home his mother has extensive knowledge about him and his preferences and could either anticipate them completely or ask the right questions which Frederick would then answer yes/no with eye blink or sounds. He had prior experiences of being away from his parents at respite care, during which he would sleep poorly and in general not be comfortable (Frederick parents1, 76). At the boarding school, he would be at the mercy of people who would not know his needs and preferences the way his mother did at home and, without a formal communication system, he had no independent way of expressing his needs and preferences. Thus, he had reason to dread the transition and lacked the means to express and share his feelings.

In the first couple of months after the transition he slept badly, got uncomfortably tense and sweaty (Frederick parents1, 78). On top of the demand to live away from his parents and home, Frederick was confronted with another new demand: he was required to express himself actively with a communication book with a particular conversational structure that he needed to learn (pragmatic organized dynamic display, see Porter, 2007). The new activity with the communication book created a crisis between the demand to express himself and Frederick's learnt, passive way of participating in communication, waiting for others to take the initiative. The demand was integrated in many activity settings, in which the professionals considered themselves as role models and demonstrated how the book worked and demonstrated the motive of the activity with the book; to express and share what was on one's mind.

During the next couple of months, Frederick adopted the particular communicational strategy required to use the book. He began to express not only statements about his immediate condition (e.g. being in pain or thirsty) but to make demands and contributions to the social setting in wholly new ways, for example, by expressing that he wanted to buy a present for his sister on her birthday (Frederick pedagogue1, 51). The activity with the book had developed the way Frederick experienced his relation to the surroundings. Thus, the resolution to the crisis of moving out of home was resolved as Frederick began to build a motive to express himself, aided by his current social support and its possibilities for independent expression. Frederick became well-integrated in his new social setting and joined many of the activities and social groups at the boarding school.

For young people with severe disabilities, the time after the transition can be difficult as they encounter new demands at the same time as they have lost the tailored support of the old setting. This is even more pronounced for young people with delay in development of communicational skills, such as Frederick and Susan. For them, the challenge of the transition to life away from their parents threatens their basic sense of being understood and feeling safe. Even though Freya and Jonathan also found the transition to the new setting demanding, they both had the capacity to express the experience of being overwhelmed from time to time and they could also take action to handle the situation, by withdrawing to their room (Freya2, 56-8), choosing to spend the weekends back home (Freya2, 76-86; Jonathan parents2, 144) and texting home (Freya parents2, 76). Frederick and Susan both needed types of support reminiscent of early childhood to reach a positive resolution of the developmental crisis into a neo-formation. The very specific form of support was necessary to help their development towards higher mental capacities for adult life outside their childhood home and stress the need for some young people to participate in extensive structured and tailored education for a period beyond the age of 18 to continue their development.

Transition beyond: Towards an imagined future of adult life

The specific institutional transitions and neo-formations are interlinked with a broader move from childhood to youth and beyond. Several of the young participants were actively positioning themselves to move towards particular futures. Some of these futures could be related to institutional transitions, for example, the transition from high school to university (Emilia). However, the considerations reach beyond the specific institution and relate to what type of adult life that is desirable – and possible. Due to their extensive impairment and their inability to carry out activities such as eating, dressing and other basic needs on their own, the transition process to adulthood needed to be seen in relation an upcoming bifurcation into one of two possible main life trajectories. As the young people move into adulthood, they can either move towards life in an institutionalized living unit or independent life in their own house or apartment with user-managed personal assistants (UPA) financed by the welfare system. To be eligible for UPA, the young adult (age 18+) must be able to plan and direct her or his own life. Being eligible for UPA, hoping to become eligible or considering the (few) possibilities among institutionalized living units figures in the transition to adult life for all the participants.

Similar to the transition to youth education, the transition towards adult life is riven with uncertainties for several of the young participants. It was or had been uncertain whether they would be considered eligible for UPA and thus able to live the independent life they were dreaming of. It is a strong motive in many of the participating parents as well as the young participants themselves to be eligible for the UPA:

Jonathan [with Tobii]: I would like to live independently (Jonathan2, 54).

The Danish context contains a particular institutionalized practice with the motive of supporting the development towards being eligible for UPA. Egmont Højskolen[3] is a unique folk high school founded in 1956 with the aim of creating more life opportunities for people with disabilities. The learning environment combines students with and without disabilities and offers subject teaching in 'life with user-managed personal assistants' and 'my life- my responsibility'. The students with disabilities hire personal assistants among the students without disabilities. Jonathan attended the second part of his adapted youth education at Egmont. The activity settings at Egmont placed new, high demands on Jonathan that were beyond what he was capable of at the beginning (Jonathan2, 10–13, 38–40). However, the presence of supportive teachers and supportive practices enabled him to engage in his new responsibilities and gradually acquire new skills and competences, thereby becoming able to participate in new and more advanced ways. Egmont is an institutional support of the preparation for the transition to adulthood that assists the individual with disabilities to prepare for adulthood in a very concrete and practical sense. Another of the participants, Sarah, who was living in her own house with UPA, linked her present ability to manage her life with the demanding environment she encountered during her time at Egmont (Sarah1, 101–19, 145–65).

After the transition to a life with UPA, the young people struggled to find a place in society. They had ideas and dreams, but felt unsure whether their dreams would be societally supported. Emilia got nothing but top grades in high school and wanted to become a science researcher in physics, but would it be possible for a person who communicates with a gaze-controlled voice-output computer?

> Emilia [email interview]: In the future I dream about going to university. Actually, I think it is more than a dream, it is beginning to seem more and more realistic. It is only in four years' time, so I am thinking about it. ... I have got a new good friend, who has infused me with additional zest for life because he is an associate professor at a university, uses Tobii [the gaze-controlled voice-output computer Emilia uses for her communication] and he is also a really sweet and pleasant person and despite his ALS, he can sustain the job. (Emilia1, 52–3)

The quote revealed both the feeling of uncertainty and the hope that arose from meeting someone in a similar situation who did what Emilia would like to do in the future and thus provided her with a concrete example of institutional and societal support for her future dream.

The eldest participants all had pensions as they had been deemed unable to hold a job that could support them economically. Thus in an age period where their peers were involved in vocational and academic education or jobs and developing their ideas about themselves as adults from being involved in different concrete practices, the young people in the study found themselves in a societal limbo without opening future opportunities. Several of the parents also expressed concern that the time after youth education would be characterized by fewer opportunities:

> Frederick's mother: We asked at the last meeting, where do the young people go when they end [the youth education at the boarding school]? They go to different places. Most return to their home municipality. And that is really a shame, because I worry that they don't know the PODD-system. And then it is not used. (Frederick parents2, 153)

The worry that Frederick was at risk of losing his communication system was real as it happens often in the transitions between institutions (Socialministeriet, 2013). Jonathan's father was also worried (Jonathan parents2, 192). William was a fourth example. William was interested in technical music production, which he could perform using his gaze-controlled computer. He had attended a local unit for adapted youth education that offered a music production line for three years. At the time of the first interview, he was unsure about his future and how he would be able to use his skills as a music producer (William1, 659–90). A crisis arose from the incongruence between his motive (to become a music producer) and the existing opportunities in society. Despite the societal objective of education for all, including young people with severe disabilities, there is a lack of opportunities to use the education afterwards. The individual crisis was solved by William's father, who negotiated and created a new opportunity for William to work as an assistant at his former adapted education unit. However, this solution hinged on William's father and his extensive experience and knowledge about negotiating with social workers in the municipal administration (William father1, 147–9). Even though it demonstrates the important cultural-historical point that people place demands on the practices based on their motives (Hedegaard, 2014), it also reveals how the developmental conditions of children and young people with severe disabilities are very dependent on their parent's ability to struggle for improvements and adaptations. Children and young people without resourceful parents will be left with poorer conditions. The transition processes to adulthood for young people with disabilities were challenged by a mismatch between services during childhood and youth aimed at supporting learning and development and services after the age of 18 in which the motives of continued learning and development seem less institutionalized.

Discussion

For young people with severe disabilities, the transition to youth education created tension and crisis that fuelled the deconstruction of earlier competences and motives and led to the development of neo-formations. This was especially clear in the case of Susan and Frederick, for whom the transition to a boarding school was extremely difficult, but also facilitated important developmental gains in their psychological development. The demands and support from the professionals with specialized expertise in young people with severe disabilities and development of AAC created new motives and skills for communication that led further development in social relations and social participation. For Sarah and Jonathan, the transition to Egmont was similarly demanding, but also supported development of subjective organizational ability to organize their own life, thus supporting them in their development towards their dream and hope of being eligible for UPA. For Emilia, the transition to high school was already led by her motive to become a science researcher, but this leading motive was supported in the demanding environment of mainstream high school and her successful integration in it.

Institutional transitions are part of broader life transitions

Still, the institutional transition to youth education was also part of the broader transition from child to young person and adulthood. The preparations before, as well as neo-formations and possibilities for integration into the youth education setting after, the transition are part of the larger preparation for adulthood. The choice between different types of youth education forces young people to start considering what type of adult life they consider desirable. For many of the young people in the study, the youth education activity settings contained activities pointing towards possible futures, living away from one's parents, practising managing one's own life or learning subject matter for a desired future as a scientist or music producer.

At the same time, the interweaving between the transition to youth education and the transition to life as an adult implies that the uncertainty and societal resistance associated with access to desired educational units spill out to the wider developmental opportunities they expect and imagine. Jonathan felt unsure about whether he would be granted UPA. Emilia did not yet know whether she would be allowed to study at the university in an adapted way as she did at high school or whether she will be accepted as a researcher in a more distant future. William was unsure of how he could get the opportunity to continue to develop his skills in music production. For young people with severe disabilities, the transition to adulthood seems riddled with uncertainties between desired futures and possible futures. While uncertainty about the future is probably a common feature of this life period for most young people in Western countries in the twenty-first century, the uncertainty seems more pronounced for young people with severe disabilities. They experience societal resistance and fewer opportunities both at the transition to youth education and in the transition to adult life in general. The impairment of the young people in the study – not being able to walk and not having (intelligible) verbal language – partly explains the different set of opportunities, but not all. Discriminative ideas about people with disability, lack of provision of financial support and geographical availability of services and educational units created a restricted set of life trajectories to aim for. The uncertainty about the future and future opportunities enters as concern about how future activity settings will not support the leading motives of the young participants.

The closing of a social developmental window

As the young person's time at the youth education closes in, a social developmental window is also about to close. On the one hand, there is no age limit on when to begin with UPA and thus the age period is not necessarily associated with a final decision between independent life with UPA and life at an institution. On the other hand, without institutional support, young people like Frederick and Susan will not be able to develop the higher mental functions and communicational skills necessary to be eligible for UPA. The time after youth education is associated with a decrease in support of learning and development. Institutional living units have fewer resources compared to, for example, the boarding school in the study and offer leisure activities rather than actual education. Young adults with severe disabilities and delayed development need continued possibilities for education understood as systematic, supported development of higher mental functions to integrate into their adult life (Clarke et al., 2011).

For the more resourceful participants eligible for UPA, the time after youth education was also a time of shrinking opportunities compared to childhood. They were in youth education or had attended youth education, but employment prospects were scant. Jonathan, Emilia, William and Freya all imagined themselves in professional positions but feared or experienced societal resistance rather than support. Contrary to earlier transitions, there is no clear position for them to image as part of the preparation for the transition to adulthood.

Conclusion

For young people with severe disabilities, the transition to youth education and towards adulthood can foster positive developmental crises. However, the incongruence between the young person with disability and societal demands suddenly increases as the young person approaches chronological adulthood and is met with common sociocultural expectations such as being able to leave home and manage their own life. To access institutions that supported the motives and motive development of young people, they and their parents had to struggle. The continued motive development is impeded by shrinking social opportunities and a pressure to be regarded as an adult around the time of chronological legal age, when key decisions about their future life track are about to be made. For all the young participants, their developmental leaps during this transitional period were possible through their meeting with institutional motives and demands. At a societal level, there is a need to loosen up the institutionalized demand of young people with severe disabilities to be regarded – at least in an administrative, financial and institutional sense – as adults at the age of 18. Some will be ready, some will not. Service offers – especially with regard to continued possibilities for education understood as systematic, supported development of higher mental functions – need to be open to the slower developmental speed of young adults with severe disabilities by cooperation across service agencies responsible for children and youth and for adults.

Managing transitions and creating alternative developmental trajectories often require a lot of work from parents and professionals. For many families, imagining and creating a future for their adolescent and young child with disabilities presents a complex set of challenges and problems without a clear pre-existing solution. To find a solution calls for networks of professionals that, along with the young people themselves and their parents, formulate long-term developmental goals for adult life and the type of support that is needed. It calls for the building of relational expertise (Edwards, this volume) that involves families and professionals building an expanded understanding together of the challenge related to creating an adult developmental trajectory for young people with severe disabilities.

Note

1. https://www.retsinformation.dk/Forms/R0710.aspx?id=191895
2. The 1993 objective was for 95 per cent of a cohort to complete a youth education before they turned 40; in 2017, the objective was revised to 90 per cent of a cohort to complete a youth education before they turned 25.
3. https://www.egmont-hs.dk

References

Bele, I. V., and Kvalsund, R. (2016). A longitudinal study of social relationships and networks in the transition to and within adulthood for vulnerable young adults at ages 24, 29 and 34 years: Compensation, reinforcement or cumulative advantages? *European Journal of Special Needs Education, 31*(3), 314–29.

Bøttcher, L., and Dammeyer, J. (2016). *Development and learning of young children with disabilities. A Vygotskian perspective.* New York: Springer.

Clarke, S., Sloper, P., Moran, N., Cusworth, L., Franklin, A., and Beecham, J. (2011). Multi-agency transition services: Greater collaboration needed to meet the priorities of young disabled people with complex needs as they move into adulthood. *Journal of Integrated Care, 19*(5), 30–40.

Dammeyer, J. (2010). Parents' management of the development of their children with disabilities: Incongruence between psychological development and culture. *Critical Practice Studies, 1*, 42–55.

Davies, M. D., and Beamish, W. (2009). Transitions to school for young adults with intellectual disability: Parental perspectives on 'life as an adjustment'. *Journal of Intellectual and Developmental Disability, 34*(3), 248–57.

Dyke, P., Bourke, J., Llewellyn, G., and Leonard, H. (2013). The experiences of mothers of young adults with an intellectual disability transitioning from secondary school to adult life. *Journal of Intellectual and Developmental Disability, 38*(2), 149–62.

Hedegaard, M. (2008). A cultural-historical theory of children's development. In M. Hedegaard and M. Fleer (Eds), *Studying children. A cultural-historical approach.* Maidenhead: Open University Press.

Hedegaard, M. (2014). The significance of demands and motives across practices in children's learning and development: An analysis of learning in home and school. *Learning, Culture and Social Interaction, 3*, 188–94.

Hedegaard, M., and Edwards, A. (2014). Transitions and children's learning. *Learning, Culture and Social Interaction*, 3, 185–7.

Hedegaard, M., and Fleer, M. (2008). *Studying children. A cultural-historical approach.* Maidenhead: Open University Press.

Pallisera, M., Fullana, J., Puyaltó, C., and Vilà, M. (2016). Changes and challenges in the transition to adulthood: Views and experiences of young people with learning disabilities and their families. *European Journal of Special Needs Education, 31*(3), 391–406.

Porter, G. (2007). *PODD Kommunikationsbøger* [Translated from Pragmatic Dynamic Organised Display. Communication books.] Handikram: Gistrup.

Salamanca Declaration (1997). http://static.uvm.dk/Publikationer/1997/salamanca.pdf.

Shakespeare, T. (2006). *Disability rights and wrongs*. London and New York: Routledge.

Socialministeriet (2013). *Mennesker med komplekse kommunikationsbehov – en analyse af tilbud og barrierer for indsatsen på området* [Persons with complex communicational needs – an analysis of service offers and barriers]. http://kommunikation.socialstyrelsen.dk/.

Vygotsky, L. S. (1993). The fundamentals of defectology. In R. W. Rieber and A. S. Carton (Eds), *The collected works of L.S. Vygotsky: Volume 2*. New York: Plenum Press.

Winn, S., and Hay, I. (2009). Transition from school for youth with a disability: Issues and challenges. *Disability and Society, 24*(1), 103–15.

Winther-Lindqvist, D. (2019). Becoming a schoolchild – A positive developmental crisis. In M. Hedegaard and M. Fleer (Eds), *Children's transitions in everyday life and across institutions* (pp. 47–70). New York: Bloomsbury.

13

Supporting the Transitions to Work of Autistic Young People: Building and Using Common Knowledge

Anne Edwards and Yvette Fay

Introduction

Knowing about my diagnosis has really helped as I get support. Being able to tell people what is different about me makes a huge difference.
– Young person with ASC in Wittemeyer et al. (2011), p. 26.

An Autistic Spectrum Condition (ASC) is commonly described along the lines of 'a behavioral disorder that includes deficits in communication and social interaction, and a series of behaviors described as "repetitive, restricted, and stereotyped patterns of behaviors, activities and interests"' (Schall, Wehman, and McDonough, 2012, p. 190), which also leads to increasing levels of anxiety throughout adolescence (Chen et al., 2015). Partly because there is a growing understanding of the condition and a broadening of the definition, recent evidence from the United Kingdom and the United States reveals its high incidence, with a UK estimate of 1 in 100 children affected in some way (Baird et al., 2006) and a US estimate of 1 in 68 (Chen et al., 2015). There are economic as well as personal and social consequences arising from the prevalence of autism. A report on transition to adulthood for the UK All-Party Parliamentary Group on Autism (Allard, 2009) referred to an estimation that autism costs the UK in the region of £28 billion a year and argued that improving transitions into adulthood could help reduce that figure. There is much to be done: in the United Kingdom only 15 per cent of adults with ASC are in full-time employment (National Autistic Society, 2018); in the United States young people with ASC have the lowest employment rate among young people with disabilities (Chen et al., 2015), while transitions into post-16 further education (FE) can also be problematic (Shepherd, 2015).

These problems are recognized. In the UK, there have been a series of national strategies for adults with autism, which aim at ensuring that they are supported to get a job and stay in work (National Autistic Society, 2015). The breadth of the problem that these strategies have been attempting to address was laid out in an Autism Education Trust report on outcomes for young people with ASC (Wittemeyer et al., 2011): only 17 per cent of young people with ASC indicated they had the help they needed in finding a job; only 15 per cent had the support and help they needed to stay in a job; while, encouragingly, 53 per cent reported that other people's understanding of ASC had made a difference in enabling them to do the things they wanted to do. But progress towards developing that kind of understanding in the workplace is slow. In 2016, Autistica, a major UK charity that supports research into autism, listed transition to work as eighth in a list of 10 autism research priorities on its website: 'How can we encourage employers to apply person-centred interventions and support to help autistic people maximize their potential and performance in the workplace?'. To date, Autistica has yet to address this priority.

The wording of the Autistica priority, with a focus on person-centred support, is nonetheless useful. National government-led strategies that encourage employers to create conditions to enable the contributions of workers with special needs can help change mindsets, not least by highlighting the social responsibilities of the industrial and commercial world. But current research shows that employers' understanding of ASC needs developing (Chen et al., 2015), and even the most well-intentioned employer is likely to benefit from specific guidance on the nature of person-centred interventions for potential employees with ASC, primarily because ASC presents itself in so many different forms. From this perspective, the idea of a spectrum is itself a little misleading: it is more accurate to think of profiles of strengths and needs for each individual with ASC. The smartphone app that we will discuss later is an attempt to respond to an individual profile in ways that will ease both the transition into the workplace and transitions between tasks that occur once in employment. In addition, we shall suggest that an app which is controlled by the young person becomes a resource, or second stimulus in Vygotskian terms, for solving the problems of independent and interdependent adjustments to workplace demands and learning.

The conceptual framing

A number of interrelated terms that are commonplace within cultural-historical approaches to human learning need to be rehearsed briefly at this point: practice, demand, transition, motive orientation, common knowledge and agency (they are explained at greater length in Chapter 1). From a cultural-historical perspective, practices are made and inhabited by people. Practices are loaded with the history and values of previous actors in the practice and, at the same time, are open to change through the intentional actions of current actors who bring other histories and also respond to changing external demands. There is, therefore, potentially at least, a dialectical relationship between person and practice: people may shape and be shaped by the practices they inhabit. Institutions such as schools and workplaces are made up of practices where what matters, or the motives, in each institution gives shape to the practice and where institutions mediate external demands, such as good examinations results in schools and profitability in workplaces. These higher order motives or purposes are translated to a more micro level where they become recurrent demands. Practices therefore carry demands that arise from both the histories of the practice 'this is the way we do it here' and from institutional responses to new external demands 'the new safety regulations mean you must always wear a helmet'.

Hedegaard, mindful of the dialectic just outlined, has cautioned us that, when trying to understand how people learn by propelling themselves forward in activities in practices, we need to attend as much to the recurrent demands that learners meet in a practice as we do to what the learner brings to an activity (Hedegaard, 2012). This analysis, as Hedegaard notes (Hedegaard and Edwards, 2014 and Chapter 1), opens up a helpful way of thinking about transitions. Learners usually become familiar with the recurrent demands in activities in one institution, such as family life, and then have to re-orient themselves to new demands when they enter a different practice with different activities and different demands. Key to their being able to make adjustments to engage with what matters in the new activities, in the practices of the new institution, is the ability to recognize the new demands presented by the activities.

When a recurrent demand is correctly identified, the learner can begin to orient themselves towards it and respond to it by acting in ways that are expected in the practice, such as by wearing a safety helmet. In doing so, the learner creates a new personal motive orientation. Hedegaard explained the development of a new motive as follows: 'Motive development can then be seen as a movement initiated by the learner's emotional experience related to the activity setting'

(Hedegaard, 2012, p. 21). The development of a person's motive orientation in a practice is therefore connected to their sense of who they are and what they can do in the practice. The development of a productive motive orientation may therefore be impeded by excessive anxiety or by an unrealistic sense of one's position within a practice. If we return to the definition of ASC which opened this chapter, we can see how challenging making a transition into work might be for a young person with the condition.

Our argument is that a young person with ASC, who is making the transition from school to college or the workplace, can be helped in making adjustments and develop a productive motive orientation. In order to do so, they need to make clear what matters to them, the motive orientations they are bringing to the new setting, and they must be explicitly told about what matters in the new activity setting. This point brings us to the idea of 'common knowledge', explained in Chapter 1. In her analyses of collaboration across practice boundaries (Edwards, 2010, 2011, 2012, 2017), Edwards has explained that common knowledge consists of what matters in those practices, that is, the motives that shape the practices and the activities within them. These different motives are understood by all the collaborators and the resulting common knowledge becomes a resource that enables collaboration.

For example, we could see that one motive for a teacher might be achieving a high attendance rate for pupils so that the students can access the curriculum, learn and get qualifications; while for a social worker an important motive might be strengthening the family to give support to the child. Common knowledge consists of mutual knowledge of both sets of motive and, when used as a resource, it helps professionals from different practices to negotiate joint action in their work with a vulnerable child. In those circumstances, common knowledge can be used to mediate a carefully calibrated joint response to the complex problems presented by a child's developmental trajectory. Edwards's studies have therefore shown that by using common knowledge professionals are able to exercise a relational form of professional agency when tackling a problem. Equally, professionals working alongside a family member can do so relationally, drawing on the insights of the family to help them develop their agentic responses to the problem (Edwards, 2005). These responses are likely to be new purposeful activities.

Here we come to agency, the final term to be explained, which for us is evident in the unfolding of intentional actions in purposeful activities. We are not suggesting that agency should invoke the idea of the heroic individual. Rather, our premise is that agency can be strengthened when working alongside another person, as in the example of the teacher and social worker or professional and client just discussed. Cooperation to strengthen individual agency is captured in Edwards's notion of 'relational agency' (Edwards 2005, 2010, 2017, and Chapter 1, this volume). In brief, relational agency is the capacity to work agentically alongside another person to both interpret a demand and respond to it. As we have just explained, this kind of relational work is mediated by common knowledge, knowledge of what matters to each other when interpreting and responding. Exercising relational agency therefore involves a capacity to communicate with others, to be able to discuss what matters for oneself and to be aware of what matters for the other person. For young people with ASC the development of this relational form of agency involves building and using common knowledge and developing new motive orientations in the new practices.

In the present study, we have taken the idea of common knowledge as a resource and partially stabilized it within the design of a smartphone app. The app, containing the captured common knowledge, then operates as a tool that allows the young person with ASC to recognize the demands in the new setting. At the same time, it makes explicit their current motive orientations and reveals to others what will enable them to respond agentically to recurrent demands. A key feature of the app is that it is a tool that is controlled by the young person when in the workplace. We want to emphasize the point about control, as we shall argue that providing a young person with the app as a tool allows them to take some control over their own actions, to work both in independent and interdependent ways with others and so develop new motive orientations that enable them to engage with the demands of college or the workplace and learn how to participate in and contribute to the practices they are entering.

Young people with ASC and the use of technology

Our focus on technological support for the transition from school for young people with ASC is not unique. Chen et al.'s (2015) review of research on autism and employment pointed to the value of assistive technologies such as iPads in the workplace, increasing independence and successful employment outcomes. One UK example of assistive technology for ASC is the Brain in Hand app, which offers a number of anxiety reducing features including a detailed diary, and users also have the opportunity to pay for 50 hours per month of text or telephone support from an autism expert. It is not cheap: the app together with the support feature costs slightly more than £100 per month. It also differs from the app we are developing, despite a laudable primary focus on anxiety reduction, with a lack of attention to building common knowledge about what matters to the young person and the employer as a way of assisting the young person's engagement with workplace demands. Another difference is that the 50 hours of support shifts the focus from developing interdependence at college or work to a reliance on someone outside the workplace.

The emphasis on in(ter)dependence, control and engagement is central to a review of US research and practice on successful transitions into the workplace for young people with ASC (Schall et al., 2012). Schall and colleagues also recognize how digital technologies can assist in the development of self-determination: 'Youth with ASD [Autistic Spectrum Disorders] can be empowered in the workplace with the use of equipment such as smart-phones and personal digital assistants' (p. 194). They continue: 'Self-determination requires that the teenager with ASD learn the knowledge, demonstrate the competency, and identify the opportunities necessary to exercise freedom and choice in ways that are valuable to him or her' (p. 195). They are not arguing for the creation of a self-absorbed individual, indeed they tie self-determination to a work ethic in employment. Rather, they point to how digital technologies can help young people with ASC demonstrate what they are capable of and identify the demands and possibilities within workplace practices.

Schools have also long regarded technology-enhanced environments to be helpful to support the learning of students with autism (Guldberg, Parsons, Porayska-Pomsta and Keay-Bright, 2017); yet there remain concerns that the use of technology such as tablets and smartphones can increase the social isolation of young people with ASC in and beyond school. A recent seminar series funded by the UK Economic and Social Research Council (ESRC) examined the threat and potential of 'digital bubbles' by reviewing the research evidence on the uses of technology for people with ASC (Parsons, Yuill, Brosnan and Good, 2015).

One contributor to the ESRC seminar series, Barnabear, who himself has ASC, in part addressed some of these benefits by discussing how technologies can be bridges helping people to communicate. He suggested that they can be buffers allowing information to be read when convenient rather than in real time and they can be filters by limiting information to key points. The research team summarized Barnabear's presentation as asking the key question: what technologies are needed to help people with autism in understanding, navigating and interacting in and with the world (Parsons et al., 2015). Another young person with ASC has, at least in part, answered Barnabear's question by designing an app, the MiContact, which helps similar young people to make eye contact when interacting with others. The 2017 team winner of the BT Ireland Young Scientist Business Bootcamp, Ciara Ní Ghríofa, has successfully trialled the app with a small number of students and demonstrated that it is directly addressing a need by enabling the young people to meet classroom demands by engaging with their teachers and peers.

This emphasis on how the young person with ASC can be enabled to navigate practices and interact effectively, as we have already indicated, is also central for us. We aim at overcoming the dependency that is often encouraged by those who support people with learning disabilities when they engage with technology (Seale, 2014). Our intention is to help prepare the young person for their entry into a new practice and engagement in and with changing activities in the practice. Barnabear spoke of technology as a potential bridge between the young person with ASC and others in relation to how communication occurs. We recognize the value of these points and have incorporated them in the app we are developing. But with our attention to motive orientation and common knowledge, we are strengthening the bridge to include the opportunity for a growing sense of what matters in the workplace and how these recurrent demands can be recognized and approached by the young person, where useful with the person-centred support of co-workers.

The study

The study is in three stages and is planned to run over three years: we are writing at the start of year two. The three stages are as follows: *Year 1*: An interview study with key stakeholders and review of literature on autism, transitions to work and technology. *Year 2*: The design and development of the app and small-scale field testing leading to modifications of the app. *Year 3*: (subject to funding) A large-scale trial of the app.

The aim of the interviews in the first year was to elicit what mattered for students with ASC and a degree of learning difficulties and their parents and for employers and educators in relation to the transition of the young person. The insights gleaned were to inform the development of the app so that the questions and prompts on the app were fit for the purpose of helping the young person navigate the demands of the practices they were entering.

Edwards interviewed people identified by Fay in her role as assistant head teacher at a special school with responsibility for securing work placements for the older students. The following people were interviewed: teachers working with older students at a special school where 42 per cent of the intake has ASC ($n = 3$); an FE college tutor working with ASC students; young people with ASC who were about to leave special school ($n = 4$ as a group); parents of young people with ASC who were about to make the transition to college or work ($n = 3$); employers who took young people with ASC on work placements ($n = 5$); and young people in employment ($n = 2$). The latter were accessed via a large national company which supports and employs people with ASC. Confidentiality was assured and the ethics of the methods employed were approved through the committee system of the special school. Involvement with the project was entirely voluntary as potential participants were all given the opportunity to decline the invitation to engage (opt out) and parental permission for involvement was sought for the four students (opt in).

The interviews were all digitally recorded and notes were also taken. The recordings were not transcribed, but the notes allowed the researcher to trace back to the actual terminology used in the recorded interviews. The interviews with the teachers and students were carried out at the school; the FE tutor, the employers and the two employed young people were seen in their workplaces; and parents were visited in their homes. The interviews with all the participants each lasted around an hour and, with the exception of the four students, focused on eliciting expectations for the transition, what they thought mattered for young people making the transition, how the transition was and could be supported, what their own concerns were, and how parents, school, college and workplace worked together. Interviewees were asked to be concrete in their responses, focusing on actions in activities wherever possible and were asked to identify what mattered for them, what were their motives as they explained their actions.

The four students were sent a short outline of what would happen when Edwards visited the following day and the note included a picture of her. When they met, Edwards explained to them that she needed their help with the study and they were given two prepared worksheets: one asking them to identify what they wanted other people to know about them at college or work and the other asking them to identify what they wanted to know about starting college or work. There was considerable variation in writing ability in the group so Edwards had prepared small cards with likely phrases written on them, such as 'How do I get there?' and 'I like to do things one at a time'. She also wrote phrases on blank cards, which were dictated by the students during the one hour session such as 'I have a sense of humour'. The students discussed the options as they selected them and wrote them down, frequently providing clear rationales for their decisions.

The findings

In this section, we focus on what we discovered mattered most for the different participants. It was important for us to elicit this strand from the interview data as we needed to be sure that we would be designing an app that could capture these concerns and aspirations.

The young people

The majority of responses from the students to the opener 'I want people to know these things about me' were positive statements: 'I am good [at] helping and fixing stuff'; 'I like computers'; 'I'm good with animals'; 'I enjoy doing art and I am good at it'; and 'I play football on Sunday'. Each student also mentioned at least one way in which the environment could be structured to help them: 'Sometimes I need to go somewhere quiet'; 'I need clear instructions'; and 'I like to do things one at a time'. The latter statements were all on the cards supplied by the researcher and did not spontaneously arise in the students' conversation. The opener 'When I go to work or college I want to know' predictably elicited long lists of areas where the students were anxious about the details of the first day. Responses included questions about break time and lunch time and who will be there to help them and tell them what to do? They also asked if there were places where they could go to be quiet and questions about finding their way around, such as 'Where is the canteen?' Also, predictably, they wanted to know how to get to the workplace and when to leave. There were, additionally, quite a few personal interests, such as 'Will I need a membership card to use the gym?' It was clear that they had projected themselves forward to the new situation and needed some certainty about the spatial and ordinal parameters of their day. They were also asked about the jobs they would like to have and responses included bricklaying, car washing and hairdressing. No one had questions to ask about what was expected of them in those roles, what they would be doing and how they should do it. This gap in their responses suggested that their anxieties about the practicalities had perhaps created a barrier to thinking about what they would actually do and why they would do it.

The two young men in employment were interviewed together. They had been on a short work placement in the department before being offered jobs there. The person responsible for supporting young people with ASC in the department had prepared a short YouTube clip showing how they would walk from the underground station to the building in which they would work, who they would first meet and what the department looked like. They found this very helpful. They also felt supported by the whole team and not just the key person. Adjustments to the environment had been made, so that they had headphones to cut out noise, were seated next to each other and knew where they could go for a quiet period. They were doing data transfer tasks, which they enjoyed and were very good at, thereby easily earning the very fair salaries they were being paid. They had not wanted to be overloaded with demands at first: they reported that they had been worried about getting overwhelmed emotionally if that happened. But once they grasped the demands of the job, they did not want to be 'underwhelmed'. Their task demanded considerable accuracy, but the demands were consistent, indeed repetitious, and they apparently quite quickly oriented themselves to its regular demands and disliked 'slow days'. They thought the idea of the app was useful and suggested adding something about young people's lives outside work to its format.

The parents

The parents (all mothers) were very clear about the strengths and needs of their children and welcomed the prospect of the app as a resource for them to support their children's transition by also helping them to understand the demands of the workplace. One mother spoke of how useful it had been for her to visit the workplace where her son was undertaking a work placement organized by the school. They were all anxious about their children's anxiety. However, while the young people were focused on the details of transport and the order of the day, the parents were more concerned about how others would react to their children's 'aggression to himself' or dislike of being 'told off'. They all talked of how their child could be best supported: 'He is obsessed about time, we use an egg timer'; 'He needs prompts to be able to do anything'. In brief, these responses suggested that parental/carer involvement in populating the app is likely to be useful, bringing their insights about what matters for the young person into the common knowledge held in the app.

The employers

The conversations with the employers consistently demonstrated considerable empathy for how the young person was able to make sense of the work environment. They were aware that each young person was different, some needing 'a safety blanket around them' to begin with and all recognized that they needed routine and to be able 'to get into the swing of things'. They were also clear about what they wanted to see in the work of the young person. As well as 'punctuality', they also wanted them 'to show some interest in coming into the workplace, ask questions, get involved, enjoy what they are doing'. 'We want people to progress themselves.' These are quite high demands requiring some degree of agency, when compared with the expectations and concerns of the young person. As we have seen, the focus group students could envisage themselves in a role such as bricklayer or hairdresser, but didn't indicate any awareness of the demands of the role or how it might change over time.

This apparent inability to envisage the actual demands of the workplace was also noted by one of the parents: '[Name's] sense of who he is and what he needs doesn't match reality.' This lack of sensitivity to the actual demands of a job was brought out very clearly by an employer who had been a teacher and was now running a charity that created a supported work environment. He described the problem of young people who 'adopt a presentation of person in a supervisor role, when they have missed the detail of the job ... we help them see that the key is in the task and not in mimicking the way it is done'.

The employers also paid a lot of attention to preparing the young people for entry into the workplace and liaison with both the school and the families. They all recognized the need for a key person in the workplace for immediate guidance; but they also recognized that everyone who came in contact with the young person was part of a wider workplace support system. There was a strong awareness of the need to go slowly to begin with and prevent the young people making errors as 'that can be devastating for them for a long time' and to think in terms of progression and a gradual reduction in the levels of support 'we need to see that someone is progressing'. Also thinking of learning over the longer term, the employers all spoke in favour of starting preparation for work as early as possible in the young person's school career.

The educators

The school teachers noted the extent to which the students were supported and 'nurtured' at school. All three teachers also used terms that indicated student fearfulness about the move to college or work describing it as 'scary' or 'terrifying'. They explained the school's attention to students' life skills through students taking on increasing responsibility within the school in order to grow their confidence and independence in preparation for the transition. They were therefore aware that they needed to prepare young people for work, but recognized that they could only do it in general terms. They observed that the role of parents and carers in helping with the young person's applications for college or work needed to be encouraged: 'Sometimes they stand back and think we are the experts.' It was also noted that as the students have few recognized qualifications they need to prove that they have other qualities. They all agreed with the employers that preparation for leaving the school should start early in their secondary school careers.

The FE tutor welcomed the individual student profiles that special schools supplied and found it important that the students contributed to the profiles. Demands on students included a much faster pace of work, no consistent pedagogic style across the tutors and the need to move around the college building to attend specialist classes. She also noted how helpful it was if teachers from the schools spent time in FE to better understand the demands and brought students with them prior to their making the transition to help reduce student anxiety. Liaison with parents arose only when there was a problem.

Overview of the findings

In summary, the transition into college or the workplace called for a way of capturing the motives of both the young people and the employers or FE providers to keep the young persons' anticipations grounded in the reality of the demands in the new setting. The employers and FE tutors particularly noted the need for the young people to develop new motive orientations, which would allow them to recognize and respond to new demands and to navigate the practices in the new environment. The employers and FE tutors also expected the young person to become increasingly independent as learners in the new settings. The school teachers were limited in their capacity to prepare the young person for the specific demands of the new settings, while the parents appeared to be an underused resource in supporting the transition.

The demands on the design of the app were therefore quite wide-ranging; but above all it needed to be a resource or tool that would reduce the young person's anxiety; enable them to make sense of what was required of them in the study situation or job; help them clarify what mattered for them in and out of the workplace, be able to ask for support when needed and capture their growing understanding of college or workplace practices. There was also a need to enable the relational engagement of parents and carers in supporting the young person.

Developing the app Me at Work

Table 13.1 indicates the broad categories of what mattered for each set of interviewees in relation to the common knowledge to be stored on the app. In identifying the key topics, we found ourselves in agreement with the point about focusing on demands and actions made by Silver and Parsons, when discussing adults with high-functioning autism rather than the group we were focusing on. They suggested that these adults should be encouraged 'to consider questions like: "What might happen to me?", "What do I need to know in this situation?" and "What do I need to do?" rather than questions about the other, for example, "What is he or she thinking?" or "What will he or she do next?"' (Silver and Parsons, 2015, pp. 93–97).

Table 13.1 Demands on the app mentioned in the interviews

Sources of ideas	Demands on the app
The young people at school	I need to know details about the day and the workplace
You need to know things about me to help me at college or in the workplace
I am good at some things
The young people at work	These are things that are interesting about me outside work
The parents	It can be helpful if parents can be part of the transition process
The employers	The young person needs to know what we expect of them in the job they will be doing
We expect to see some progress over time and a lessening of dependency
The educators	The school can help prepare the young person through developing life skills, but can't focus on specific demands in specific work places
The young person and family need to have some control over the transition
The students should present a rounded profile showing their capabilities

The next stage was to design a wireframe or framework for the app. This is shown in Figure 13.1.

```
┌─────────────────────────────────────┐
│ Front Page with six tiles/tabs: This is me; where I │
│ work; what you need to know about me; what I        │
│ want to know about working here; what I already     │
│ know about working here; what my employer wants     │
│ me to know about working here.                      │
└─────────────────────────────────────┘
```

| This is me I am…… I like to….. I am good at.. | Where I work | These are things I want you to know about me | This is what I want to know about working here | This is what I know about working here | This is what my employer wants me to do at work |

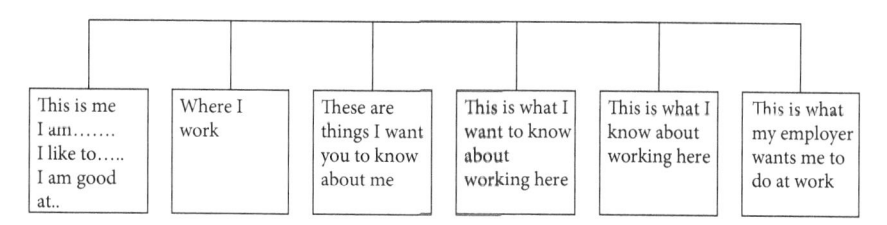

Figure 13.1 The outline design for the app Me at Work.

Each tab takes the user to a page which the young person will populate with the help of a template. The college tutor or employer will provide content for the second and sixth pages. This will be regularly emailed to the young person or their parent/carer, and they will upload it. This process helps address the need for increased parental contribution to the transition as they are to be asked to check that the content is up-to-date and discuss the content with the young person. The second page could include the following information in preparation for the first day at college or work: the bus stop, walking from the bus stop to the entrance, maps, video clips or photographs of the exterior and interior of the building (reception, work space, etc.), a picture of the person who will meet them, where they will sit, safety clothes and so on. The page can be updated as demands change, for example, moving from sweeping the warehouse to going on deliveries, working with Joe instead of Jane and so on.

The remaining pages are to be populated by the young person, perhaps with the help of parent or carer. Each page offers an 'ideas bank' gleaned from the interviews and the research literature, from which the young person can select. In addition, they can add their own statements. There will be notes for guidance to support the use of the app and again there is a role for parent or carer here. Figure 13.2 is an example of the content for the third page of the app.

We are currently in negotiation over the production of the app and will evaluate it though a small-scale trial to enable initial amendments and then are planning a national trial. Evaluation will focus both on its feasibility and feedback from users; but we are also interested in the extent to which it supports

> **The ideas bank**
>
> I need clear instructions
>
> I need a timetable for the day
>
> I like to do things one at a time
>
> I don't like lots of noise
>
> I sometimes need to go somewhere quiet
>
> I like to get things right
>
> I need time to think
>
> I get lost easily
>
> I have a sense of humour

Figure 13.2 Outline of ideas for 'These are things I want you to know about me'.

the growing agency and learning of the young people as, using the app, they develop their motive orientations and become expert in navigating the demands of new practices.

Final reflections

The chapters in this book are examining how challenging transitions are accomplished. The contributions explain how new motive orientations are created by people as they enter new settings, and what part of common knowledge, in our study comprising what matters for the young person and for the workplace, plays in creating what Barnabear, in his contribution to the digital bubbles seminar series, had called a bridge (Parsons et al., 2015).

The bridge we have attempted to stabilize within the design of an app consists of common knowledge: (i) what the young person loads onto the app about what is important for them both permanently (I need to be told one thing at a time) and in relation to the next day or week (Will I need to bring a packed lunch?), and (ii) the employers' information about what is important for them in the college or workplace, the demands that the young person needs to recognize and respond to in activities within workplace practices. As newcomers, at least initially, the young people need to recognize these demands. They need to see that, as one employer put it, 'the key is in the task and not in mimicking the way it is done'. In brief, they need to develop motive orientations that allow them to meet the demands of the organization.

The intention, as we have already explained, is that the app acts as a second stimulus, a resource to help the young person agentically recognize and respond to the expectations embedded in the practices of the organization they are entering and, over time, to adjust to fresh demands when their tasks also change. But the app is not meant to be a replacement for support from others. It is designed to enable relational working and interdependence, both with the young person's family and with college or workplace colleagues. As already indicated, Edwards has written at length about relational agency as a powerful form of joint action, which can strengthen the agency of participants and which is mediated by common knowledge. We would want to emphasize here the app's potential for engaging the parents in relational work as part of the support system, at least initially. The content of the app is also intended to reduce the anxiety that previous research has pointed to (Chen et al., 2015) and our informants confirmed.

For all of these reasons, we suggest that the app may be of use beyond the ASC community for young people with other learning challenges as they make the transition into college or work. Indeed, in all our discussions about the use of the app with other researchers, special needs experts, employers and educational psychologists, its wider utility is always raised as a topic.

We started the chapter with an overview of the challenges faced by those who are aware of the need to find ways of supporting the engagement of adults with ASC in workplaces. There is still a very long way to go, as the figures we quoted suggest, but the strategies, reports and research reviews we have referred to indicate a willingness to tackle the challenges. We hope that the resource we are currently creating proves useful in these endeavours.

Acknowledgements

Thanks to the following people for extremely helpful conversations: Professor Sarah Parsons, Professor Liz Todd and Dr Nicola Yuill. Also thanks to the Educational Psychology Research Interest Group at the University of Sussex for their feedback on the ideas in this chapter.

References

Allard, A. (2009). *Transition to adulthood: Inquiry into young people with autism*. For the All-Party parliamentary group on Autism. London: National Autistic Society.
Baird, G., Simonoff, E., Pickles, A., Chandler, S., Loucas, T., Meldrum, D., and Charman, T. (2006). Prevalence of disorders of the autism spectrum in a population cohort of children in South Thames: The Special needs and Autism Project (SNAP). *The Lancet, 368*(9531), 210–15.

Chen, J. L., Leader, G., Sung, C., and Leahy, M. (2015). Trends in employment for individuals with autism spectrum disorder: A review of the research literature. *Review Journal of Autism and Developmental Disorders, 2*(2), 115–27.

Edwards, A. (2005). Relational agency: Learning to be a resourceful practitioner. *International Journal of Educational Research, 43*(3), 168–82.

Edwards, A. (2010). *Being an expert professional practitioner: The relational turn in expertise*. Dordrecht: Springer.

Edwards, A. (2011). Building common knowledge at boundaries between professional practices. *International Journal of Educational Research* (50), 33–9.

Edwards, A. (2012). The role of common knowledge in achieving collaboration across practices. *Learning, Culture and Social Interaction, 1*(1), 22–32.

Edwards, A. (Ed.) (2017). *Working relationally in and across practices: A cultural-historical approach to collaboration*. New York: Cambridge University Press.

Guldberg, K., Parsons, S., Porayska-Pomsta, K., and Keay-Bright, W. (2017). Challenging the knowledge transfer orthodoxy: Knowledge co-construction in technology-enhanced learning for children with autism. *British Educational Research Journal, 43*(2), 394–413.

Hedegaard, M. (2012). The dynamics aspects in children's learning and development. In M. Hedegaard, A. Edwards and M. Fleer (Eds), *Motives in children's development: Cultural-historical approaches*, pp. 9–27. Cambridge: Cambridge University Press.

Hedegaard, M., and Edwards, A. (2014). Transitions and children's learning. *Learning, Culture and Social Interaction, 3*(3), 185–7.

National Autistic Society. (2015). Adult Autism Strategy: Statutory guidance. http://www.autism.org.uk/about/strategy/statutory-guidance.aspx (accessed 13 February 2018).

National Autistic Society. (2018). http://www.autism.org.uk/.

Parsons, S., Yuill, N., Brosnan, M., and Good, J. (2015). Innovative technologies for autism: Critical reflections on digital bubbles. *Journal of Assistive Technologies, 9*(2), 116–21.

Seale, J. (2014). The role of supporters in facilitating use of technologies by adolescents with learning disabilities: A place for positive risk-taking? *European Journal of Special Needs Education, 29*(2), 220–36.

Schall, C., Wehman, P., and McDonough, J. (2012). Transition from school to work for students with autism spectrum disorders: Understanding the process and achieving better outcomes. *Pediatric Clinics, 59*(1), 189–202.

Shepherd, J. (2015). Experiences of transition from special school to mainstream college for young people with autism. Thesis for the Degree of Doctor of Philosophy, University of Sussex.

Silver, K., and Parsons, S. (2015). Noticing the unusual: A self-prompt strategy for adults with autism. *Advances in Autism, 1*(2), 87–97.

Wittemeyer, K., Charman, T., Cusack., Guldberg, K., Hastings, P. R., Howlin, P., McNab, N., Parsons, S., Pellicano, E., and Slonims, V. (2011). *Educational provision and outcomes for people on the autism spectrum*. London: Autism Education Trust.

Index

action(s)   5, 12, 16, 30, 46, 55, 60, 140, 159, 165, 167, 184–7, 202, 214, 229, 231, 265, 269, 274
activity(ies)   2, 3, 5, 9, 10, 12, 27, 29, 31, 34, 37, 38, 45, 46, 62, 72, 76, 83, 85, 86, 91–110, 121, 125, 139, 144, 154–7, 159, 160, 165, 170, 176, 203–5, 221–39, 244, 252, 253, 255, 264, 276
activity setting   2, 6, 11, 45, 86, 87, 203–5, 209, 211, 214, 243, 244, 253, 255, 257
adult   7, 11, 17, 39, 77, 99, 106, 107, 108, 163, 170, 181, 185, 198, 202, 221, 222, 223, 224, 230, 231, 236, 237, 238, 241–60, 262, 274
adulthood   1, 7, 221–39, 241–60, 262
agency   1–17, 45, 61, 67, 115–27, 133, 221–39, 264, 265
areas of concern   21–40, 101
ASC (Autistic Spectrum Condition)   1, 12, 262, 263, 265, 266–8, 269, 277
Australia   14, 77, 88, 136
autistic   262–77

bioecological   199–201, 214

care   8, 68, 94, 102, 122, 135, 175–91, 196, 197, 212, 243
carer(s)   22, 94, 107, 120, 273
cerebral palsy   1, 7, 14, 17, 246
challenge(s)   4, 8, 23, 27–8, 34, 40, 68, 77, 82, 97, 98, 124, 127, 134, 135, 137, 140, 145, 148, 154, 157–61, 178, 198, 212, 215, 221–39, 241–60, 277
child/children   1–17, 21–40, 43–63, 68, 71, 72, 74, 75, 76, 77, 81, 91–110, 115–27, 135, 138, 140, 142, 146, 153–71, 175–91, 195–215, 241, 242, 243, 244, 257, 259, 265, 271
children's perspective(s)/child's perspective   16, 22, 23, 25, 26, 35, 36, 37, 43, 45, 47, 93, 97, 104, 191, 204
Chile   13, 14, 16, 131–49

collaborate   4, 10, 11, 16, 28, 93, 124, 166, 168, 186, 224, 237
collaboration(s)   5, 8, 10, 11, 21, 28, 35, 36, 39, 44, 73, 83, 85, 133, 138, 166, 170, 171, 184, 187, 209, 213, 214, 225, 228, 233, 265
common knowledge   4, 8, 11, 12, 16, 17, 21, 23, 26, 28, 34, 36, 40, 43–63, 67, 71, 73, 74, 75, 80, 82–8, 107, 108, 109, 119–23, 126, 127, 137, 138, 141, 142, 146, 154, 171, 175–91, 204, 205, 212–14, 215, 262–77
communication   54, 97, 106, 107, 146, 213, 251, 252, 253, 256, 257, 262
competence(s)   6, 9, 10, 12, 38, 44, 45, 61, 62, 91, 94, 97, 98, 100, 101, 102, 110, 117, 118, 123, 158, 170, 181, 202, 203, 221, 223, 242, 245, 246, 251, 255, 257
consultancy   93, 104
consultant   22–4, 25, 27, 30, 32, 34, 35, 36, 37, 38, 39, 40
consultee   23, 24, 26, 27, 35, 36, 37, 38, 39, 40
cross-cultural   195–215
cultural conditions   93, 95
cultural-historical   39, 43, 44, 46, 69, 93, 109, 119, 126–7, 153, 157, 176, 199, 201–3, 206, 214, 222, 225, 237, 242, 243–5, 256, 264
culture   5, 9, 96–8, 99, 118, 120, 154, 159, 160, 161, 164, 169, 170, 195, 202, 204, 206, 209, 211, 212, 223
daycare   1, 3, 11, 21, 23, 25, 36, 92, 94, 98, 101, 102, 107, 108, 110, 122, 123, 175–91, 179, 180, 183, 187, 189, 190
demands   1, 2, 6, 7, 9, 12, 23, 25, 36, 45–6, 67, 75, 76, 85, 87, 98, 115–27, 189, 204, 211, 214, 215, 230, 243, 249, 253, 264, 271, 273, 274
Denmark   1, 7, 8, 11, 14, 16, 22, 23, 100, 179, 246, 248

development (child)   3, 8, 27, 28, 35–8, 36, 39, 44, 91, 92–4, 95, 96–7, 98, 100, 101, 104, 108, 117, 118, 125, 126, 178, 204, 241, 243
dialectic   45, 46, 96, 126, 127, 201, 202, 206, 243–5, 264
disability(ies)   7, 97, 198, 210, 213, 241–60, 263, 268
disaster(s)   195–9, 202, 215
disconnecting activities   221–39
double move   28–9, 30, 34

early childhood   9, 67, 68, 69, 72, 74, 87, 92, 94, 98, 100, 131–49, 253
Early Childhood Environmental Rating Scale (ECERS)   83
educator   9, 10, 13, 16, 68, 74, 116, 125, 131–49, 163, 164, 165, 166, 167, 171, 181, 184, 186, 187, 268, 272–3
everyday life   12, 22, 23, 24, 36, 76, 175, 178, 179, 180, 181, 184, 186, 203, 221, 222, 223, 224, 229, 233, 235, 236, 237, 238, 243
exclusion   116, 117, 119, 127, 177, 179, 181, 226

family(ies)   1–17, 36, 38, 43, 44, 47, 53, 58, 61, 62, 68, 71, 72, 77, 78, 92, 108, 115–27, 131–49, 153, 154–7, 160, 163, 164, 165, 166, 168, 171, 179, 183, 187, 188, 196–7, 199, 201
funds of knowledge   82, 85, 137, 139, 140, 141, 142, 143, 144, 146, 147, 171

Greenland   1, 9, 14, 16, 91, 92–4, 95, 97, 98, 100, 102, 108, 109

Haiti   8, 16, 197–9, 208–9, 210, 212
home   3, 25, 36, 43, 76, 92, 98, 101, 107, 108, 118, 120, 121, 123, 124, 125, 126, 127, 143, 144, 156, 158, 164, 177, 178, 179, 185, 187, 209, 213, 229, 251, 252, 253, 269

inclusion   147, 153, 158, 166, 169–71, 179, 246, 252
inclusive   73, 157, 169
institutional practice(s)   5, 8, 13, 15, 21, 23, 37, 45, 61, 76, 96, 98, 100, 140, 203–5, 212–14, 223, 245

institutional settings   43, 202, 221, 222–4, 230, 234, 241, 242, 245
institutional transition   242, 248, 254, 257–8
interaction observation   24, 27–8, 37–8
inter-professional   14, 175, 176, 177
intervention   8, 16, 27, 32–3, 46, 59, 61, 71, 72, 76, 88, 117, 126, 127, 198

learn   2, 9, 11, 54, 84, 97, 99, 100, 107, 119, 121, 122, 142, 144, 147, 148, 163, 176, 190, 191, 203, 229, 253, 264, 265, 266, 267
learning   5, 6, 7, 8, 10, 22, 27, 29, 30, 34, 36, 37, 43, 44, 45, 47, 50, 62, 67, 71, 72, 74, 75, 76, 79, 91, 93, 96, 98, 99, 100, 107, 108, 109, 110, 116, 118, 119, 121, 123, 125, 131, 132, 133, 135, 136, 137, 138, 140, 142, 143, 144, 145, 146, 147, 149, 155, 156, 159, 161, 162, 166, 168, 170, 190, 202, 242, 245, 255, 256, 257, 258, 264, 268, 277
Leontiev, Alexei   44, 45, 46, 96, 158, 226
literacy   75, 110, 137, 138, 139, 143, 145, 147, 159
Literacy Café   13, 140, 141–2

mental health   17, 195, 196, 198–9
mental illness   221–3, 225–7, 230, 234, 235, 236, 237, 238
motivated   5, 87, 123, 158, 168, 214, 234, 235, 249
motive orientation   2, 4–11, 13, 15, 25, 30, 37, 45, 46, 76, 83, 87, 91, 98, 120, 121, 122, 125, 126, 133, 148, 222, 223, 224, 225, 227, 228, 230, 232, 233, 234, 236, 237, 238, 264, 265, 266, 268, 273, 276
motive(s)   4, 5, 6, 10, 11, 12, 13, 21, 24, 36, 44, 45, 46, 47, 51, 60, 61, 62, 67, 68, 71, 73, 74, 75, 76, 77, 82, 83, 84, 85, 86, 88, 96, 119, 120, 121, 122, 138, 142, 144, 148, 149, 154, 158, 159, 161, 162, 163, 164, 165, 170, 171, 176, 202, 205, 213, 222, 224, 226, 228, 229, 231, 234, 241, 245, 249, 252, 253, 254, 256, 257, 258, 259, 264, 265, 269, 273

need   1, 2, 3, 4, 5, 6, 7, 8, 9, 10, 12, 14, 17, 22, 23, 34, 35, 36, 38, 39, 40, 45, 46, 47,

49, 50, 51, 52, 53, 54, 58, 61, 67, 68, 75, 82, 83, 84, 85, 91, 95, 97, 98, 99, 104, 108, 115, 117, 118, 119, 120, 121, 122, 123, 125, 126, 127, 135, 138, 153, 158, 159, 160, 167, 168, 176, 177, 180, 183, 184, 188, 189, 197, 198, 199, 201, 204, 206, 208, 209, 210, 211, 213, 214, 215, 223, 225, 227, 228, 229, 230, 232, 233, 234, 236, 237, 238, 239, 242, 243, 244, 245, 248, 249, 250, 251, 252, 253, 254, 258, 259, 263, 264, 265, 267, 268, 269, 270, 271, 272, 273, 274, 275, 276, 277

out-of-home care   178, 179

parenting   12, 14, 52, 118, 119, 120, 125, 127
parent(s)   5, 7, 8, 10, 11, 12, 13, 14, 15, 16, 23, 34, 38, 43, 44, 45, 46, 47, 48, 51, 52, 53, 54, 55, 56, 57, 59, 60, 61, 62, 67, 69, 72, 77, 99, 104, 107, 108, 116, 117, 118, 120, 123, 124, 125, 126, 127, 132, 133, 134, 135, 138, 139, 140, 141, 142, 143, 144, 145, 146, 147, 155, 156, 162, 163, 166, 167, 175, 177, 178, 179, 180, 181, 182–4, 185, 186, 187, 188, 191, 197, 210, 211, 215, 226, 241, 242, 243, 245, 246, 248, 249, 250, 251, 252, 253, 254, 256, 257, 259, 268, 269, 271, 272, 273, 275, 277
participate   3, 8, 9, 10, 25, 28, 29, 34, 36, 37, 38, 45, 47, 71, 76, 78, 91, 97, 98, 100, 101, 104, 107, 133, 140, 141, 159, 163, 164, 178, 187, 188, 203, 204, 206, 210, 234, 243, 249, 254
participation   10, 13, 28, 37, 61, 86, 104, 107, 140, 144, 153, 155, 157, 158, 160, 161, 162, 165, 168, 175, 176, 181, 187, 188, 203, 214, 222, 226, 228, 229, 232, 233, 236, 237, 241, 242, 244, 245, 246, 257
partnership   68, 69, 71, 136, 138, 139
play   1, 6, 33, 44, 45, 76, 97, 99, 100, 101, 106, 107, 120, 122, 125, 135, 145, 164, 176, 180, 187, 189, 190, 200
practice development   9, 24, 25, 27, 28, 37, 40
practice(s)   1, 2, 3, 4, 5, 6, 7, 8, 9, 10, 11, 13, 15, 16, 21, 22, 23, 24, 25, 27, 28, 34, 35, 36, 37, 38, 39, 44, 45, 46, 47, 49, 51, 58, 60, 61, 62, 67, 69, 70, 71, 72, 73, 74, 75, 76, 77, 78, 80, 81, 82, 83, 84, 85, 86, 87, 93, 96, 98, 100, 102, 104, 108, 120, 121, 122, 123, 126, 127, 131, 134, 136, 137, 138, 140, 141, 145, 146, 148, 149, 153, 154, 155, 156, 157, 158, 159, 160, 161, 162, 164, 165, 166, 167, 168, 169, 170, 171, 176, 177, 178, 187, 189, 190, 191, 201, 203, 204, 205, 206, 208, 209, 211, 212, 214, 215, 222, 223, 226, 228, 229, 230, 232, 233, 235, 237, 245, 246, 248, 249, 250, 254, 255, 256, 264, 267, 268, 273, 276
practitioner   4, 5, 6, 9, 10, 14, 15, 17, 56, 84, 92, 107, 115, 122, 123, 124, 125, 136, 146, 162, 197, 199, 209
pre-school   6, 10, 36, 72, 77, 78, 80, 82, 86, 91, 92, 95, 96, 100, 107, 108, 109, 116, 118, 120, 125, 178, 203
prevention   23, 37, 116, 117, 179, 181, 196, 224, 236, 272
professional(s)   1, 2, 4, 5, 7, 8, 9, 10, 11, 12, 14, 15, 16, 21, 22, 23, 24, 36, 39, 43, 44, 47, 59, 61, 62, 67, 68, 69, 73, 74, 76, 77, 78, 79, 83, 84, 85, 86, 87, 88, 136, 138, 139, 141, 144, 146, 148, 154, 175, 176, 177, 178, 179, 180, 181, 182, 184, 185, 186, 188, 189, 190, 191, 214, 215, 228, 245, 249, 252, 253, 257, 259, 265, 266
profession(s)   1, 86, 115
psychosocial   198–9, 221, 228, 229

quality   9, 69, 71, 72, 73, 74, 78, 80, 81, 82, 83, 84, 87, 117, 133, 135, 139, 196, 199, 227, 235

radical-local   91–109
relational agency   4, 10, 11, 17, 46, 67, 71, 73, 75, 81, 82, 85, 87, 137, 140, 141, 142, 144, 148, 222, 231, 233, 236, 237, 238, 266, 277
relational expertise   4, 10, 11, 13, 21, 27, 40, 46, 67, 71, 73, 74, 75, 81, 84, 85, 88, 108, 126, 137, 138, 139, 141, 142, 144, 146, 148, 149, 166, 171, 259
relational work   1, 266, 267
relationship(s)   5, 12, 14, 24, 46, 51, 56, 57, 58, 59, 62, 96, 104, 117, 118, 119, 122, 125, 126, 127, 131, 132, 134, 138,

139, 140, 141, 142, 143, 147, 148, 154, 155, 156, 158, 159, 160, 163, 164, 165, 167, 170, 171, 178, 180, 186, 187, 188, 199, 201, 202, 203, 204, 206, 209, 221, 235, 236, 264
residential   4, 8, 10, 11, 14, 17, 175, 177, 178, 179, 180, 181, 182, 183, 184, 185, 186, 187, 189, 190
resilience   7, 15, 16, 116, 117, 118, 119, 122, 125, 126, 196, 197, 199, 200, 201, 206, 209, 212, 214, 215
Roma   13, 16, 153, 154, 155, 156, 157, 158, 159, 160, 162, 163, 164, 165, 166, 167, 168, 169, 170, 208

school   2, 3, 5, 7, 8, 9, 10, 11, 13, 14, 16, 22, 23, 24, 25, 36, 37, 72, 80, 86, 98, 100, 104, 107, 108, 119, 120, 121, 123, 127, 131, 138, 142, 146, 153, 155, 156, 157, 158, 159, 160, 161, 162, 164, 165, 166, 167, 168, 169, 242, 243, 244, 246, 248, 249, 250, 252, 257, 258, 265, 268, 269, 272, 273
screening   10, 91, 92, 93, 94, 95, 96, 99, 100, 101, 104, 107, 109, 195
smart phone   12, 17, 71, 263, 266, 267
social psychiatry   221, 222–4, 226, 231, 236
social situation of development   2, 3, 6, 7, 9, 10, 11, 24, 25, 43, 44, 45, 52, 60, 61, 62, 91, 94, 96, 101, 106, 107, 109, 119–23, 209, 210, 214, 243
social work   14, 223
society   36, 75, 97, 98, 155, 156, 160, 176, 187, 230, 242
space of reasons   47, 50, 52, 60, 61, 62
Spain   13, 16, 153–71
systemic consultation   23, 24

teacher(s)   5, 15, 23, 26, 27, 28, 29, 30, 31, 32, 33, 34, 35, 36, 38, 39, 40, 69, 70, 71, 74, 76, 77, 92, 93, 108, 123, 126, 156, 165, 166, 167, 168, 175, 178, 180, 183, 185, 186, 188, 255, 265, 266, 268, 269, 272, 273

UK   14, 116, 117, 120, 262, 263, 266, 267

Vietnam   9, 14, 16, 67, 72, 76, 77, 83, 86
vulnerable   8, 21, 23, 92, 100, 108, 134, 187, 195, 198, 234, 265
Vygotsky, Lev   2, 7, 44, 45, 47, 93, 96, 97, 120, 159, 201, 202, 203, 214, 243

wholistic   5
work   1, 2, 4, 5, 7, 8, 9, 10–13, 14, 15–16, 17, 21, 22, 23, 24, 25, 26, 27, 29, 30, 31, 32, 33, 34, 35, 36, 38, 39, 43, 44, 45, 46, 47, 48, 49, 50, 51, 55, 58, 59, 60, 62, 67, 68, 72, 73, 74, 75, 76, 77, 78, 79, 80, 81, 83, 84, 85, 86, 87, 88, 92, 93, 94, 107, 108, 115, 116, 118, 119, 122, 123, 124, 125, 126, 127, 131–49, 153–71, 175, 176, 177, 178, 180, 181, 183, 184, 185, 187, 188, 189–91, 198, 199, 212, 213, 214, 221, 223, 225, 228–9, 230, 234, 235, 236, 238, 242, 243, 245, 249, 251, 253, 256, 259, 262–77
workplace   1, 2, 12, 17, 85, 263, 264, 266, 267, 268, 269, 270, 271, 272, 273, 276, 277

young people   1, 2, 3, 4, 5, 7, 8, 10, 11, 12, 14, 15, 17, 23, 155, 191, 221, 228, 229, 242, 243, 244, 246, 248, 249, 250, 253, 254, 255, 256, 257, 258, 259, 266, 267, 268, 269, 270–1, 272, 273, 276, 277
young person   2, 5, 7, 10, 12, 13, 14, 17, 228, 248, 258, 265, 267, 268, 271, 273, 275, 276

zone(s) of concern   1, 10, 11, 17, 21, 23, 24, 28, 30, 34, 36, 37, 38, 39, 40, 43, 47, 48, 52, 56, 59, 104